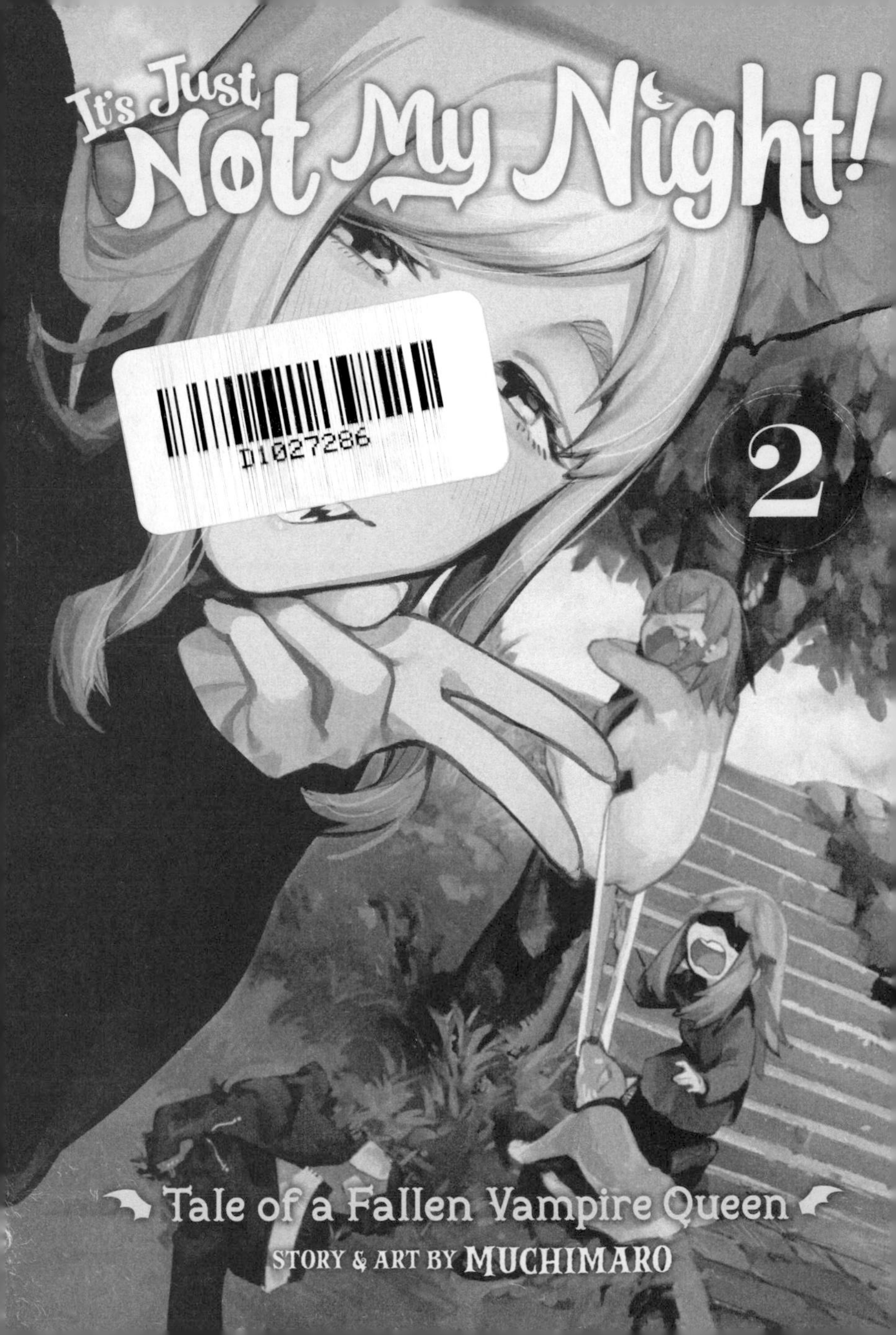
It's Just
Not My Night!
2
Tale of a Fallen Vampire Queen
STORY & ART BY MUCHIMARO

CONTENTS
2

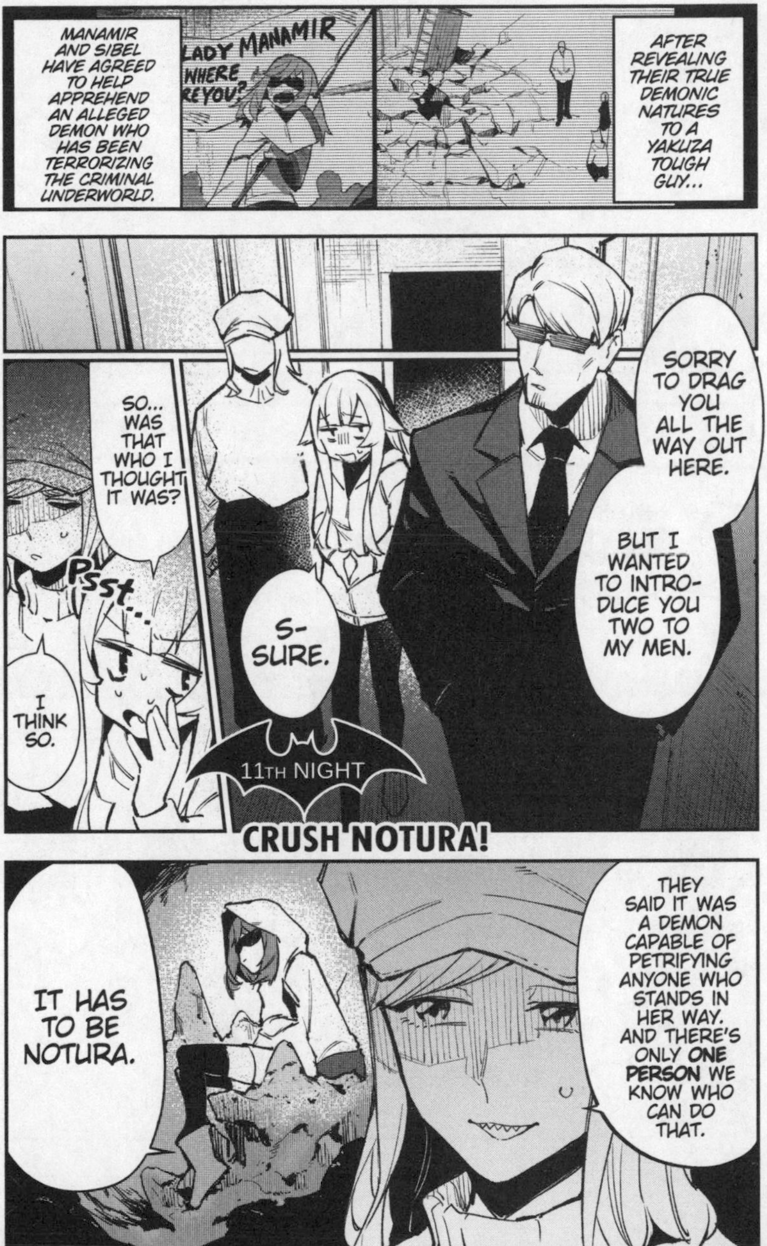
AFTER REVEALING THEIR TRUE DEMONIC NATURES TO A YAKUZA TOUGH GUY...
LADY MANAMIR WHERE ARE YOU?
MANAMIR AND SIBEL HAVE AGREED TO HELP APPREHEND AN ALLEGED DEMON WHO HAS BEEN TERRORIZING THE CRIMINAL UNDERWORLD.
SORRY TO DRAG YOU ALL THE WAY OUT HERE.
BUT I WANTED TO INTRODUCE YOU TWO TO MY MEN.
S-SURE.
SO... WAS THAT WHO I THOUGHT IT WAS?
Psst...
I THINK SO.
11TH NIGHT
CRUSH NOTURA!
THEY SAID IT WAS A DEMON CAPABLE OF PETRIFYING ANYONE WHO STANDS IN HER WAY. AND THERE'S ONLY ONE PERSON WE KNOW WHO CAN DO THAT.
IT HAS TO BE NOTURA.

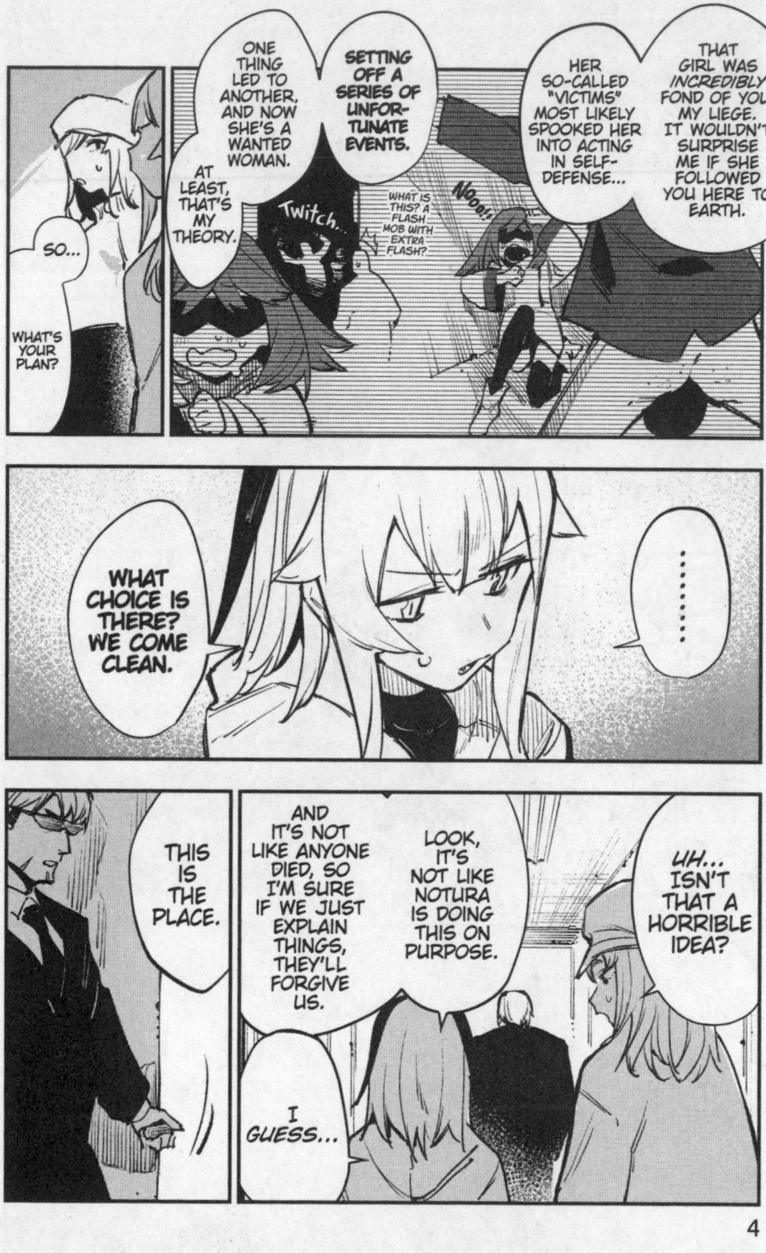
THAT GIRL WAS *INCREDIBLY* FOND OF YOU, MY LIEGE. IT WOULDN'T SURPRISE ME IF SHE FOLLOWED YOU HERE TO EARTH.
HER SO-CALLED "VICTIMS" MOST LIKELY SPOOKED HER INTO ACTING IN SELF-DEFENSE...
Nooo!!
WHAT IS THIS? A FLASH MOB WITH EXTRA FLASH?
SETTING OFF A SERIES OF UNFORTUNATE EVENTS.
ONE THING LED TO ANOTHER, AND NOW SHE'S A WANTED WOMAN.
AT LEAST, THAT'S MY THEORY.
Twitch...
SO...
WHAT'S YOUR PLAN?
....
WHAT CHOICE IS THERE? WE COME CLEAN.
UH... ISN'T THAT A HORRIBLE IDEA?
LOOK, IT'S NOT LIKE NOTURA IS DOING THIS ON PURPOSE.
AND IT'S NOT LIKE ANYONE DIED, SO I'M SURE IF WE JUST EXPLAIN THINGS, THEY'LL FORGIVE US.
I GUESS...
THIS IS THE PLACE.

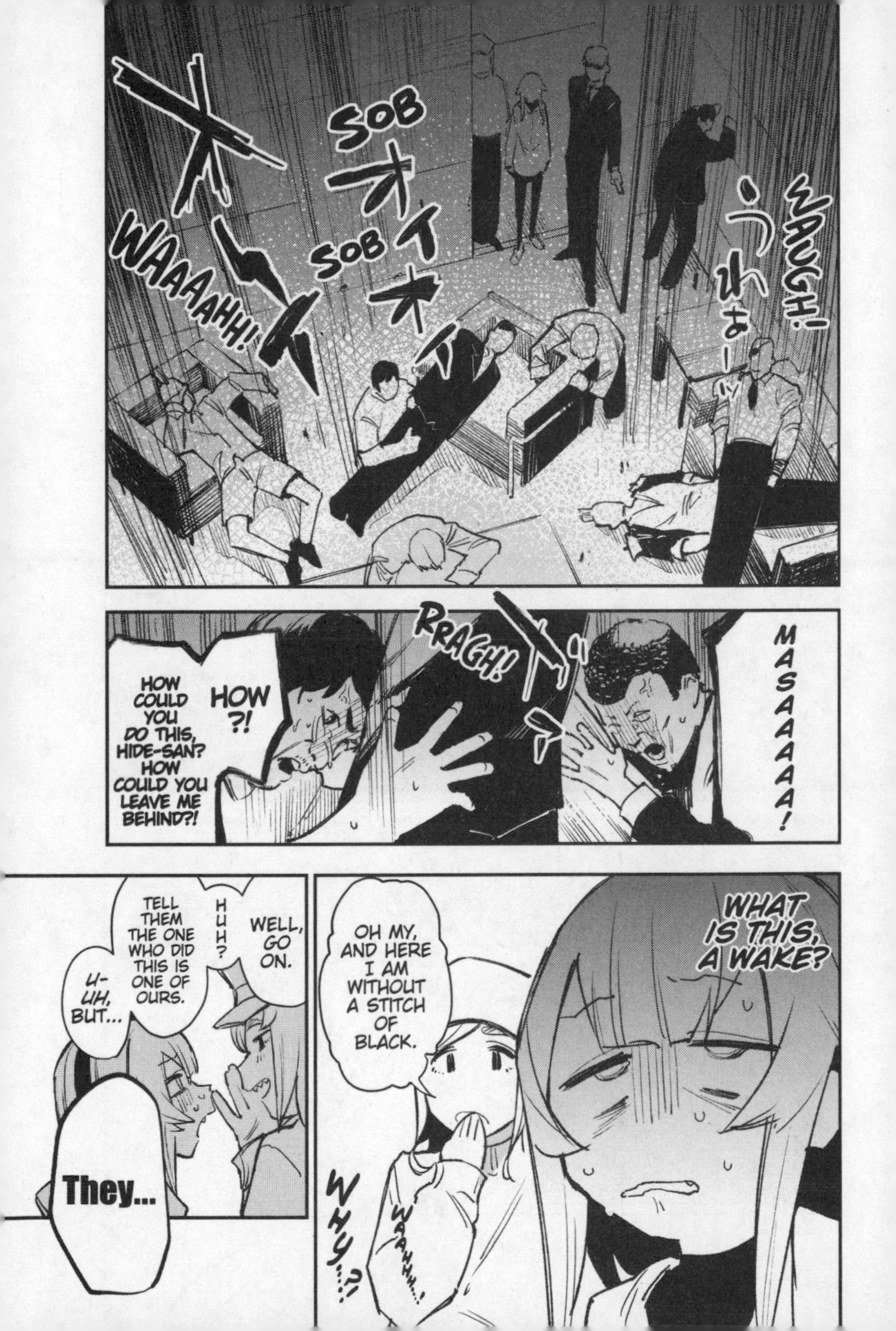
WAUGH!
SOB
SOB
オイオイ
WAAAAAHH!
MASAAAAAAA!
RRAGH!
HOW ?!
HOW COULD YOU DO THIS, HIDE-SAN? HOW COULD YOU LEAVE ME BEHIND?!
WHAT IS THIS, A WAKE?
OH MY, AND HERE I AM WITHOUT A STITCH OF BLACK.
WHY...?!
WAAHHH...!
WELL, GO ON.
HUH?
TELL THEM THE ONE WHO DID THIS IS ONE OF OURS.
U-UH, BUT...
They...

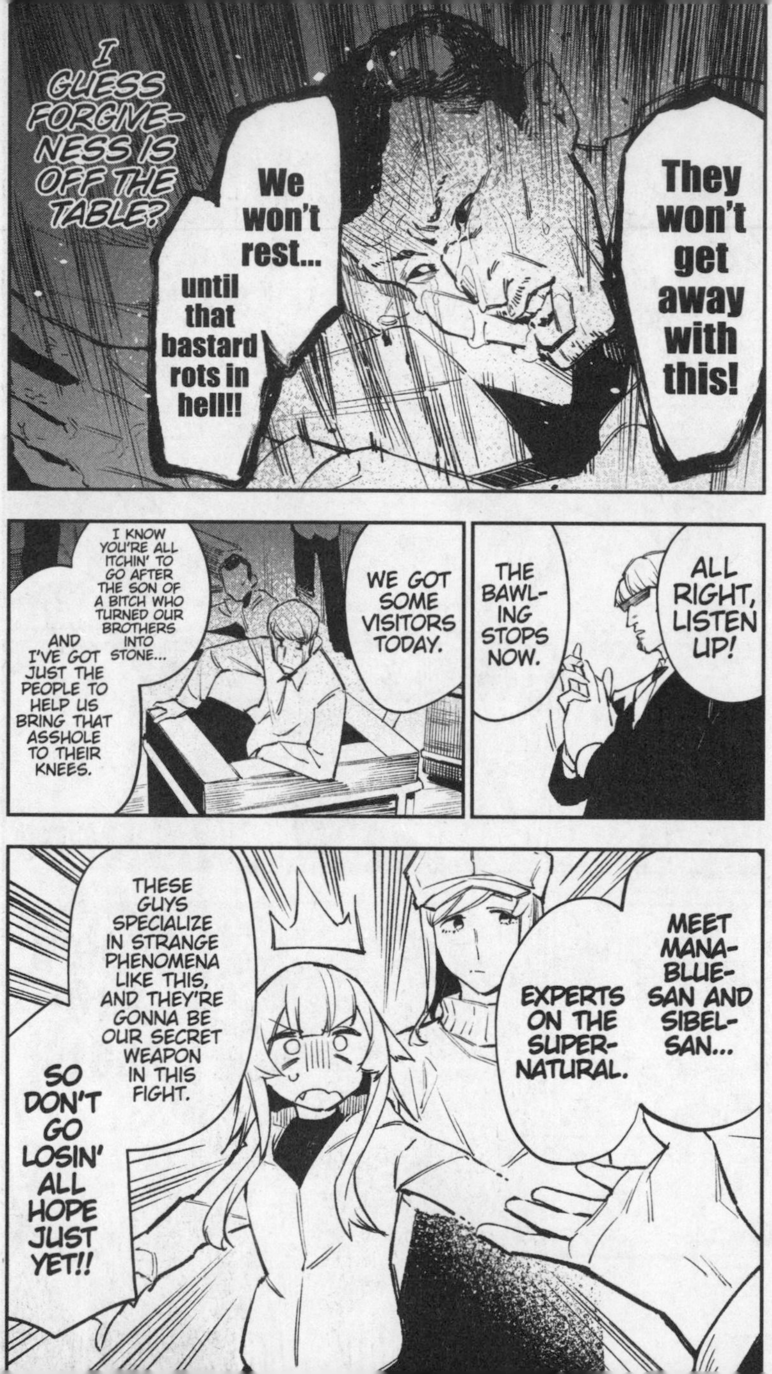
They won't get away with this!
We won't rest... until that bastard rots in hell!!
I GUESS FORGIVENESS IS OFF THE TABLE?
ALL RIGHT, LISTEN UP!
THE BAWLING STOPS NOW.
WE GOT SOME VISITORS TODAY.
I KNOW YOU'RE ALL ITCHIN' TO GO AFTER THE SON OF A BITCH WHO TURNED OUR BROTHERS INTO STONE...
AND I'VE GOT JUST THE PEOPLE TO HELP US BRING THAT ASSHOLE TO THEIR KNEES.
MEET MANABLUE-SAN AND SIBEL-SAN...
EXPERTS ON THE SUPERNATURAL.
THESE GUYS SPECIALIZE IN STRANGE PHENOMENA LIKE THIS, AND THEY'RE GONNA BE OUR SECRET WEAPON IN THIS FIGHT.
SO DON'T GO LOSIN' ALL HOPE JUST YET!!

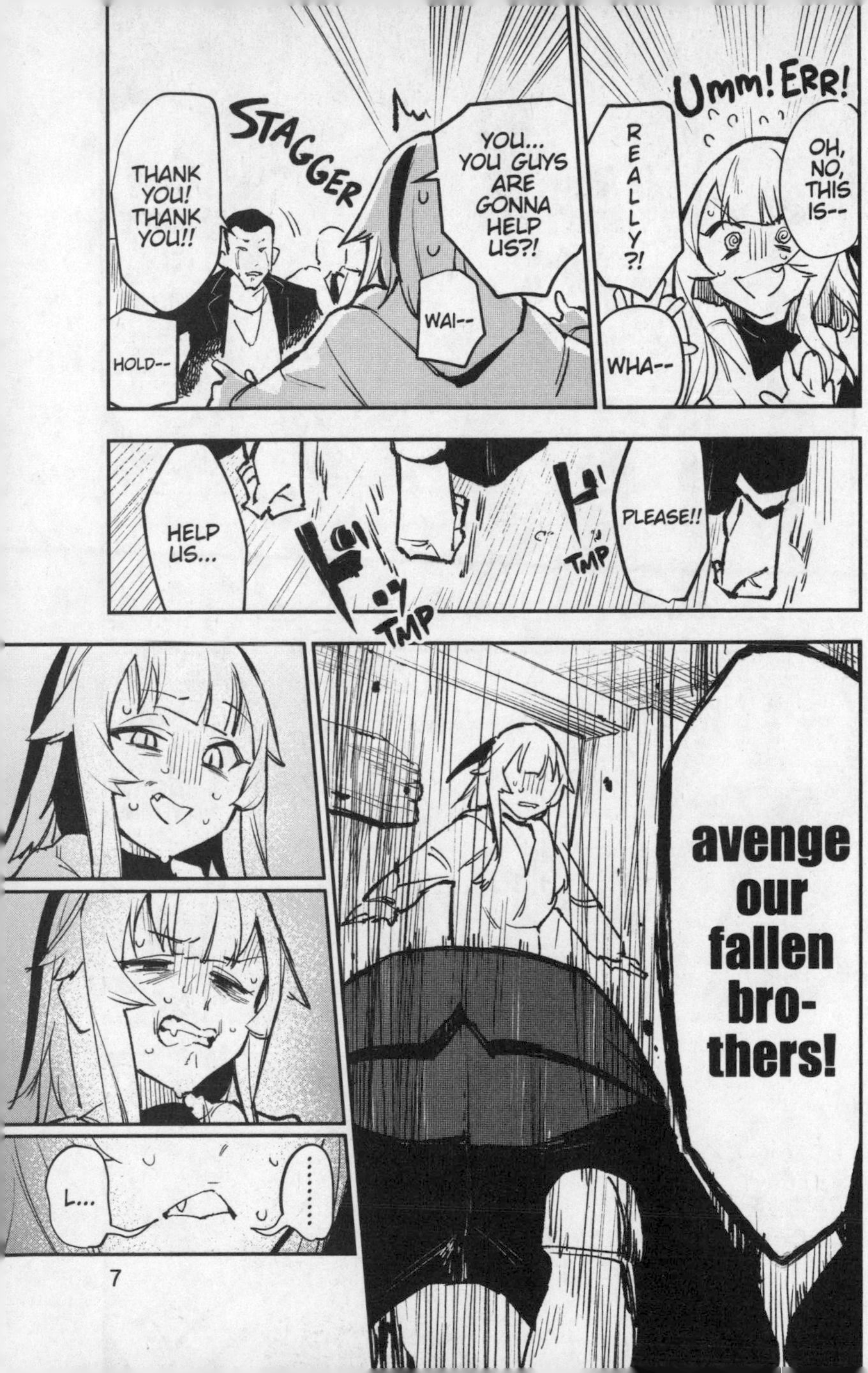
Umm! ERR!
OH, NO, THIS IS--
REALLY?!
WHA--
YOU... YOU GUYS ARE GONNA HELP US?!
STAGGER
THANK YOU! THANK YOU!!
WAI--
HOLD--
PLEASE!!
TMP
HELP US...
TMP
avenge our fallen bro-thers!
L...
......

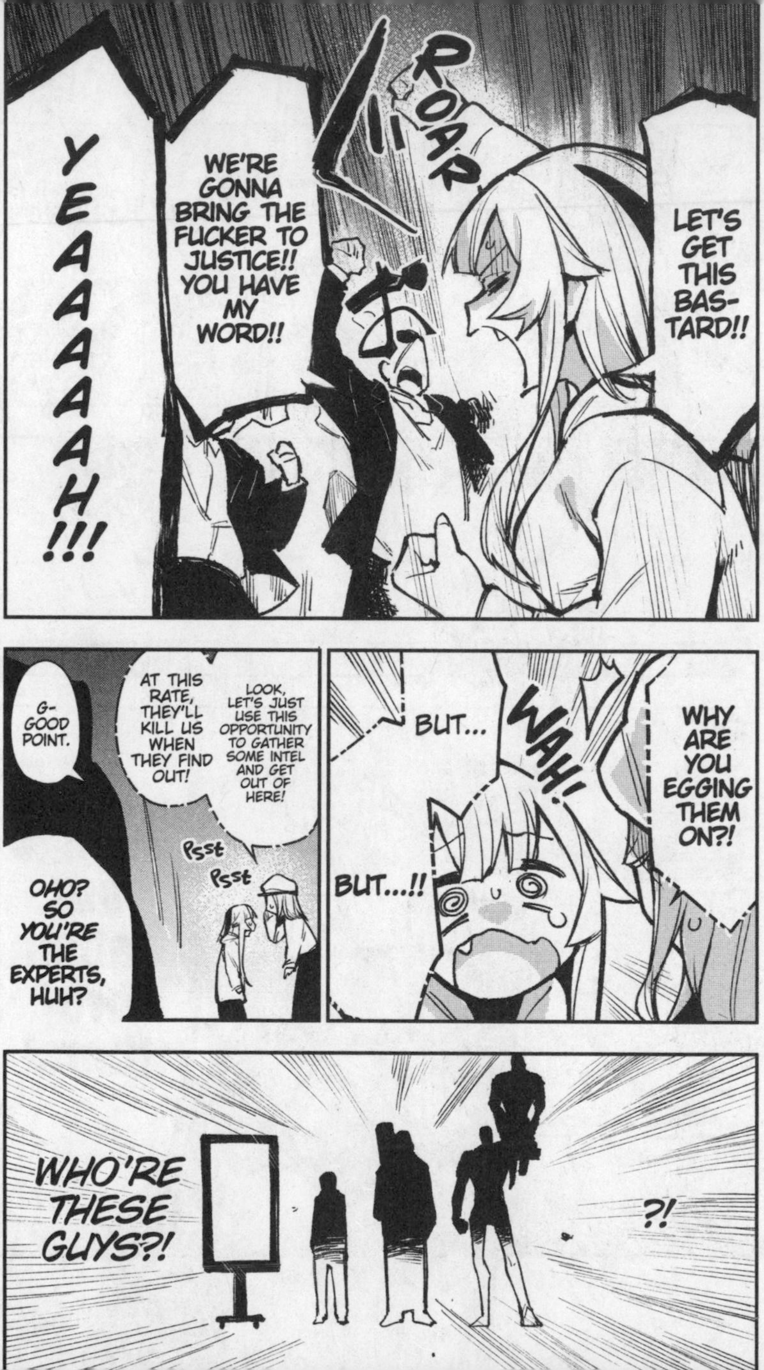
LET'S GET THIS BAS-TARD!!
ROAR
WE'RE GONNA BRING THE FUCKER TO JUSTICE!! YOU HAVE MY WORD!!
YEAAAAAAH!!!
WHY ARE YOU EGGING THEM ON?!
WAH!
BUT...
BUT...!!
LOOK, LET'S JUST USE THIS OPPORTUNITY TO GATHER SOME INTEL AND GET OUT OF HERE!
AT THIS RATE, THEY'LL KILL US WHEN THEY FIND OUT!
G-GOOD POINT.
Psst
Psst
OHO? SO YOU'RE THE EXPERTS, HUH?
?!
WHO'RE THESE GUYS?!

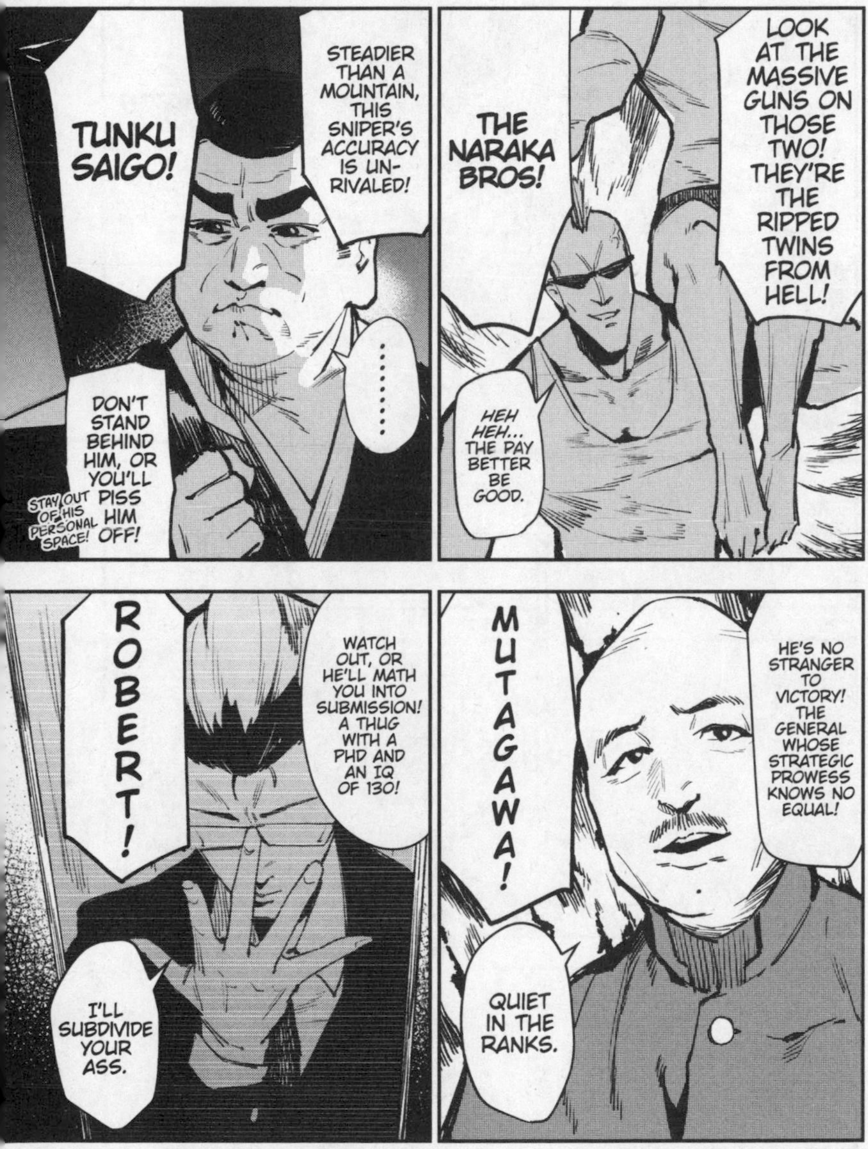

LOOK AT THE MASSIVE GUNS ON THOSE TWO! THEY'RE THE RIPPED TWINS FROM HELL!
THE NARAKA BROS!
HEH HEH... THE PAY BETTER BE GOOD.
STEADIER THAN A MOUNTAIN, THIS SNIPER'S ACCURACY IS UN-RIVALED!
TUNKU SAIGO!
......
DON'T STAND BEHIND HIM, OR YOU'LL PISS HIM OFF!
STAY OUT OF HIS PERSONAL SPACE!
HE'S NO STRANGER TO VICTORY! THE GENERAL WHOSE STRATEGIC PROWESS KNOWS NO EQUAL!
MUTAGAWA!
QUIET IN THE RANKS.
WATCH OUT, OR HE'LL MATH YOU INTO SUBMISSION! A THUG WITH A PHD AND AN IQ OF 130!
ROBERT!
I'LL SUBDIVIDE YOUR ASS.

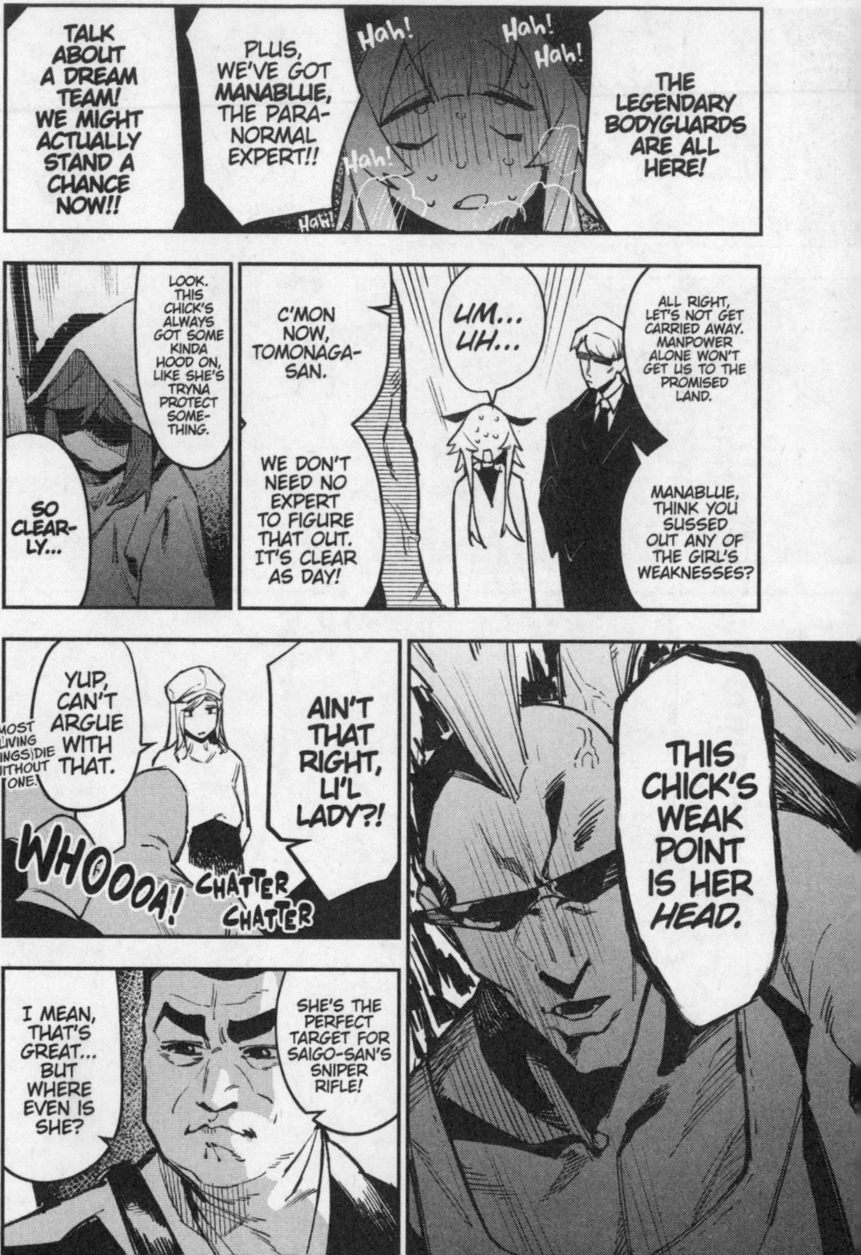
THE LEGENDARY BODYGUARDS ARE ALL HERE!
Hah! Hah!
Hah!
PLUS, WE'VE GOT MANABLUE, THE PARA-NORMAL EXPERT!!
Hah!
Hah!
TALK ABOUT A DREAM TEAM! WE MIGHT ACTUALLY STAND A CHANCE NOW!!
ALL RIGHT, LET'S NOT GET CARRIED AWAY. MANPOWER ALONE WON'T GET US TO THE PROMISED LAND.
MANABLUE, THINK YOU SUSSED OUT ANY OF THE GIRL'S WEAKNESSES?
UM... UH...
C'MON NOW, TOMONAGA-SAN.
WE DON'T NEED NO EXPERT TO FIGURE THAT OUT. IT'S CLEAR AS DAY!
LOOK. THIS CHICK'S ALWAYS GOT SOME KINDA HOOD ON, LIKE SHE'S TRYNA PROTECT SOME-THING.
SO CLEAR-LY...
THIS CHICK'S WEAK POINT IS HER HEAD.
AIN'T THAT RIGHT, LI'L LADY?!
YUP, CAN'T ARGUE WITH THAT.
MOST LIVING THINGS DIE WITHOUT ONE.
WHOOOA!
CHATTER CHATTER
SHE'S THE PERFECT TARGET FOR SAIGO-SAN'S SNIPER RIFLE!
I MEAN, THAT'S GREAT... BUT WHERE EVEN IS SHE?

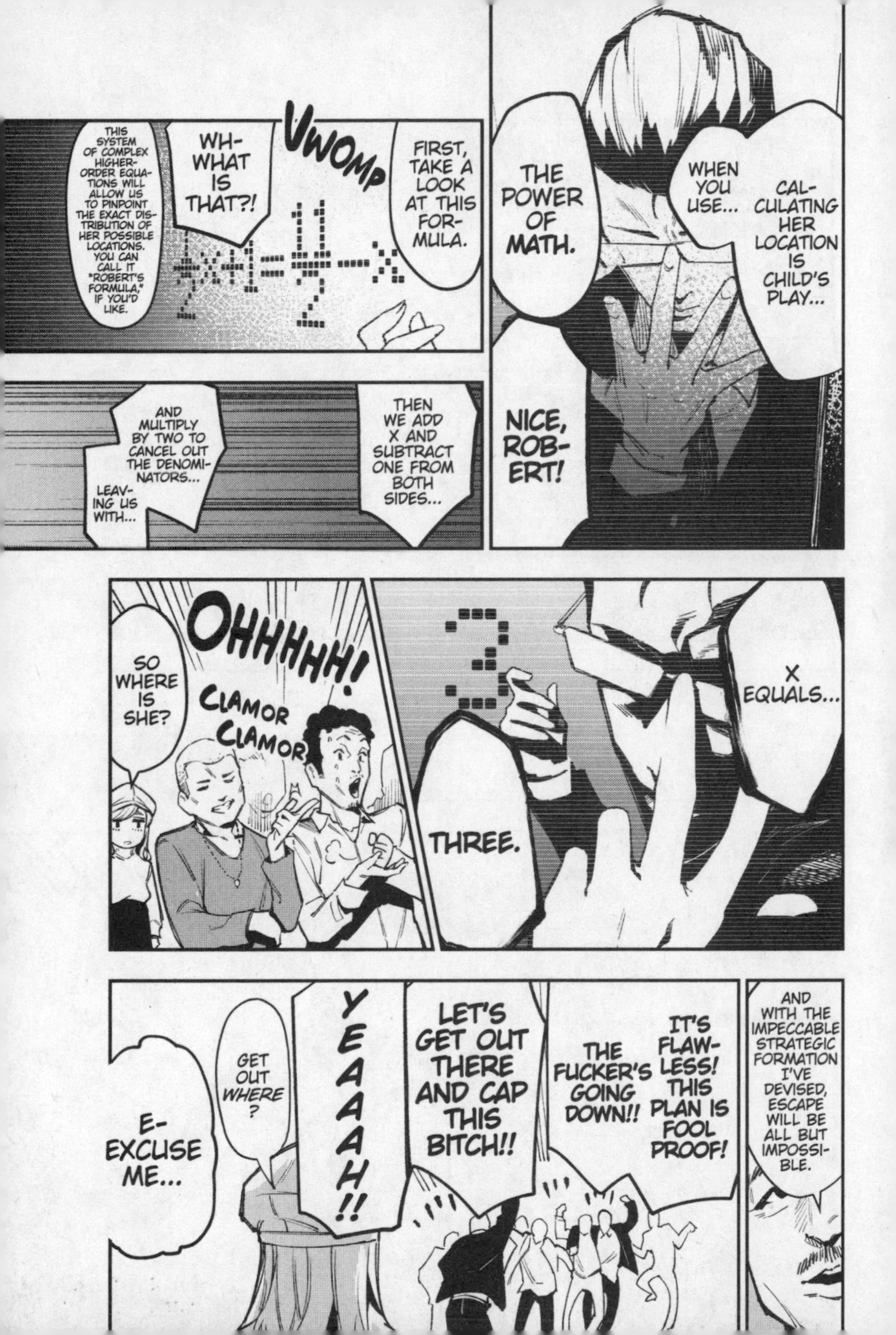
CAL-
CULATING
HER
LOCATION
IS
CHILD'S
PLAY...
WHEN YOU USE...
THE POWER OF MATH.
NICE, ROB-
ERT!
FIRST, TAKE A LOOK AT THIS FOR-
MULA.
VWOMP
WH-
WHAT IS THAT?!
THIS SYSTEM OF COMPLEX HIGHER-
ORDER EQUA-
TIONS WILL ALLOW US TO PINPOINT THE EXACT DIS-
TRIBUTION OF HER POSSIBLE LOCATIONS. YOU CAN CALL IT "ROBERT'S FORMULA," IF YOU'D LIKE.
THEN WE ADD X AND SUBTRACT ONE FROM BOTH SIDES...
AND MULTIPLY BY TWO TO CANCEL OUT THE DENOMI-
NATORS...
LEAV-
ING US WITH...
X EQUALS...
3
THREE.
OHHHHHH!
CLAMOR
CLAMOR
SO WHERE IS SHE?
AND WITH THE IMPECCABLE STRATEGIC FORMATION I'VE DEVISED, ESCAPE WILL BE ALL BUT IMPOSSI-
BLE.
IT'S FLAW-
LESS! THIS PLAN IS FOOL PROOF!
THE FUCKER'S GOING DOWN!!
LET'S GET OUT THERE AND CAP THIS BITCH!!
YEAAAAH!!
GET OUT WHERE?
E-
EXCUSE ME...

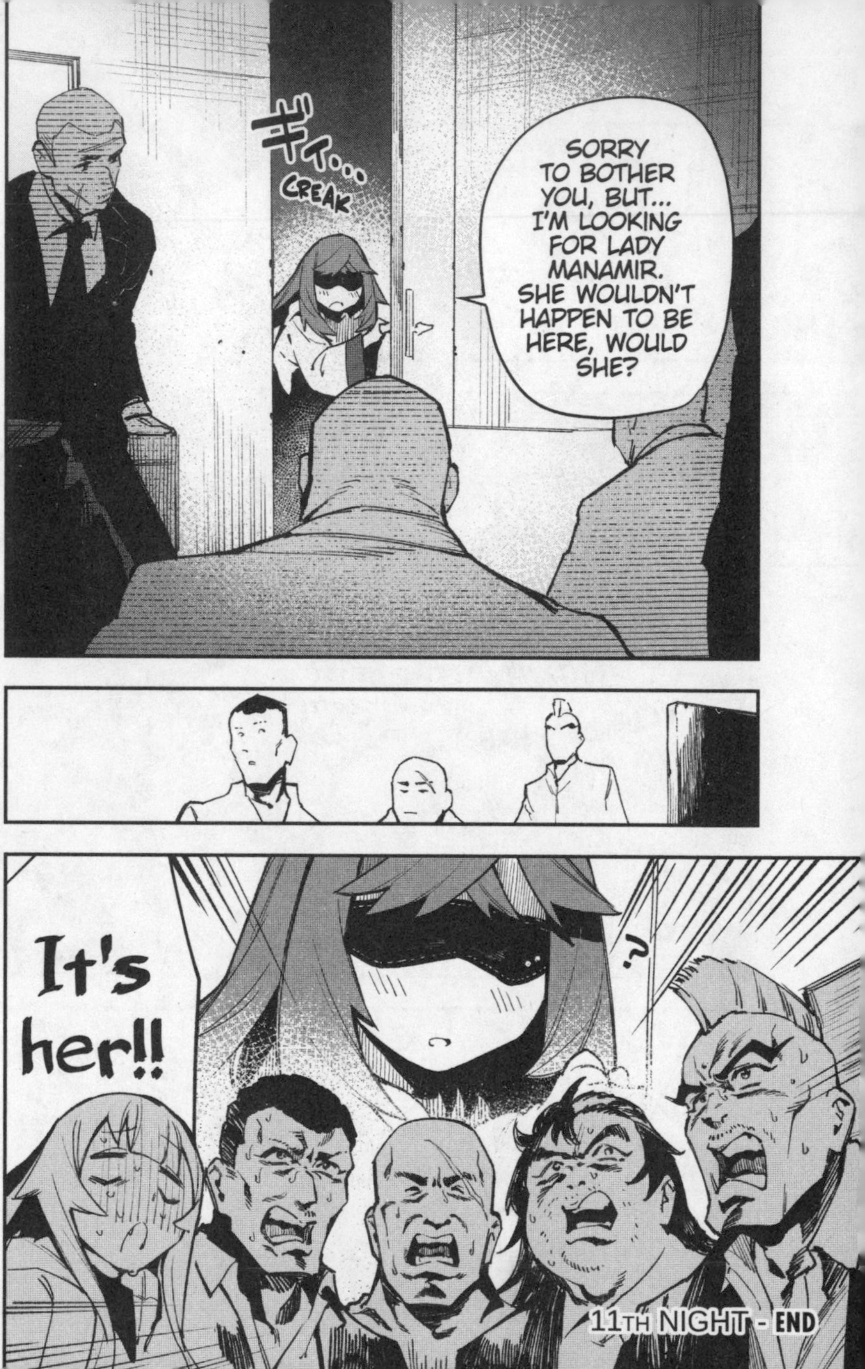
SORRY TO BOTHER YOU, BUT... I'M LOOKING FOR LADY MANAMIR. SHE WOULDN'T HAPPEN TO BE HERE, WOULD SHE?
ギイ...
CREAK
?
It's her!!
11TH NIGHT - END

I don't draw men often, so they're looking a little.. rough.
It makes the girls look cuter by comparison, doesn't it?
It's an illuuusion.
Man
Moron

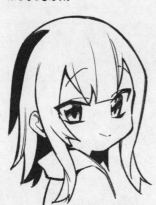

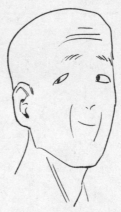

It's Just Not My Night!

Tale of a Fallen Vampire Queen

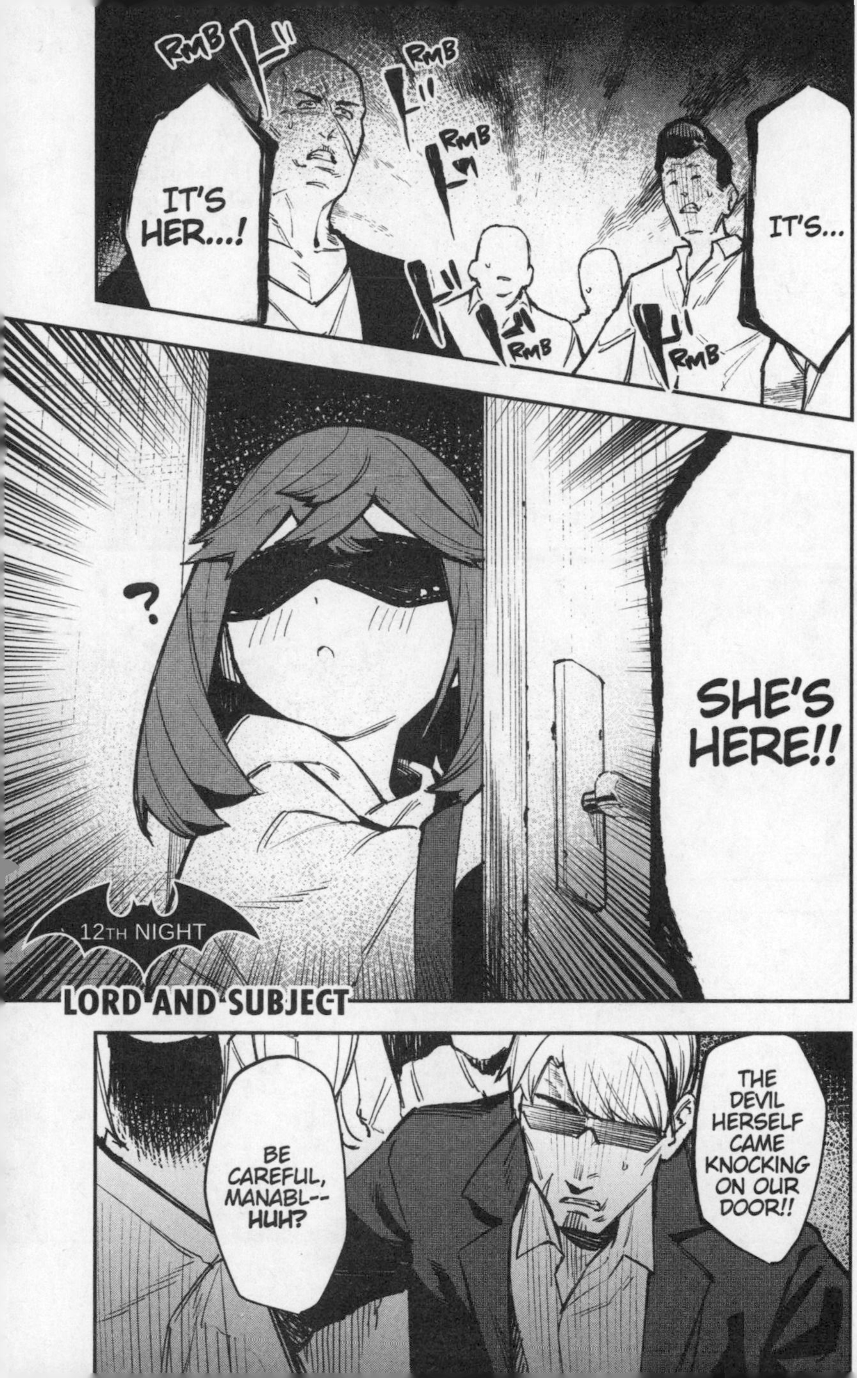
IT'S...
RMB
RMB
RMB
RMB
RMB
RMB
IT'S HER...!
SHE'S HERE!!
?
12TH NIGHT
LORD AND SUBJECT
THE DEVIL HERSELF CAME KNOCKING ON OUR DOOR!!
BE CAREFUL, MANABL-- HUH?

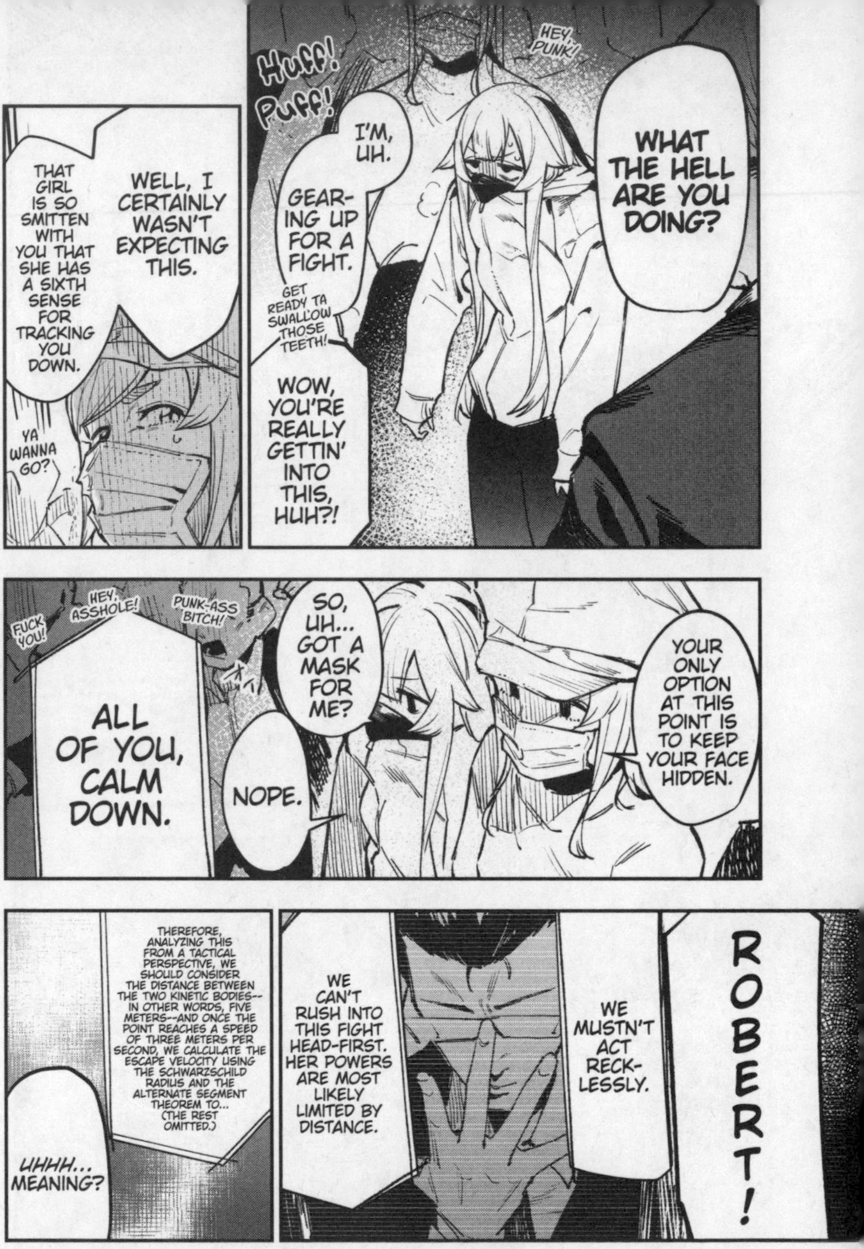
HEY, PUNK!
WHAT THE HELL ARE YOU DOING?
Huff! Puff!
I'M, UH.
GEARING UP FOR A FIGHT.
GET READY TA SWALLOW THOSE TEETH!
WOW, YOU'RE REALLY GETTIN' INTO THIS, HUH?!
WELL, I CERTAINLY WASN'T EXPECTING THIS.
THAT GIRL IS SO SMITTEN WITH YOU THAT SHE HAS A SIXTH SENSE FOR TRACKING YOU DOWN.
YA WANNA GO?
YOUR ONLY OPTION AT THIS POINT IS TO KEEP YOUR FACE HIDDEN.
SO, UH... GOT A MASK FOR ME?
PUNK-ASS BITCH!
HEY, ASSHOLE!
NOPE.
FUCK YOU!
ALL OF YOU, CALM DOWN.
ROBERT!
WE MUSTN'T ACT RECKLESSLY.
WE CAN'T RUSH INTO THIS FIGHT HEAD-FIRST. HER POWERS ARE MOST LIKELY LIMITED BY DISTANCE.
THEREFORE, ANALYZING THIS FROM A TACTICAL PERSPECTIVE, WE SHOULD CONSIDER THE DISTANCE BETWEEN THE TWO KINETIC BODIES--IN OTHER WORDS, FIVE METERS--AND ONCE THE POINT REACHES A SPEED OF THREE METERS PER SECOND, WE CALCULATE THE ESCAPE VELOCITY USING THE SCHWARZSCHILD RADIUS AND THE ALTERNATE SEGMENT THEOREM TO... (THE REST OMITTED.)
UHHH... MEANING?

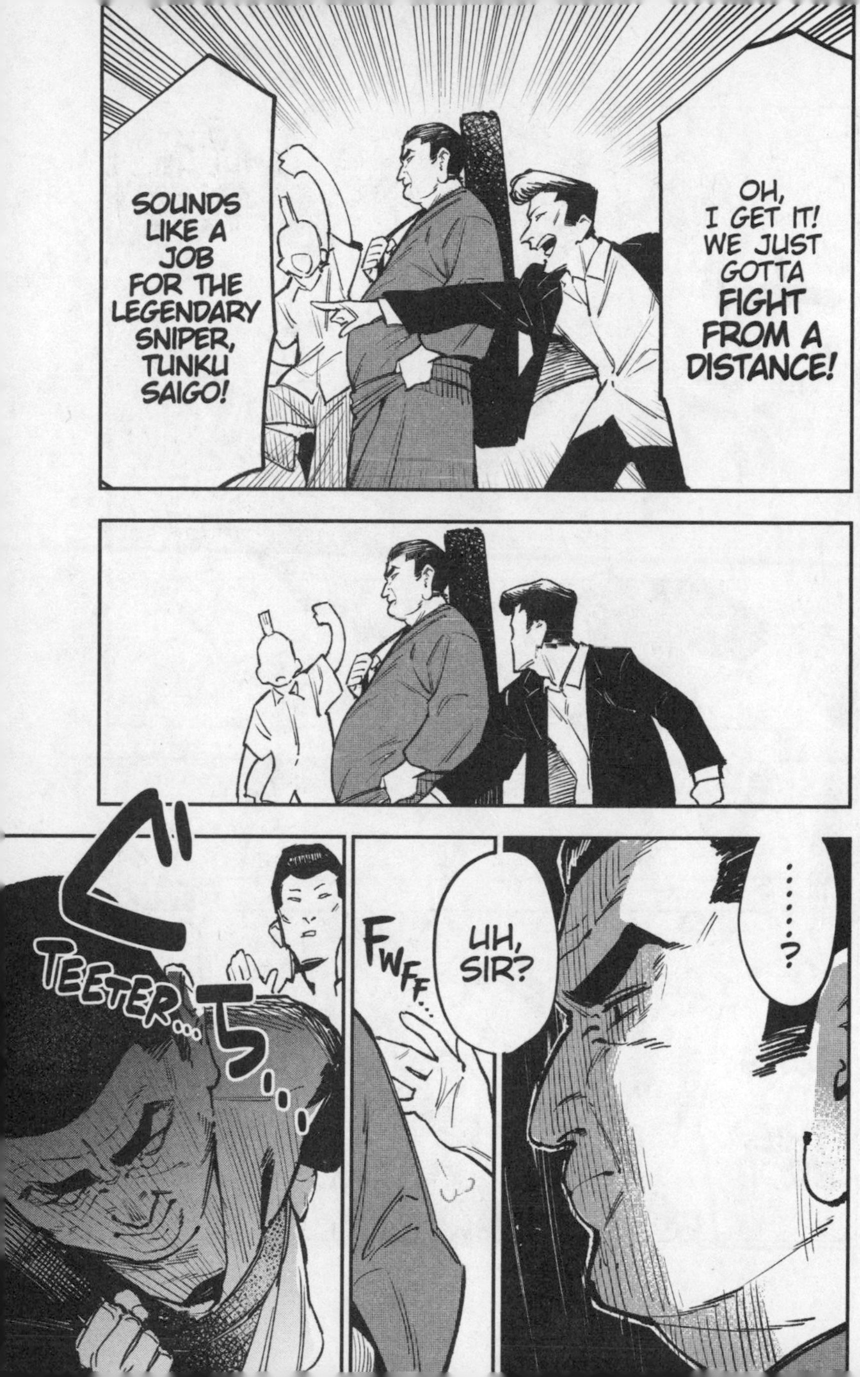
OH, I GET IT! WE JUST GOTTA FIGHT FROM A DISTANCE!
SOUNDS LIKE A JOB FOR THE LEGENDARY SNIPER, TUNKU SAIGO!
......?
UH, SIR?
FWFF...
ぐ
ら...
TEETER...

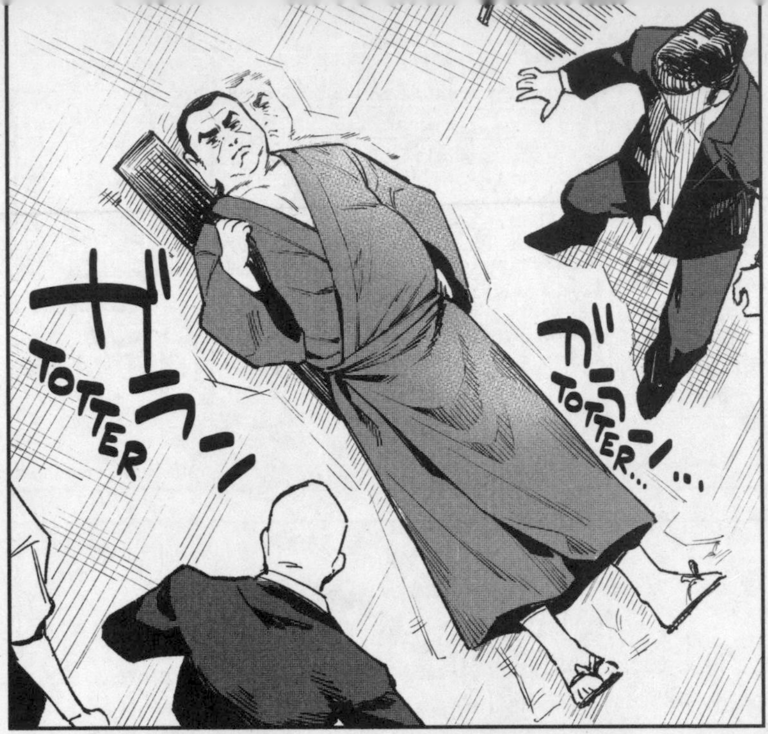
TOTTER...
TOTTER

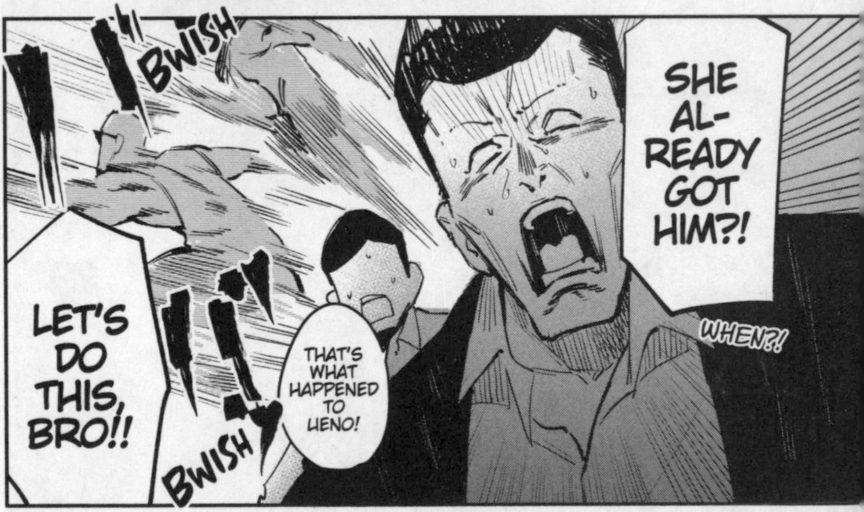
SHE AL-READY GOT HIM?!
WHEN?!
THAT'S WHAT HAPPENED TO UENO!
BWISH
BWISH
LET'S DO THIS, BRO!!

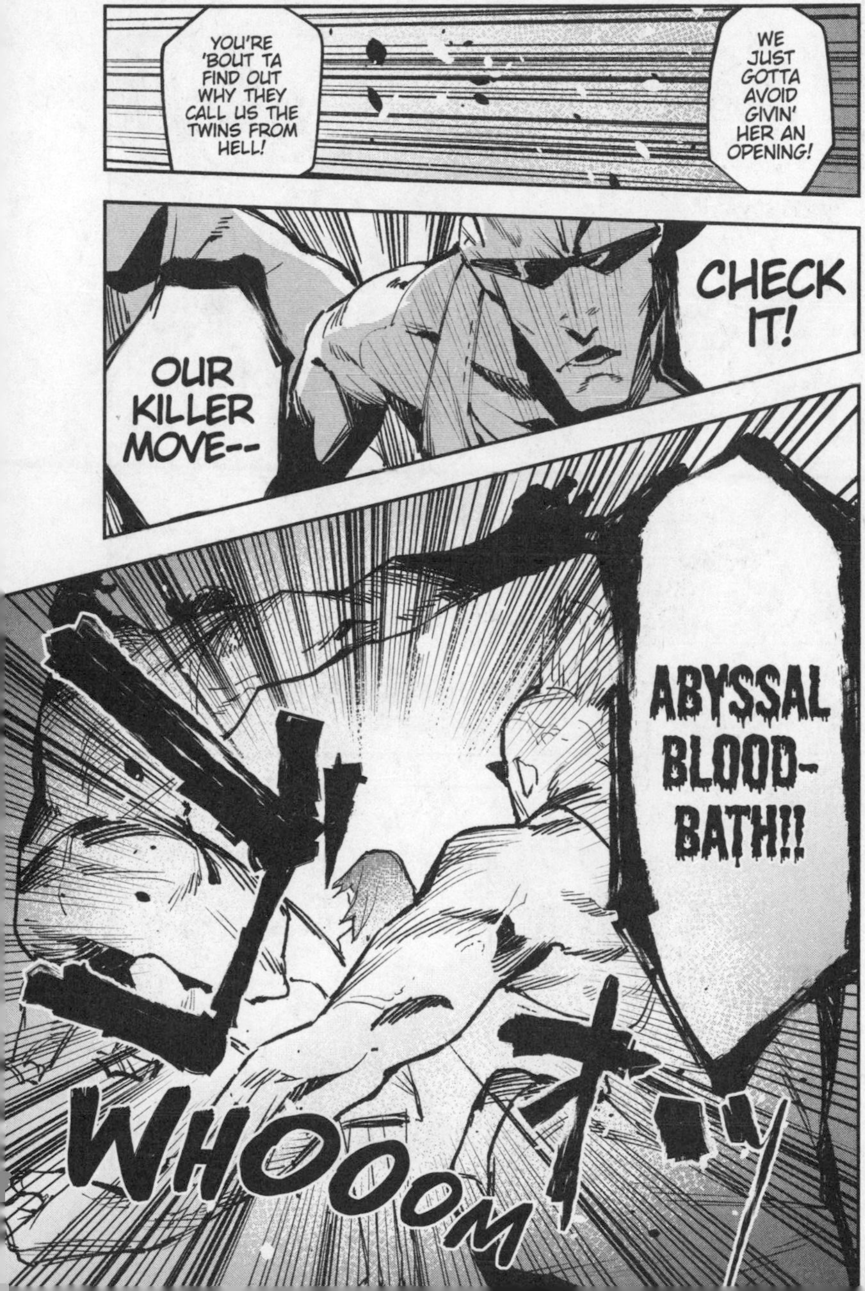
WE JUST GOTTA AVOID GIVIN' HER AN OPENING!
YOU'RE 'BOUT TA FIND OUT WHY THEY CALL US THE TWINS FROM HELL!
CHECK IT!
OUR KILLER MOVE--
ABYSSAL BLOOD-BATH!!
WHOOOOM

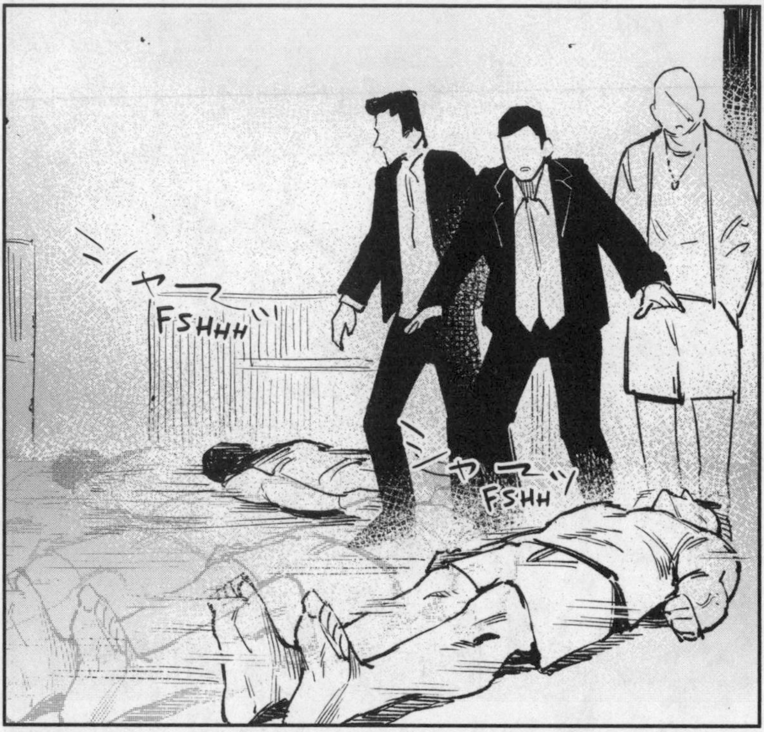
FSHHH
FSHH

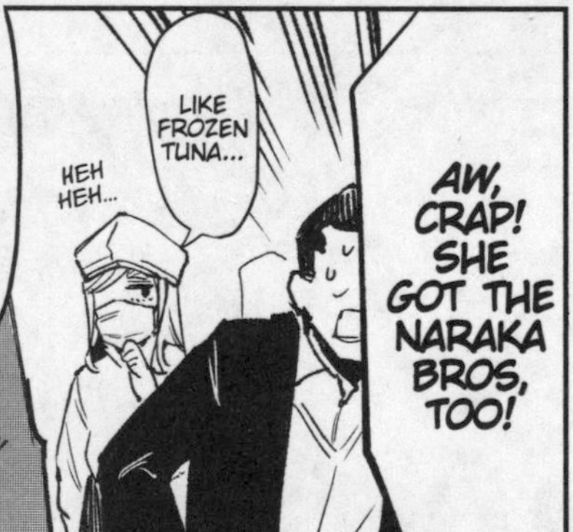
AW, CRAP! SHE GOT THE NARAKA BROS, TOO!
LIKE FROZEN TUNA...
HEH HEH...

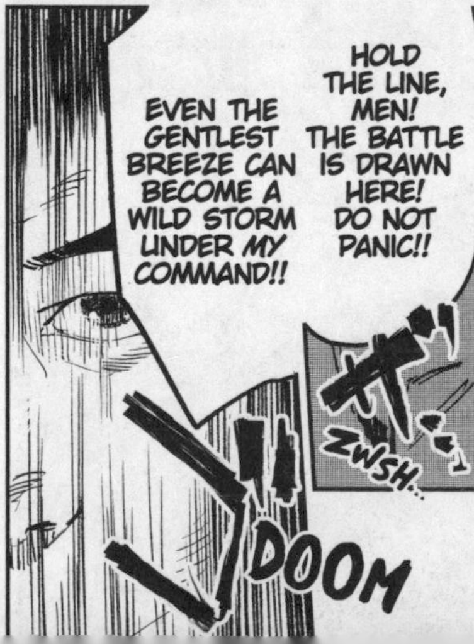
HOLD THE LINE, MEN! THE BATTLE IS DRAWN HERE! DO NOT PANIC!!
EVEN THE GENTLEST BREEZE CAN BECOME A WILD STORM UNDER MY COMMAND!!
ZWSH...
DOOM

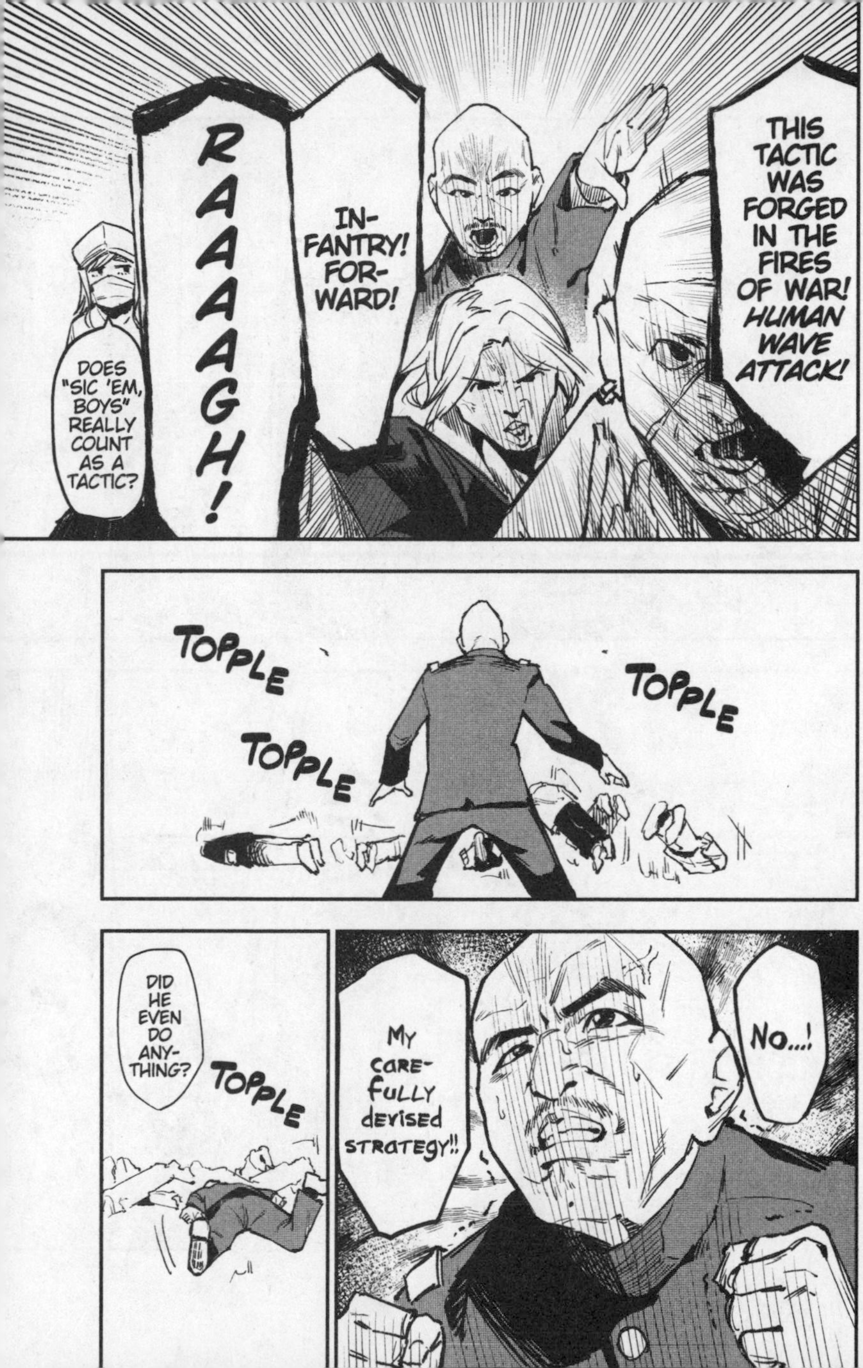
THIS TACTIC WAS FORGED IN THE FIRES OF WAR! HUMAN WAVE ATTACK!
IN-FANTRY! FOR-WARD!
RAAAAGH!
DOES "SIC 'EM, BOYS" REALLY COUNT AS A TACTIC?
TOPPLE
TOPPLE
TOPPLE
No...!
My care-fully devised strategy!!
DID HE EVEN DO ANY-THING?
TOPPLE

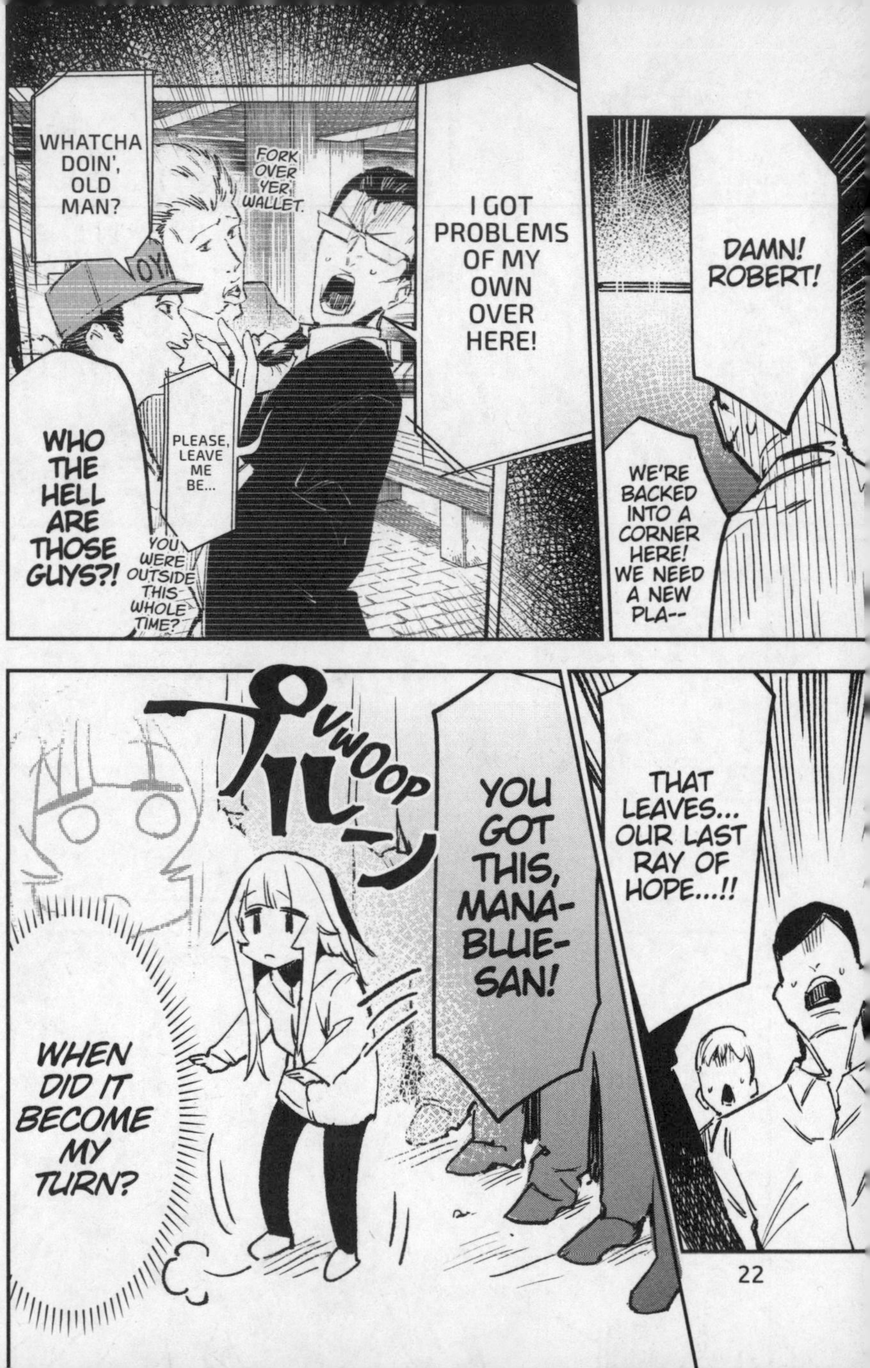
DAMN! ROBERT!
WE'RE BACKED INTO A CORNER HERE! WE NEED A NEW PLA--
I GOT PROBLEMS OF MY OWN OVER HERE!
FORK OVER YER WALLET.
WHATCHA DOIN', OLD MAN?
PLEASE, LEAVE ME BE...
WHO THE HELL ARE THOSE GUYS?!
YOU WERE OUTSIDE THIS WHOLE TIME?
THAT LEAVES... OUR LAST RAY OF HOPE...!!
YOU GOT THIS, MANA-BLUE-SAN!
VWOOP
WHEN DID IT BECOME MY TURN?

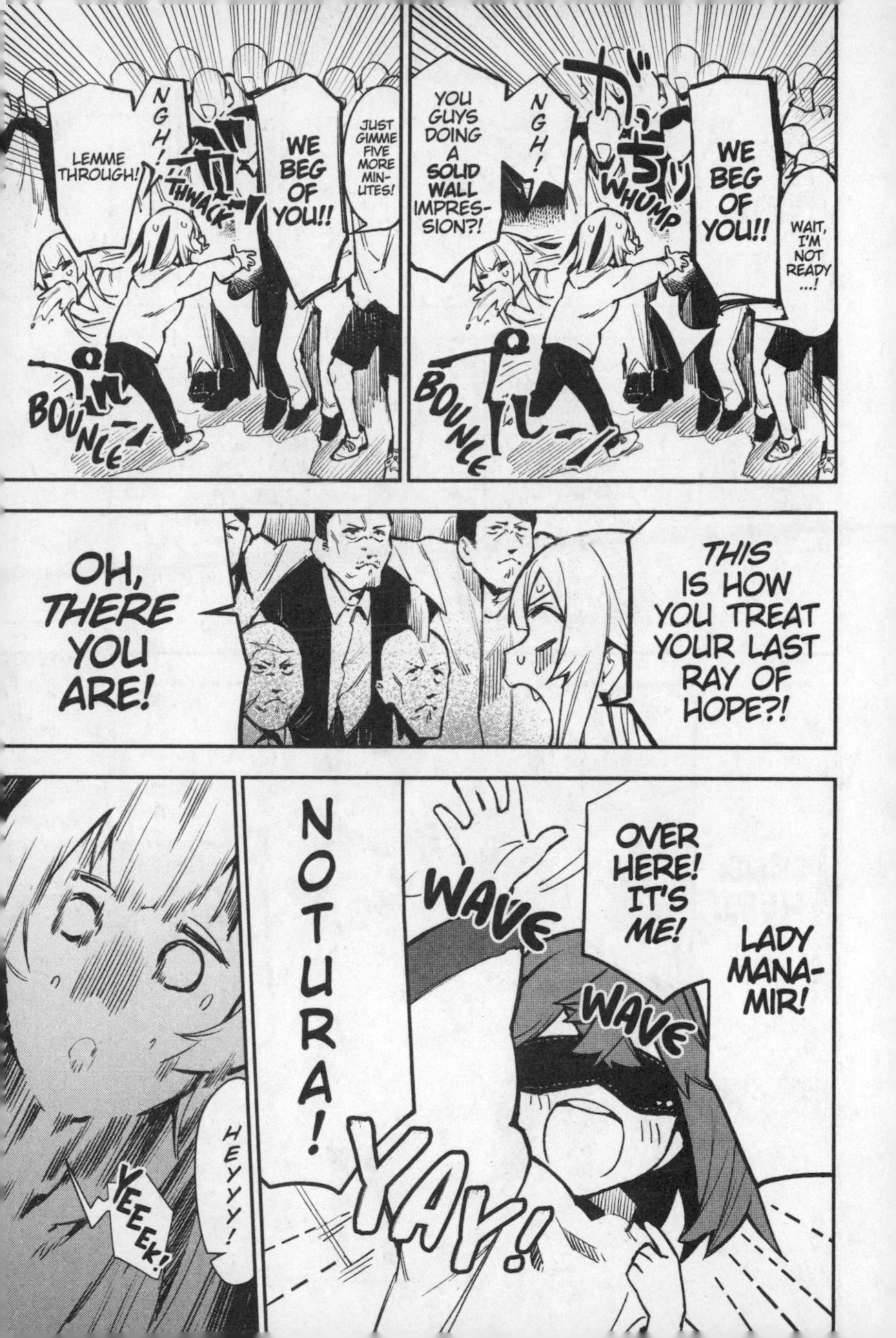
WE BEG OF YOU!!
WAIT, I'M NOT READY...!
WHUMP
NGH!
YOU GUYS DOING A SOLID WALL IMPRESSION?!
BOUNCE
JUST GIMME FIVE MORE MIN-UTES!
WE BEG OF YOU!!
NGH!
THWACK
LEMME THROUGH!
BOUNCE
THIS IS HOW YOU TREAT YOUR LAST RAY OF HOPE?!
OH, THERE YOU ARE!
OVER HERE! IT'S ME!
LADY MANA-MIR!
WAVE
WAVE
NOTURA!
YAY!
HEYYY!
YEEEK!

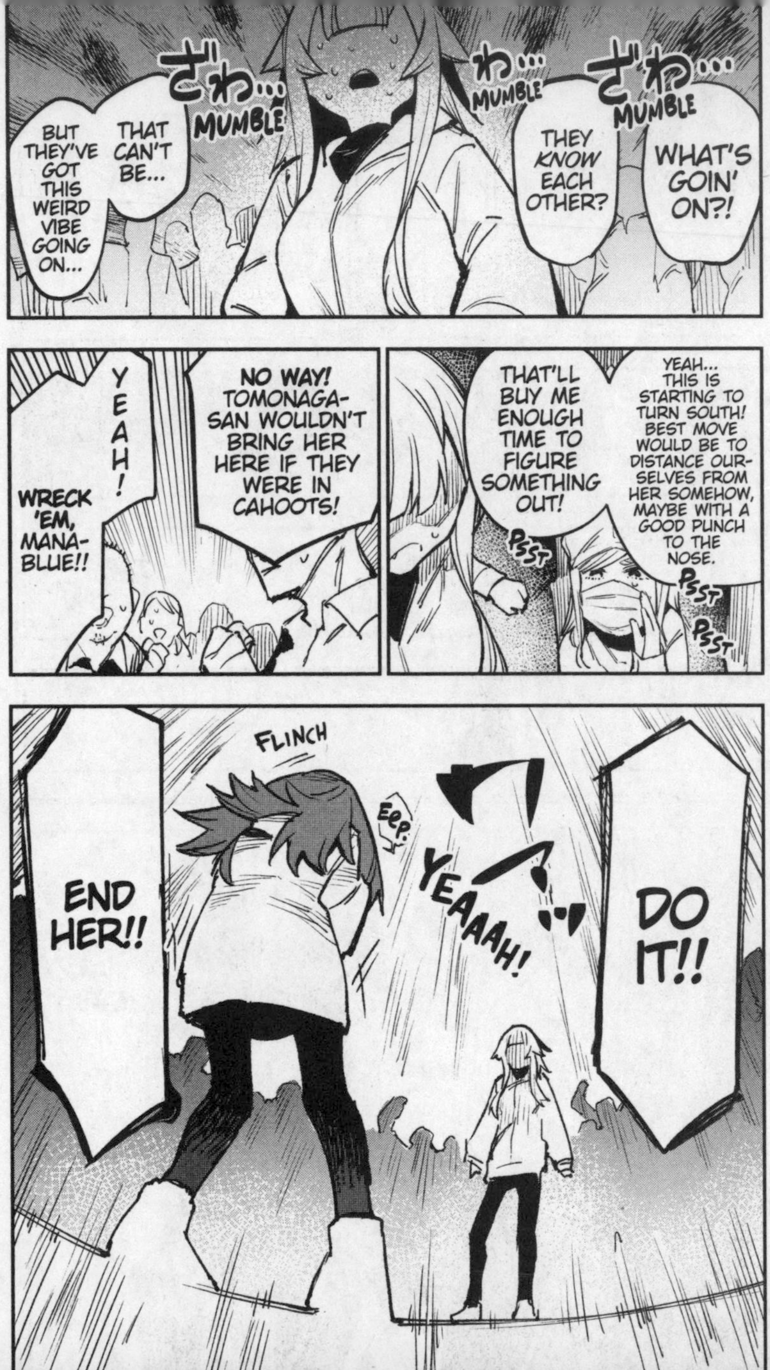

ざわ…
MUMBLE
WHAT'S GOIN' ON?!
わ…
MUMBLE
THEY KNOW EACH OTHER?
ざわ…
MUMBLE
THAT CAN'T BE...
BUT THEY'VE GOT THIS WEIRD VIBE GOING ON...
YEAH... THIS IS STARTING TO TURN SOUTH! BEST MOVE WOULD BE TO DISTANCE OUR-SELVES FROM HER SOMEHOW, MAYBE WITH A GOOD PUNCH TO THE NOSE.
PSST PSST
THAT'LL BUY ME ENOUGH TIME TO FIGURE SOMETHING OUT!
PSST
NO WAY! TOMONAGA-SAN WOULDN'T BRING HER HERE IF THEY WERE IN CAHOOTS!
YEAH!
WRECK 'EM, MANA-BLUE!!
DO IT!!
YEAAAAH!
EEP!
FLINCH
END HER!!

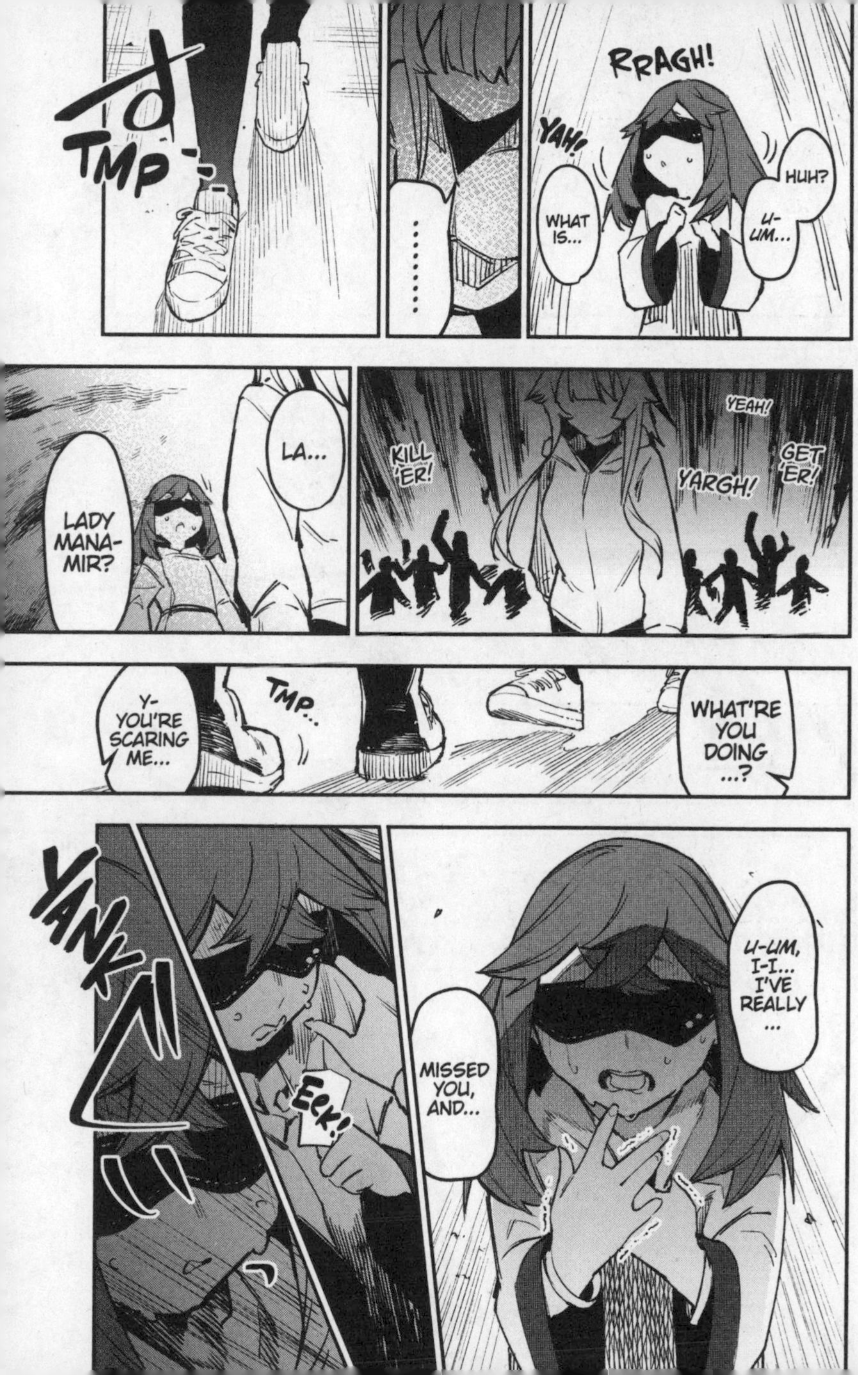
RRAGH!
HUH?
U-UM...
YAH!
WHAT IS...
....
TMP
YEAH!
GET 'ER!
YARGH!
KILL 'ER!
LA...
LADY MANAMIR?
WHAT'RE YOU DOING ...?
TMP...
Y-YOU'RE SCARING ME...
U-UM, I-I... I'VE REALLY ...
MISSED YOU, AND...
EEK!
YANK

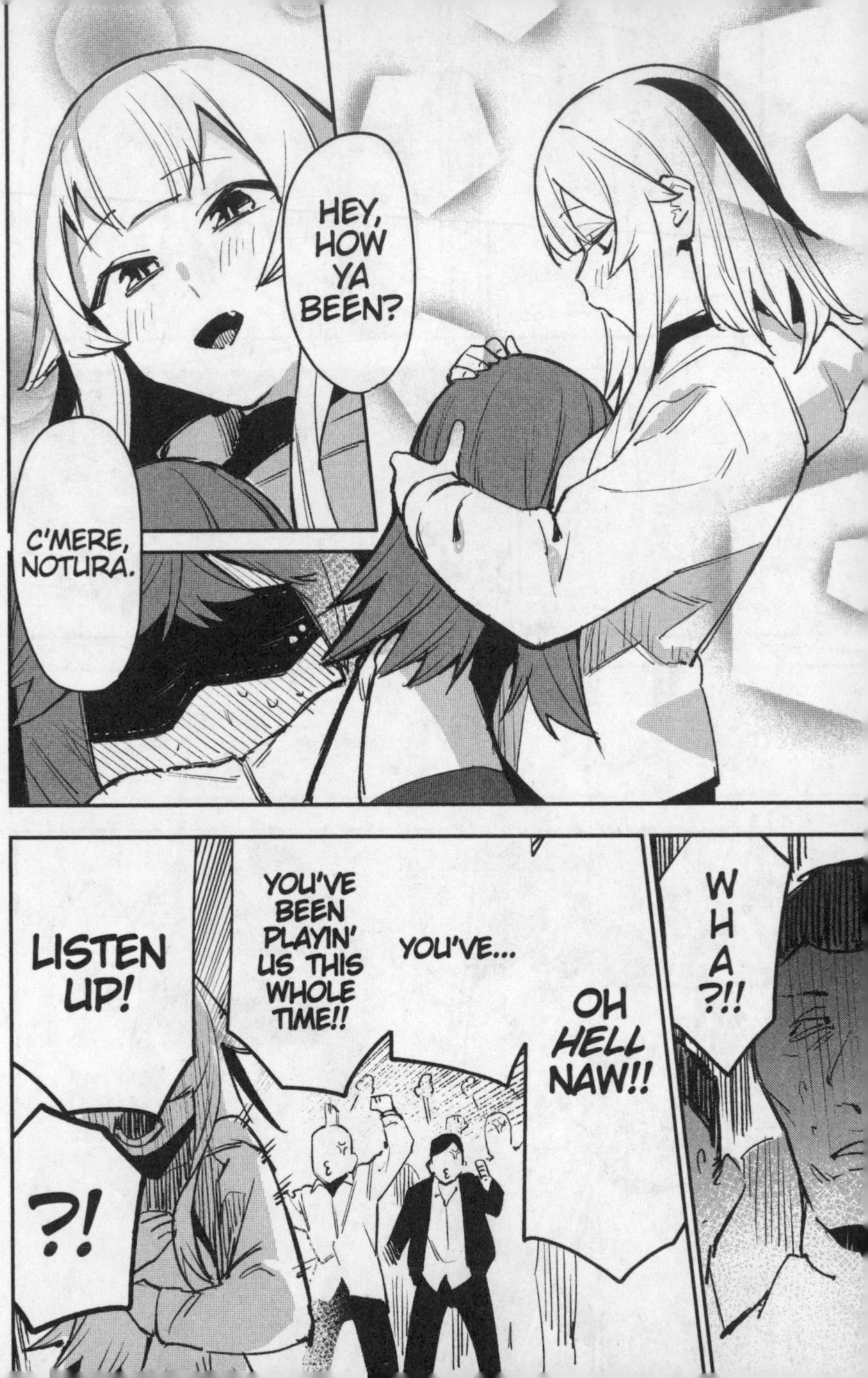
HEY, HOW YA BEEN?
C'MERE, NOTURA.
WHA?!!
OH HELL NAW!!
YOU'VE...
YOU'VE BEEN PLAYIN' US THIS WHOLE TIME!!
LISTEN UP!
?!

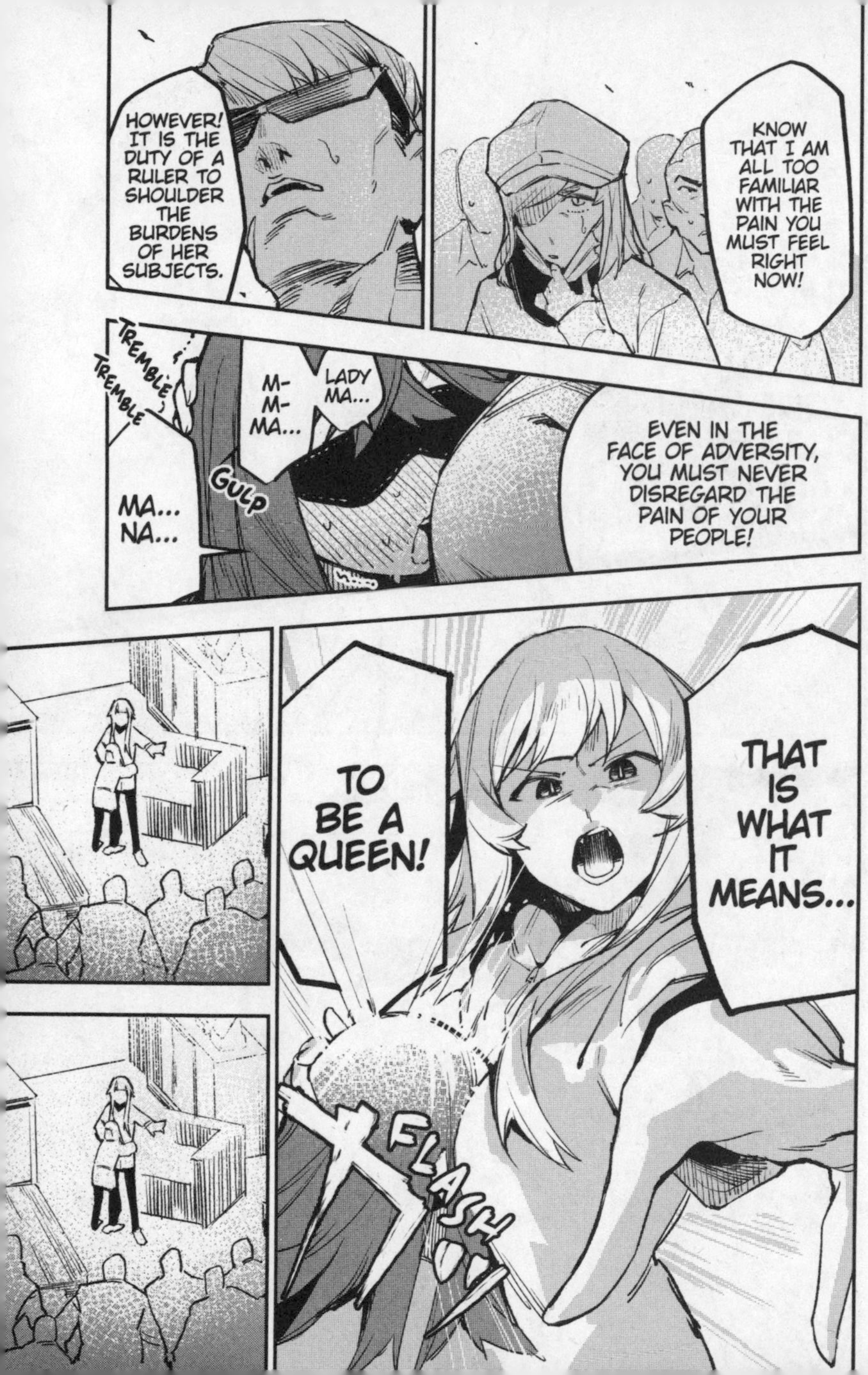
KNOW THAT I AM ALL TOO FAMILIAR WITH THE PAIN YOU MUST FEEL RIGHT NOW!
HOWEVER! IT IS THE DUTY OF A RULER TO SHOULDER THE BURDENS OF HER SUBJECTS.
EVEN IN THE FACE OF ADVERSITY, YOU MUST NEVER DISREGARD THE PAIN OF YOUR PEOPLE!
LADY MA...
M- M- MA...
TREMBLE
TREMBLE
GULP
MA... NA...
THAT IS WHAT IT MEANS...
TO BE A QUEEN!
FLASH

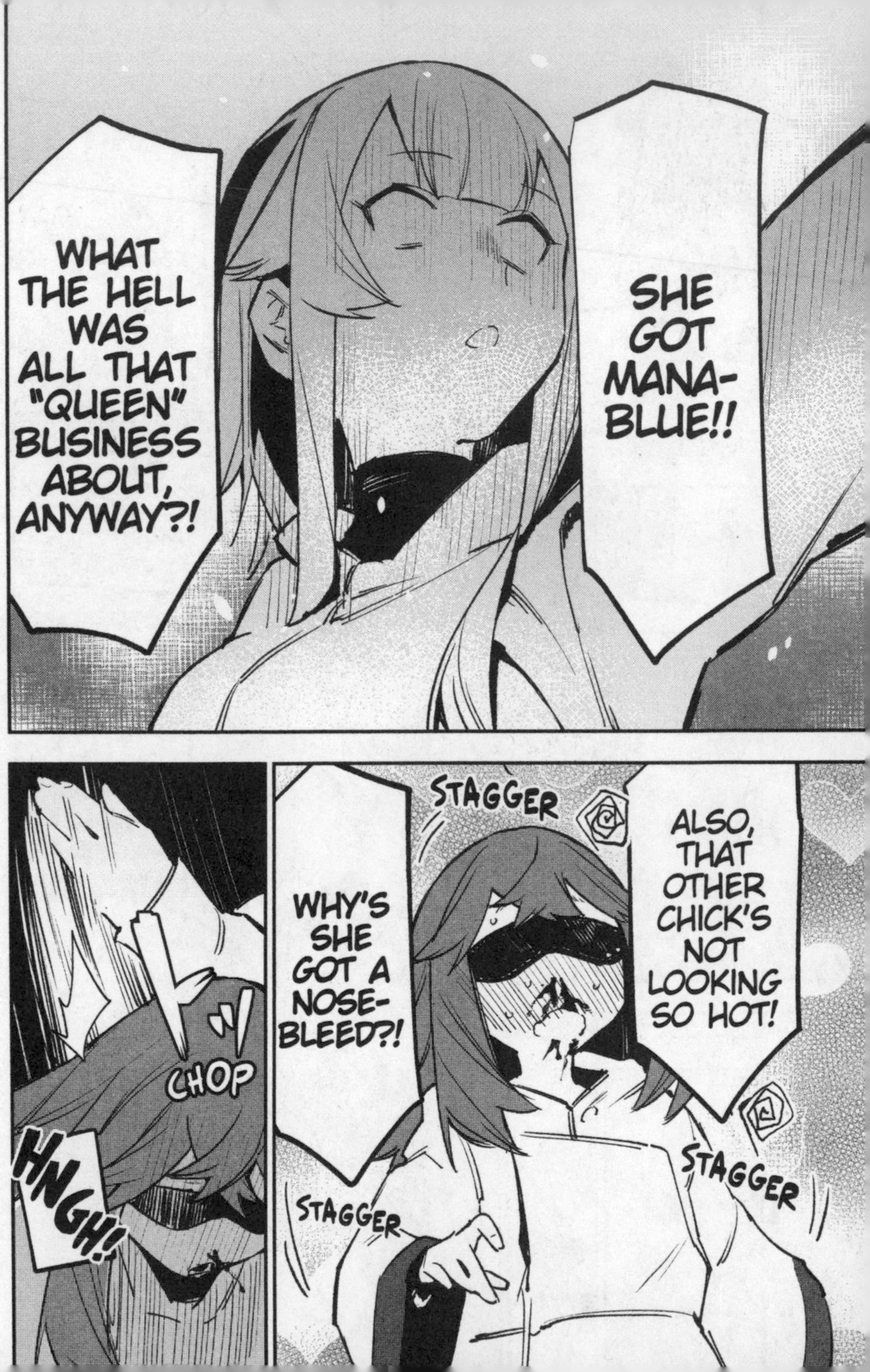
SHE GOT MANA-BLUE!!
WHAT THE HELL WAS ALL THAT "QUEEN" BUSINESS ABOUT, ANYWAY?!
ALSO, THAT OTHER CHICK'S NOT LOOKING SO HOT!
STAGGER
WHY'S SHE GOT A NOSE-BLEED?!
STAGGER
STAGGER
CHOP
HNGH!

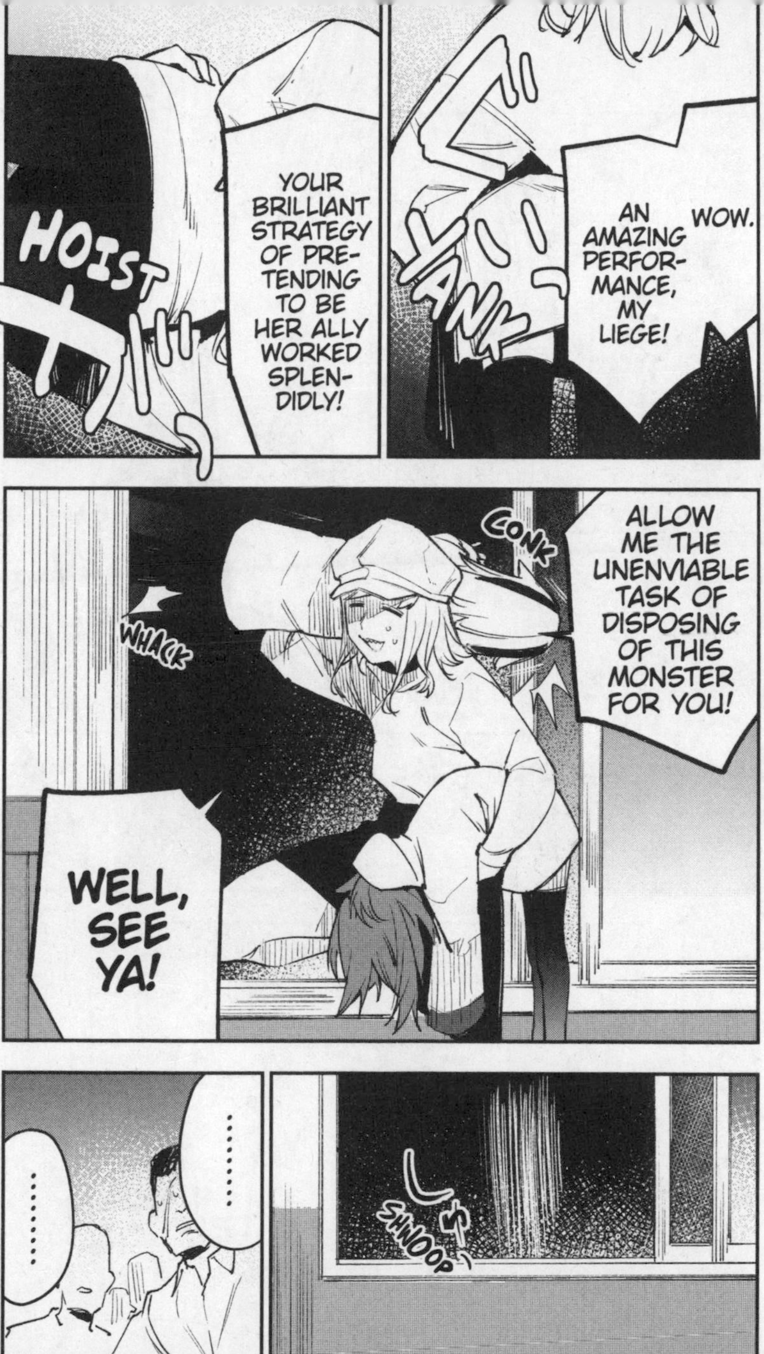
WOW.
AN AMAZING PERFORMANCE, MY LIEGE!
YANK
YOUR BRILLIANT STRATEGY OF PRETENDING TO BE HER ALLY WORKED SPLENDIDLY!
HOIST
ALLOW ME THE UNENVIABLE TASK OF DISPOSING OF THIS MONSTER FOR YOU!
CONK
WHACK
WELL, SEE YA!
SHNOOP
......
......

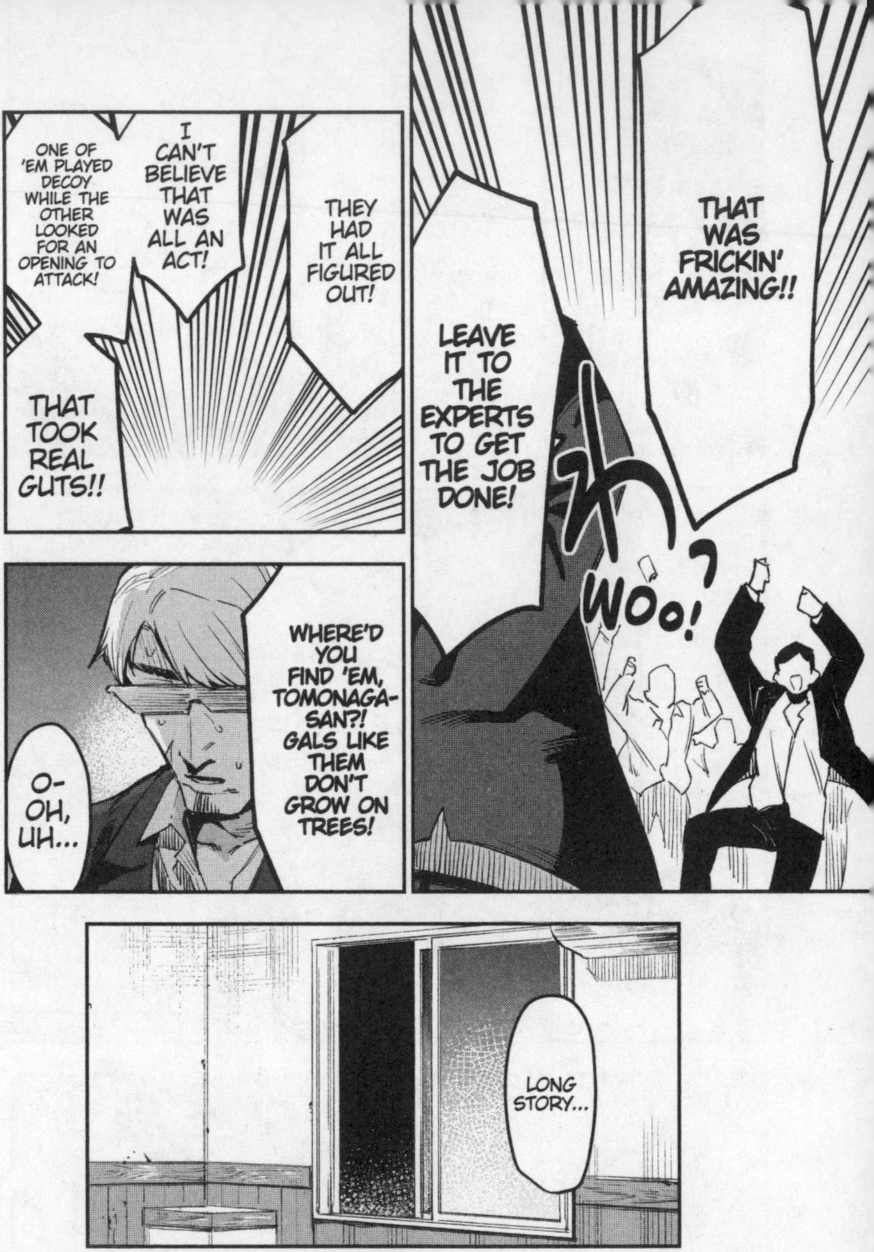
THAT WAS FRICKIN' AMAZING!!
LEAVE IT TO THE EXPERTS TO GET THE JOB DONE!
WOO!
THEY HAD IT ALL FIGURED OUT!
I CAN'T BELIEVE THAT WAS ALL AN ACT!
ONE OF 'EM PLAYED DECOY WHILE THE OTHER LOOKED FOR AN OPENING TO ATTACK!
THAT TOOK REAL GUTS!!
WHERE'D YOU FIND 'EM, TOMONAGA-SAN?! GALS LIKE THEM DON'T GROW ON TREES!
O-OH, UH...
LONG STORY...

12TH NIGHT - **END**

The variety of yakuza dudes I can draw is pretty small, so I watched some yakuza movies for inspiration.

There was even less variety in the movies.

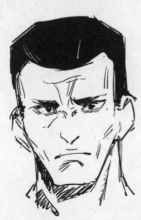

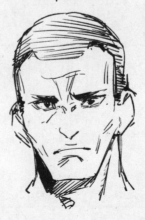

It's Just Not My Night!

Tale of a Fallen Vampire Queen

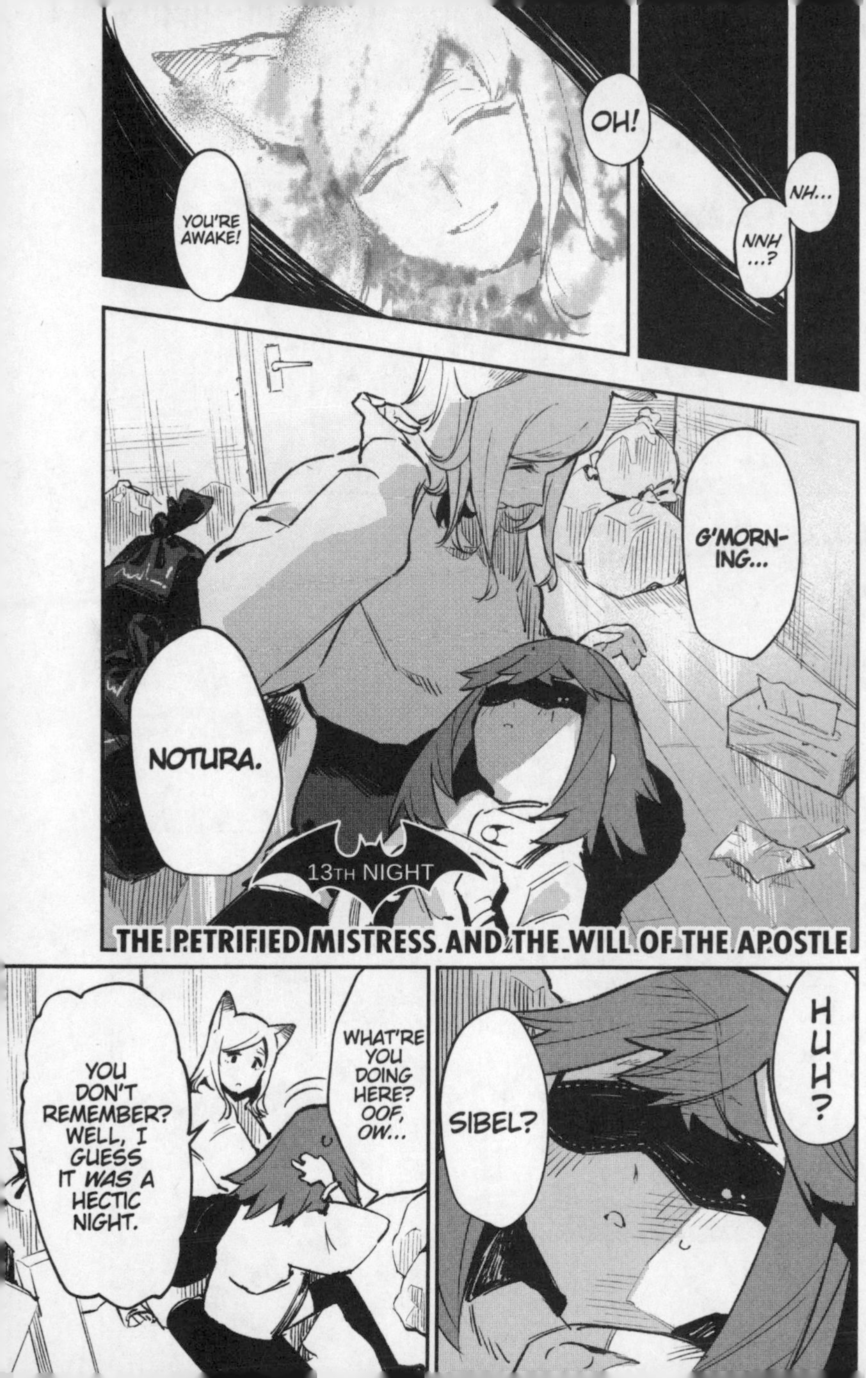
NH...
NNH ...?
OH!
YOU'RE AWAKE!
G'MORNING...
NOTURA.
13TH NIGHT
THE PETRIFIED MISTRESS AND THE WILL OF THE APOSTLE
HUH?
SIBEL?
WHAT'RE YOU DOING HERE? OOF, OW...
YOU DON'T REMEMBER? WELL, I GUESS IT WAS A HECTIC NIGHT.

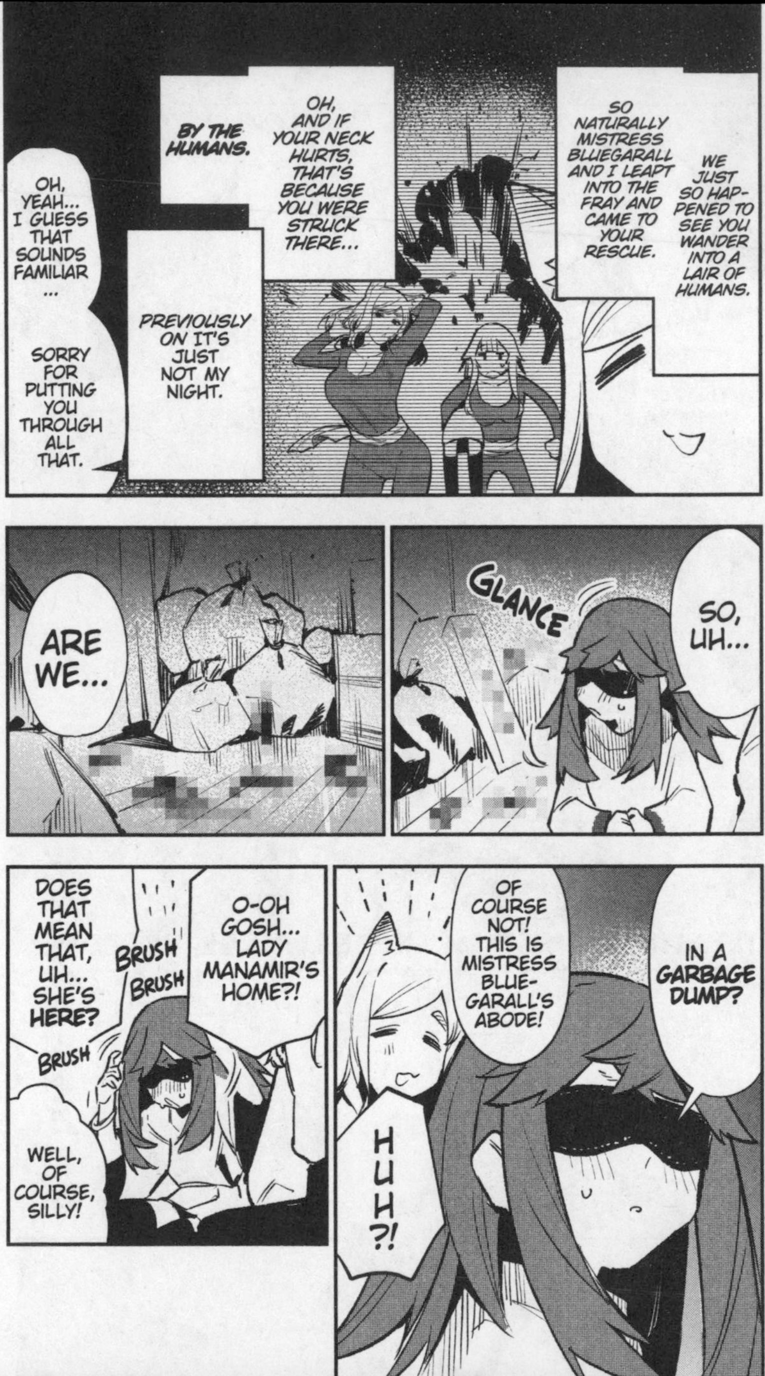
WE JUST SO HAPPENED TO SEE YOU WANDER INTO A LAIR OF HUMANS.
SO NATURALLY MISTRESS BLUEGARALL AND I LEAPT INTO THE FRAY AND CAME TO YOUR RESCUE.
OH, AND IF YOUR NECK HURTS, THAT'S BECAUSE YOU WERE STRUCK THERE...
BY THE HUMANS.
PREVIOUSLY ON IT'S JUST NOT MY NIGHT.
OH, YEAH... I GUESS THAT SOUNDS FAMILIAR ...
SORRY FOR PUTTING YOU THROUGH ALL THAT.
SO, UH...
GLANCE
ARE WE...
IN A GARBAGE DUMP?
HUH?!
OF COURSE NOT! THIS IS MISTRESS BLUE-GARALL'S ABODE!
O-OH GOSH... LADY MANAMIR'S HOME?!
DOES THAT MEAN THAT, UH... SHE'S HERE?
BRUSH
BRUSH
BRUSH
WELL, OF COURSE, SILLY!

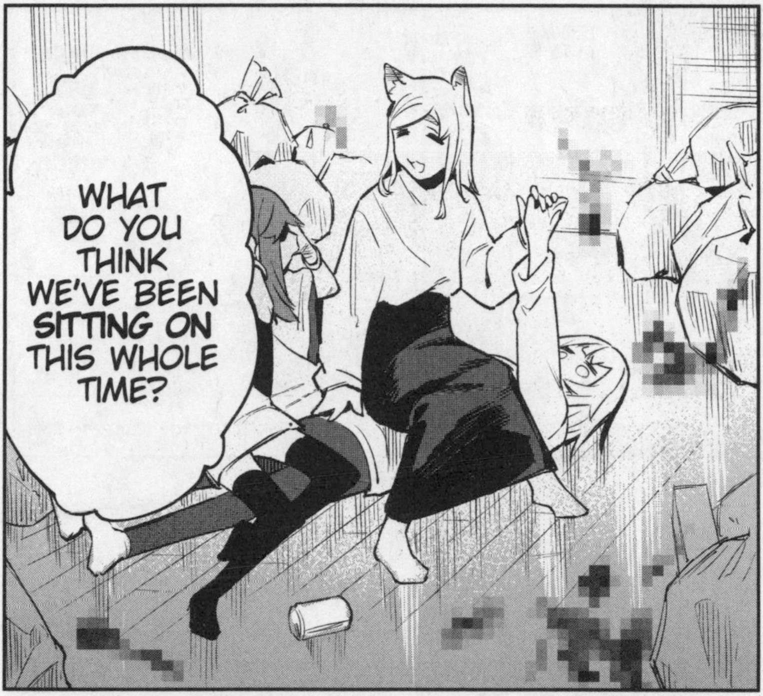
WHAT DO YOU THINK WE'VE BEEN SITTING ON THIS WHOLE TIME?

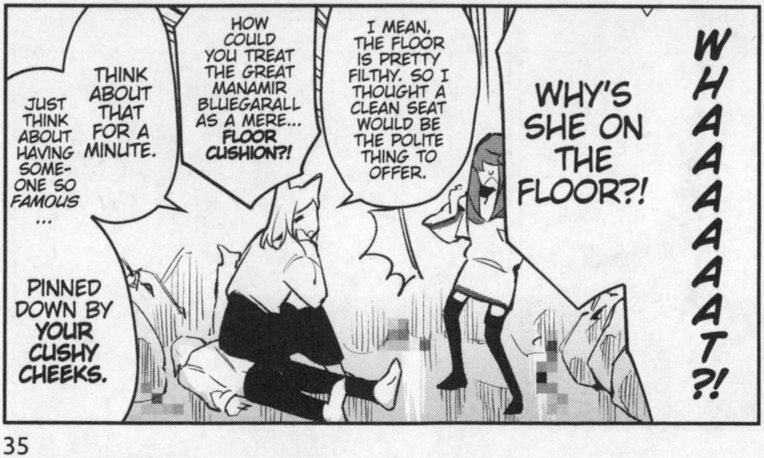
WHAAAAAAAT?!
WHY'S SHE ON THE FLOOR?!
I MEAN, THE FLOOR IS PRETTY FILTHY. SO I THOUGHT A CLEAN SEAT WOULD BE THE POLITE THING TO OFFER.
HOW COULD YOU TREAT THE GREAT MANAMIR BLUEGARALL AS A MERE... FLOOR CUSHION?!
THINK ABOUT THAT FOR A MINUTE.
JUST THINK ABOUT HAVING SOME-ONE SO FAMOUS ...
PINNED DOWN BY YOUR CUSHY CHEEKS.

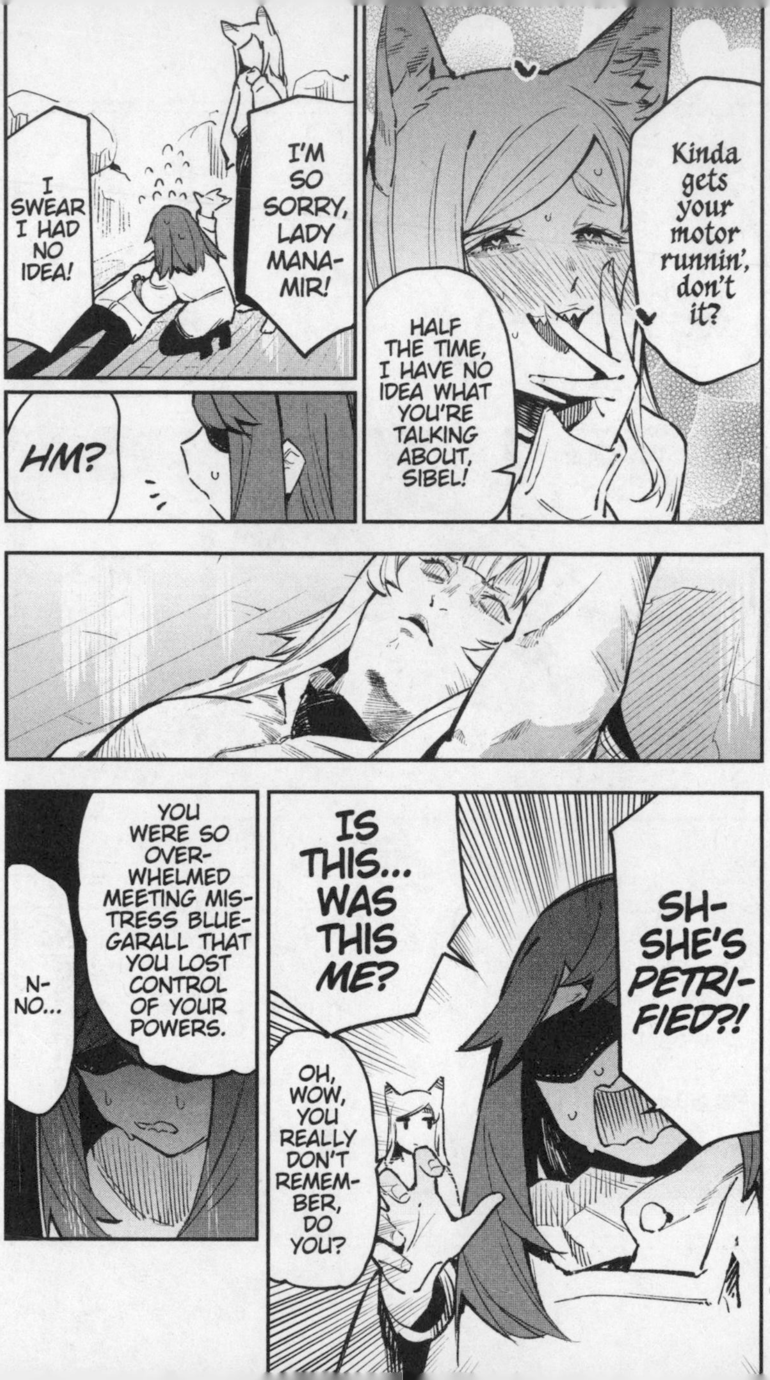

Kinda gets your motor runnin', don't it?
HALF THE TIME, I HAVE NO IDEA WHAT YOU'RE TALKING ABOUT, SIBEL!
I'M SO SORRY, LADY MANAMIR!
I SWEAR I HAD NO IDEA!
HM?
SH-SHE'S PETRIFIED?!
IS THIS... WAS THIS ME?
OH, WOW, YOU REALLY DON'T REMEMBER, DO YOU?
YOU WERE SO OVERWHELMED MEETING MISTRESS BLUEGARALL THAT YOU LOST CONTROL OF YOUR POWERS.
N-NO...

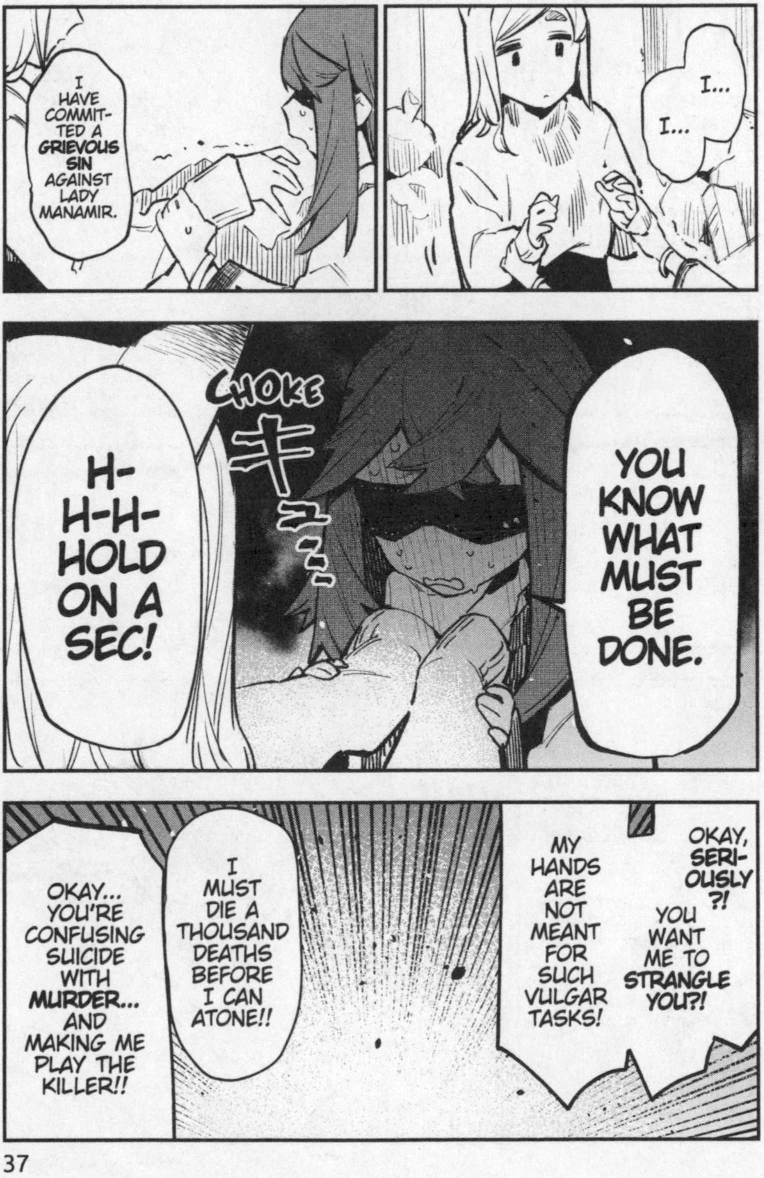
I...
I...
I HAVE COMMITTED A GRIEVOUS SIN AGAINST LADY MANAMIR.
YOU KNOW WHAT MUST BE DONE.
CHOKE
キュ
H-H-H-HOLD ON A SEC!
OKAY, SERIOUSLY?!
YOU WANT ME TO STRANGLE YOU?!
MY HANDS ARE NOT MEANT FOR SUCH VULGAR TASKS!
I MUST DIE A THOUSAND DEATHS BEFORE I CAN ATONE!!
OKAY... YOU'RE CONFUSING SUICIDE WITH MURDER... AND MAKING ME PLAY THE KILLER!!

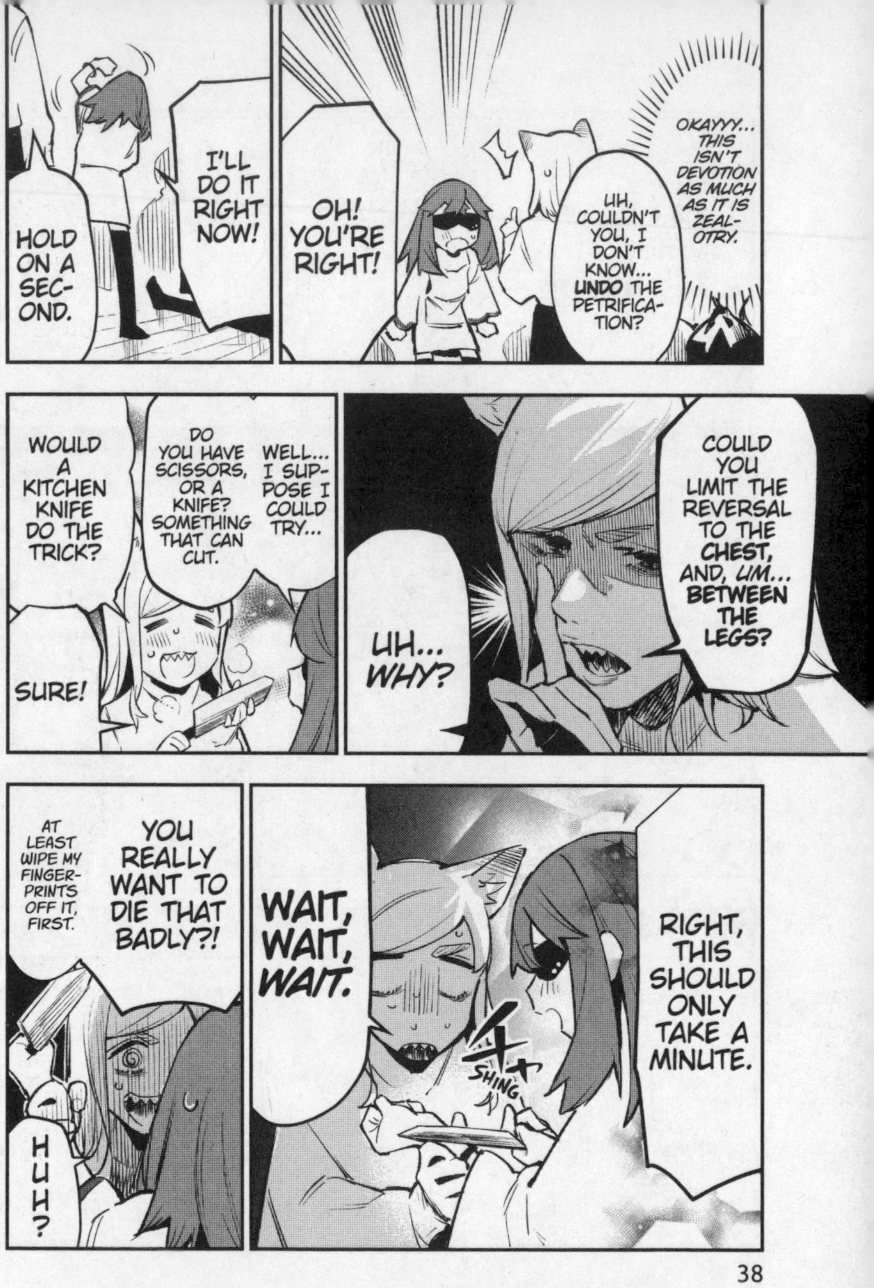
OKAYYY... THIS ISN'T DEVOTION AS MUCH AS IT IS ZEAL-OTRY.
UH, COULDN'T YOU, I DON'T KNOW... **UNDO** THE PETRIFICA-TION?
OH! YOU'RE RIGHT!
I'LL DO IT RIGHT NOW!
HOLD ON A SEC-OND.
COULD YOU LIMIT THE REVERSAL TO THE **CHEST,** AND, *UM...* **BETWEEN THE LEGS?**
UH... *WHY?*
WELL... I SUP-POSE I COULD TRY...
DO YOU HAVE SCISSORS, OR A KNIFE? SOMETHING THAT CAN CUT.
WOULD A KITCHEN KNIFE DO THE TRICK?
SURE!
RIGHT, THIS SHOULD ONLY TAKE A MINUTE.
SHING
WAIT, WAIT, *WAIT.*
YOU REALLY WANT TO DIE THAT BADLY?!
AT LEAST WIPE MY FINGER-PRINTS OFF IT, FIRST.
HUH?

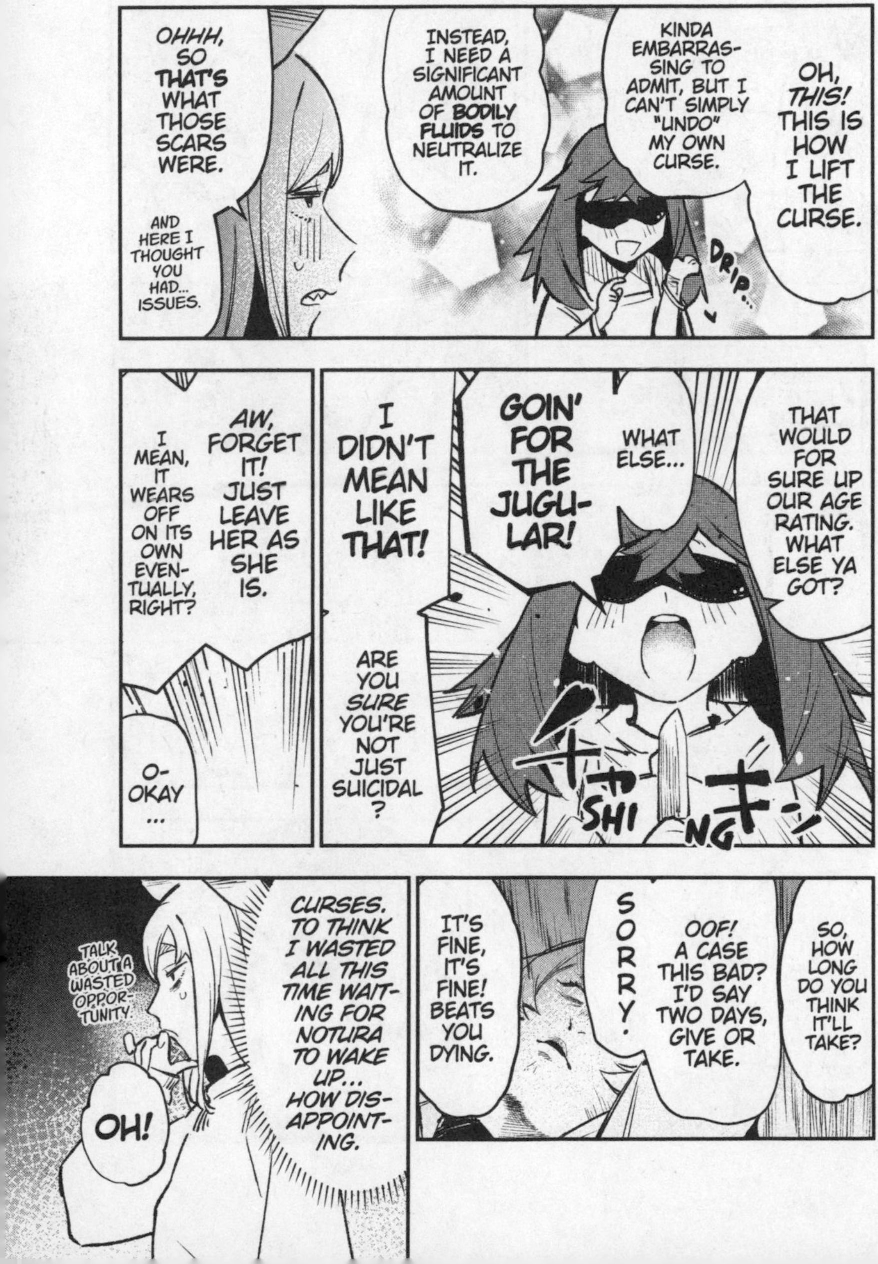

OH, THIS! THIS IS HOW I LIFT THE CURSE.
KINDA EMBARRASSING TO ADMIT, BUT I CAN'T SIMPLY "UNDO" MY OWN CURSE.
INSTEAD, I NEED A SIGNIFICANT AMOUNT OF BODILY FLUIDS TO NEUTRALIZE IT.
DRIP...
OHHH, SO THAT'S WHAT THOSE SCARS WERE.
AND HERE I THOUGHT YOU HAD... ISSUES.
THAT WOULD FOR SURE UP OUR AGE RATING. WHAT ELSE YA GOT?
WHAT ELSE...
GOIN' FOR THE JUGULAR!
I DIDN'T MEAN LIKE THAT!
SHING
ARE YOU SURE YOU'RE NOT JUST SUICIDAL?
AW, FORGET IT! JUST LEAVE HER AS SHE IS.
I MEAN, IT WEARS OFF ON ITS OWN EVENTUALLY, RIGHT?
O-OKAY...
SO, HOW LONG DO YOU THINK IT'LL TAKE?
OOF! A CASE THIS BAD? I'D SAY TWO DAYS, GIVE OR TAKE.
SORRY.
IT'S FINE, IT'S FINE! BEATS YOU DYING.
CURSES. TO THINK I WASTED ALL THIS TIME WAITING FOR NOTURA TO WAKE UP... HOW DISAPPOINTING.
TALK ABOUT A WASTED OPPORTUNITY.
OH!

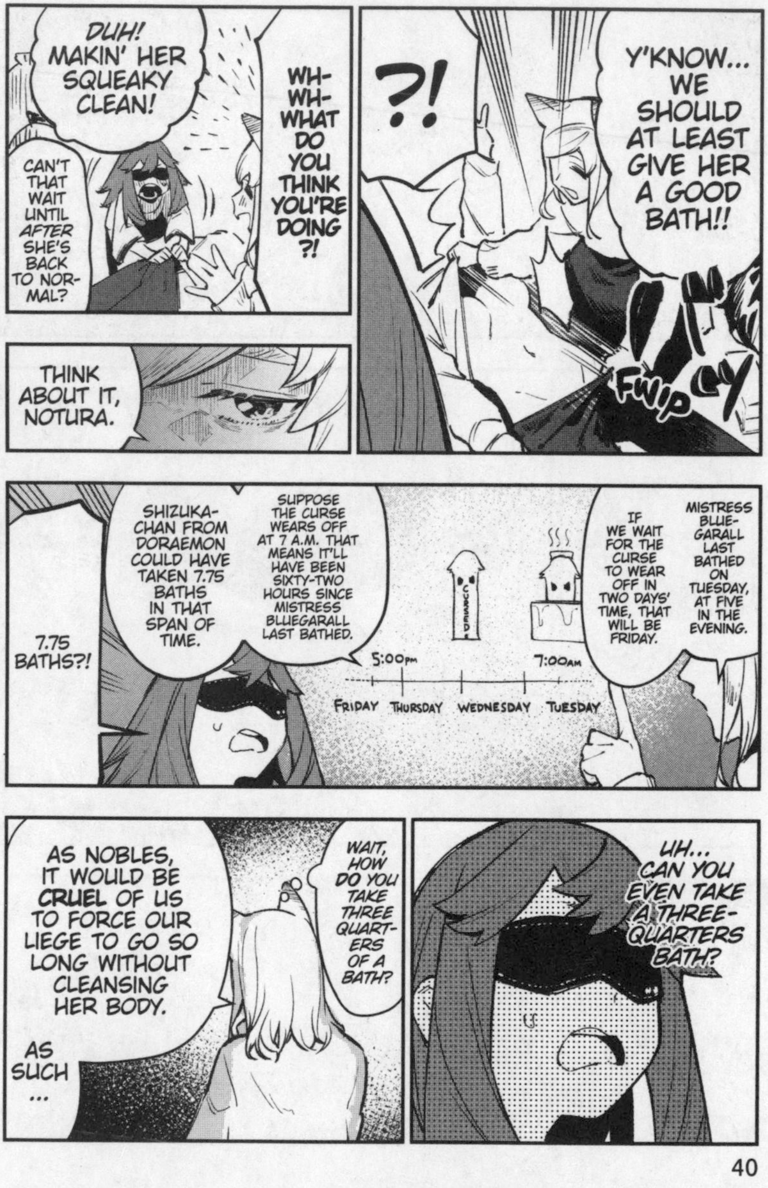
Y'KNOW... WE SHOULD AT LEAST GIVE HER A GOOD BATH!!
?!
FWIP
WH-WH-WHAT DO YOU THINK YOU'RE DOING?!
DUH! MAKIN' HER SQUEAKY CLEAN!
CAN'T THAT WAIT UNTIL AFTER SHE'S BACK TO NOR-MAL?
THINK ABOUT IT, NOTURA.
MISTRESS BLUE-GARALL LAST BATHED ON TUESDAY, AT FIVE IN THE EVENING.
IF WE WAIT FOR THE CURSE TO WEAR OFF IN TWO DAYS' TIME, THAT WILL BE FRIDAY.
CURSED
5:00PM
7:00AM
FRIDAY THURSDAY WEDNESDAY TUESDAY
SUPPOSE THE CURSE WEARS OFF AT 7 A.M. THAT MEANS IT'LL HAVE BEEN SIXTY-TWO HOURS SINCE MISTRESS BLUEGARALL LAST BATHED.
SHIZUKA-CHAN FROM DORAEMON COULD HAVE TAKEN 7.75 BATHS IN THAT SPAN OF TIME.
7.75 BATHS?!
UH... CAN YOU EVEN TAKE A THREE-QUARTERS BATH?
WAIT, HOW DO YOU TAKE THREE QUARTERS OF A BATH?
AS NOBLES, IT WOULD BE CRUEL OF US TO FORCE OUR LIEGE TO GO SO LONG WITHOUT CLEANSING HER BODY.
AS SUCH...

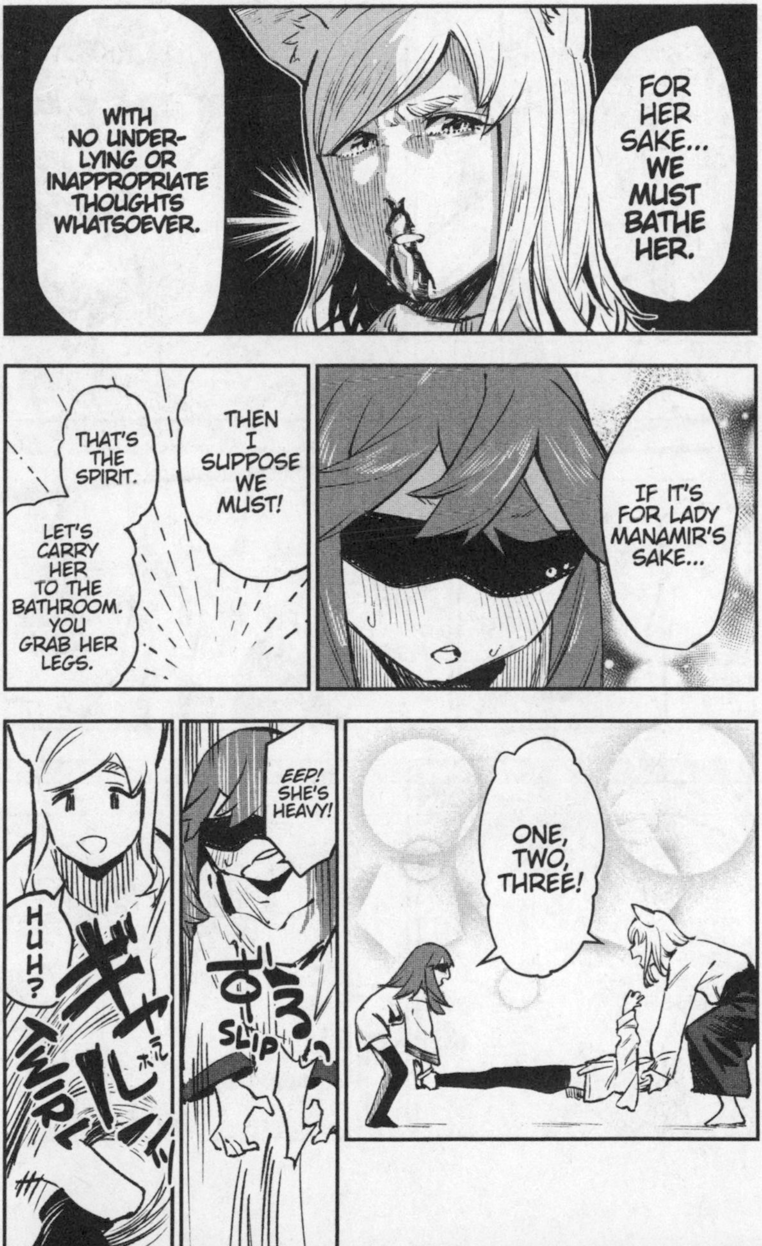
FOR HER SAKE... WE MUST BATHE HER.
WITH NO UNDER-LYING OR INAPPROPRIATE THOUGHTS WHATSOEVER.
IF IT'S FOR LADY MANAMIR'S SAKE...
THEN I SUPPOSE WE MUST!
THAT'S THE SPIRIT.
LET'S CARRY HER TO THE BATHROOM. YOU GRAB HER LEGS.
ONE, TWO, THREE!
EEP! SHE'S HEAVY!
SLIP
HUH?
TWIRL

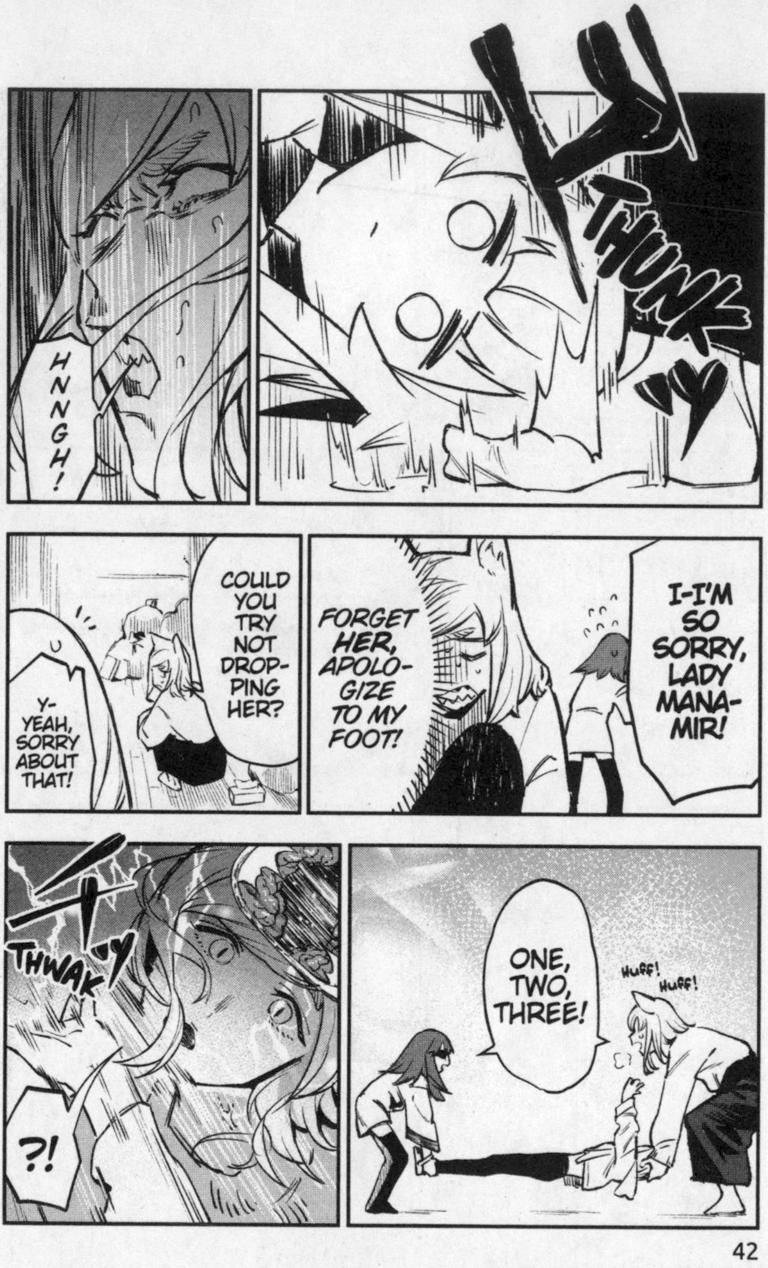
THUNK
HNNGH!
I-I'M SO SORRY, LADY MANA-MIR!
FORGET HER, APOLO-GIZE TO MY FOOT!
COULD YOU TRY NOT DROP-PING HER?
Y-YEAH, SORRY ABOUT THAT!
ONE, TWO, THREE!
Huff! Huff!
THWAK
?!

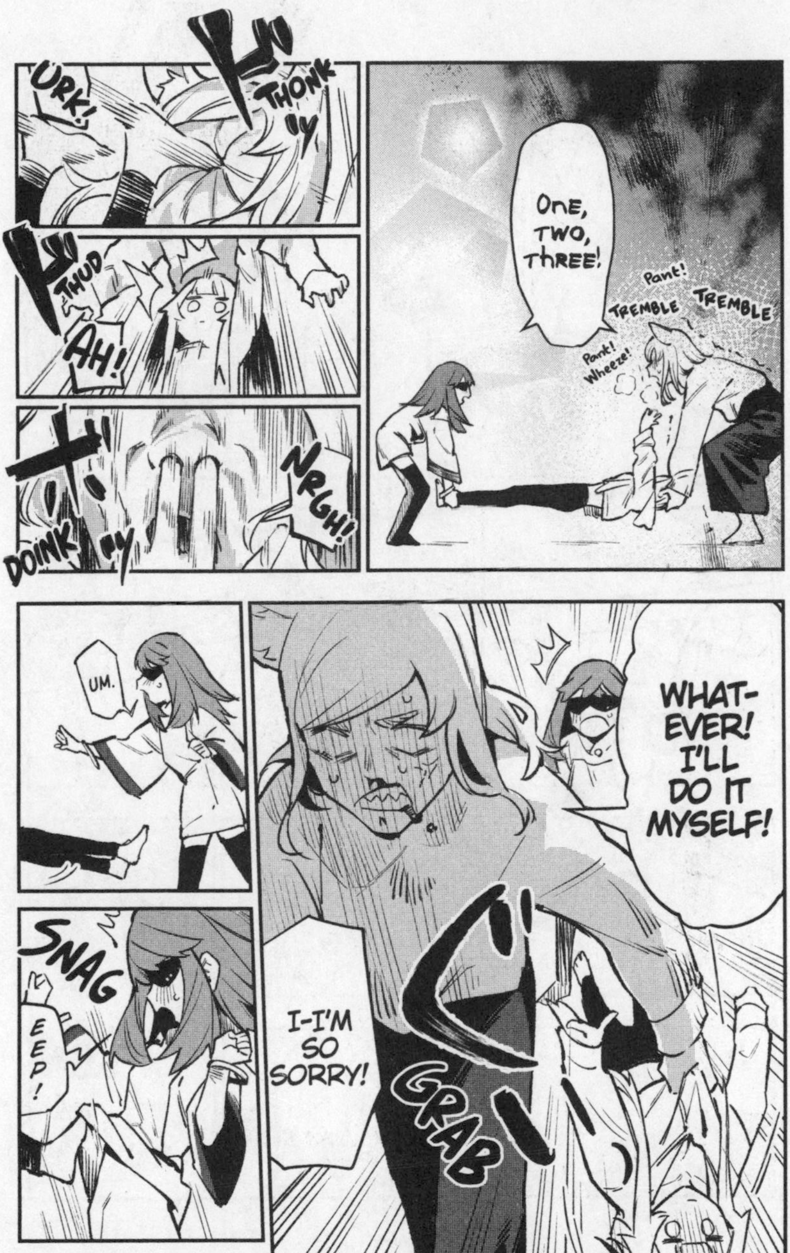

One, two, three!
Pant!
TREMBLE TREMBLE
Pant! Wheeze!
THONK
URK!
THUD
AH!
NRGH!
DOINK
WHAT-EVER! I'LL DO IT MYSELF!
I-I'M SO SORRY!
GRAB
UM.
SNAG
EEP!

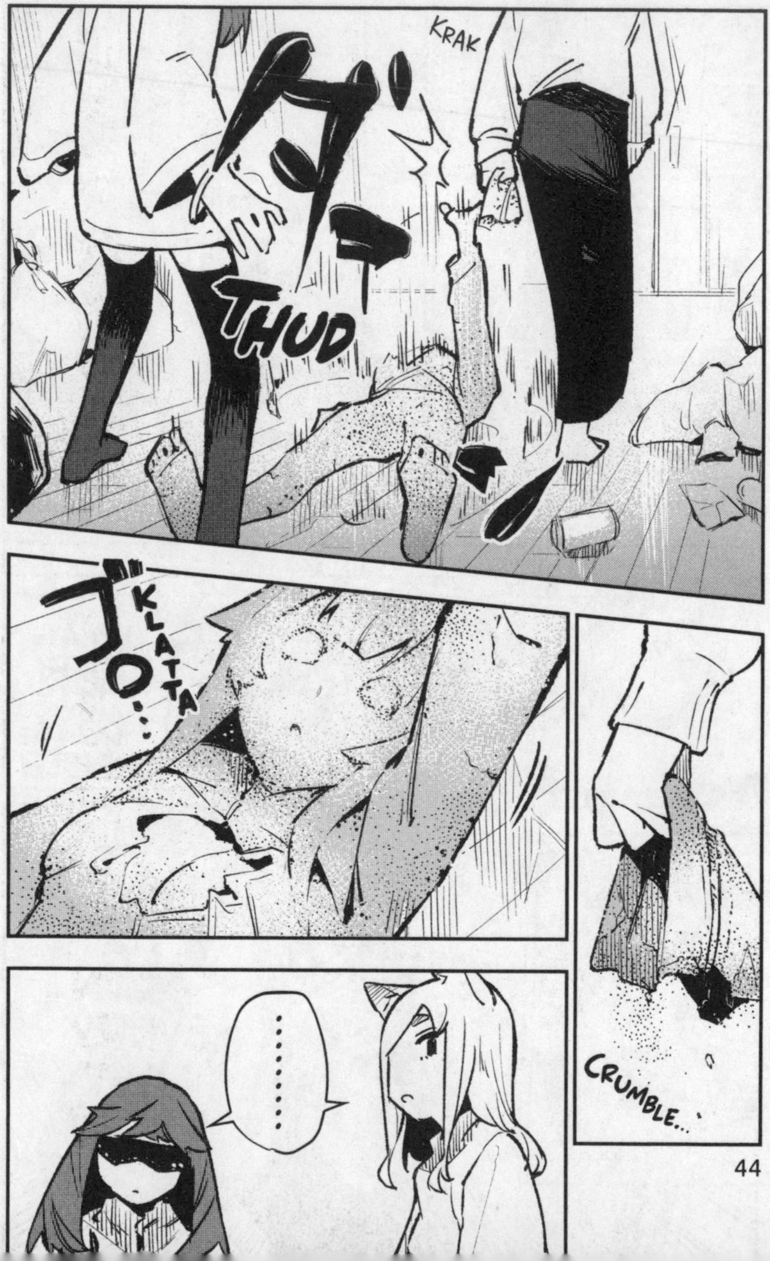
KRAK
THUD
CRUMBLE...
KLATTA
......

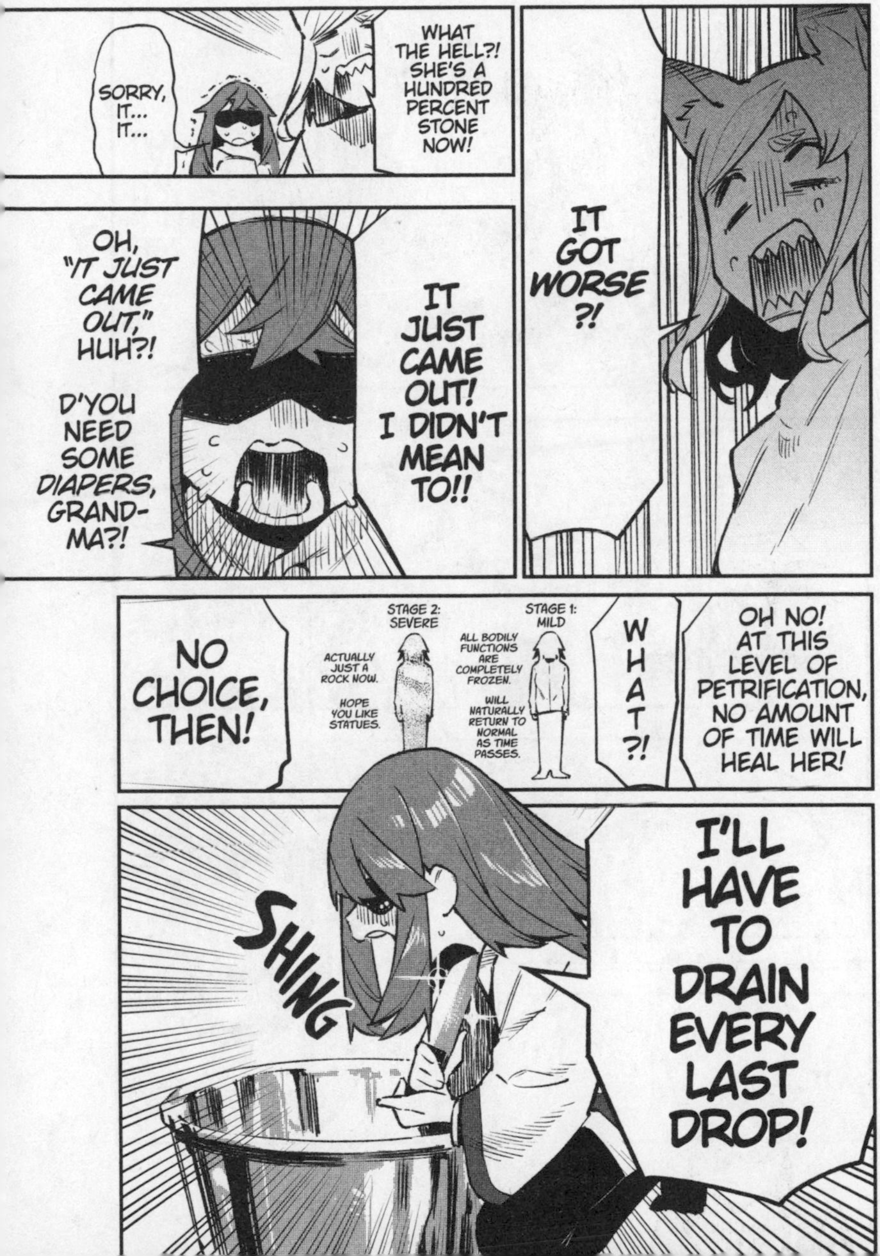
IT GOT WORSE?!
WHAT THE HELL?! SHE'S A HUNDRED PERCENT STONE NOW!
SORRY, IT... IT...
IT JUST CAME OUT! I DIDN'T MEAN TO!!
OH, "IT JUST CAME OUT," HUH?!
D'YOU NEED SOME DIAPERS, GRANDMA?!
OH NO! AT THIS LEVEL OF PETRIFICATION, NO AMOUNT OF TIME WILL HEAL HER!
WHAT?!
STAGE 1: MILD
ALL BODILY FUNCTIONS ARE COMPLETELY FROZEN.
WILL NATURALLY RETURN TO NORMAL AS TIME PASSES.
STAGE 2: SEVERE
ACTUALLY JUST A ROCK NOW.
HOPE YOU LIKE STATUES.
NO CHOICE, THEN!
I'LL HAVE TO DRAIN EVERY LAST DROP!
SHING

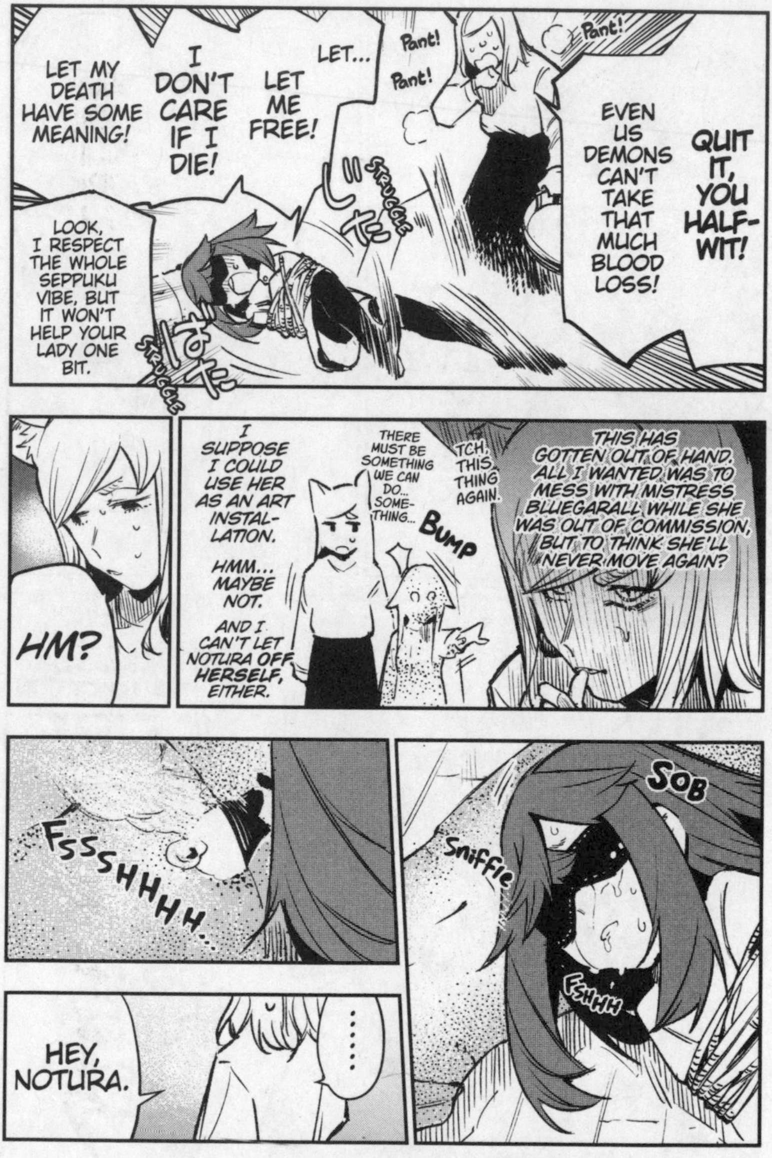
QUIT IT, YOU HALF-WIT!
EVEN US DEMONS CAN'T TAKE THAT MUCH BLOOD LOSS!
Pant!
Pant!
Pant!
LET...
LET ME FREE!
I DON'T CARE IF I DIE!
LET MY DEATH HAVE SOME MEANING!
STRUGGLE
LOOK, I RESPECT THE WHOLE SEPPUKU VIBE, BUT IT WON'T HELP YOUR LADY ONE BIT.
STRUGGLE
THIS HAS GOTTEN OUT OF HAND. ALL I WANTED WAS TO MESS WITH MISTRESS BLUEGARALL WHILE SHE WAS OUT OF COMMISSION, BUT TO THINK SHE'LL NEVER MOVE AGAIN?
TCH. THIS THING AGAIN.
BUMP
THERE MUST BE SOMETHING WE CAN DO... SOME-THING...
I SUPPOSE I COULD USE HER AS AN ART INSTAL-LATION.
HMM... MAYBE NOT.
AND I CAN'T LET NOTURA OFF HERSELF, EITHER.
HM?
SOB
Sniffle
FSHHH
FSSHHHHH...
......
HEY, NOTURA.

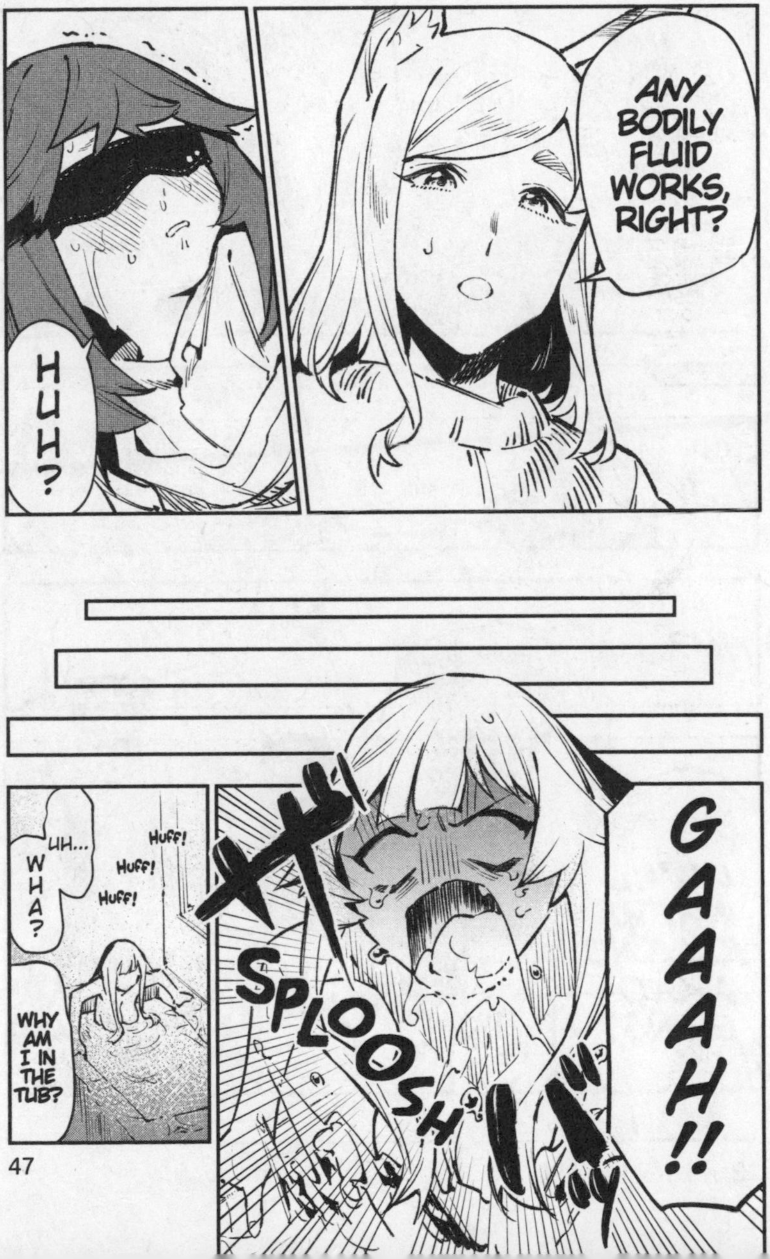
ANY BODILY FLUID WORKS, RIGHT?
HUH?
GAAAAH!!
SPLOOSH
UH... WHA?
Huff!
Huff!
Huff!
WHY AM I IN THE TUB?

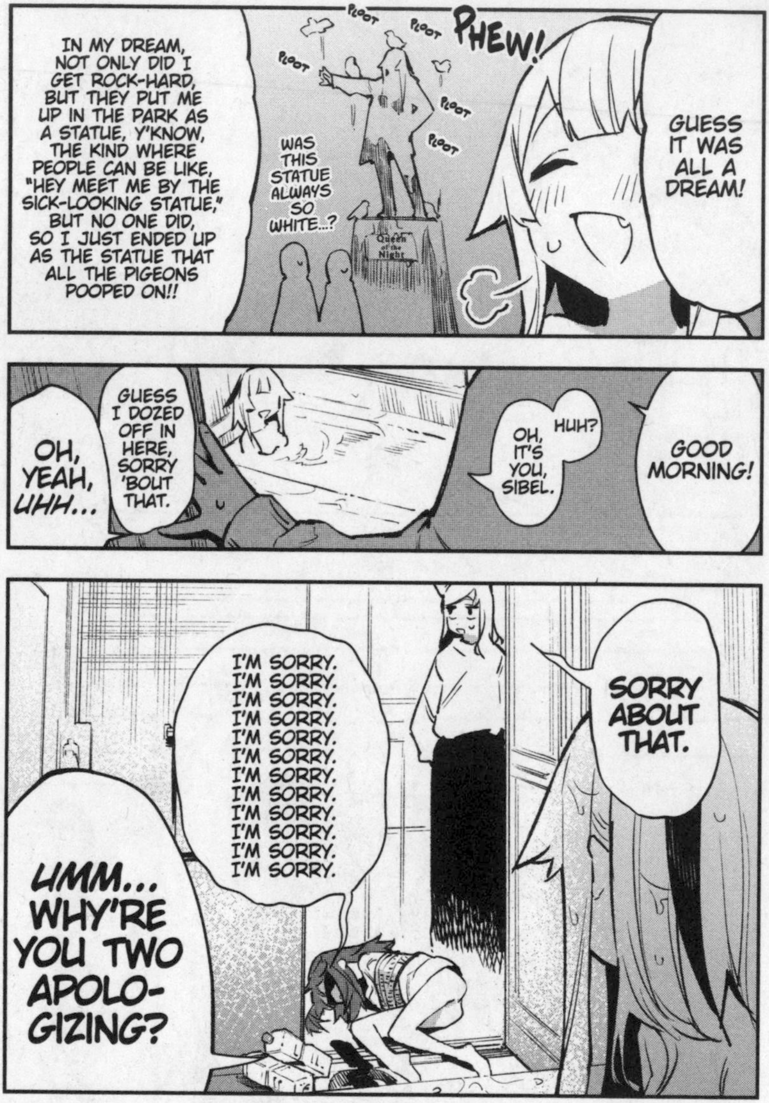

GUESS IT WAS ALL A DREAM!
PHEW!
PLOOT
PLOOT
PLOOT
PLOOT
PLOOT
WAS THIS STATUE ALWAYS SO WHITE...?
Queen of the Night
IN MY DREAM, NOT ONLY DID I GET ROCK-HARD, BUT THEY PUT ME UP IN THE PARK AS A STATUE, Y'KNOW, THE KIND WHERE PEOPLE CAN BE LIKE, "HEY MEET ME BY THE SICK-LOOKING STATUE," BUT NO ONE DID, SO I JUST ENDED UP AS THE STATUE THAT ALL THE PIGEONS POOPED ON!!
GOOD MORNING!
HUH?
OH, IT'S YOU, SIBEL.
GUESS I DOZED OFF IN HERE, SORRY 'BOUT THAT.
OH, YEAH, UHH...
SORRY ABOUT THAT.
I'M SORRY. I'M SORRY. I'M SORRY. I'M SORRY. I'M SORRY. I'M SORRY. I'M SORRY. I'M SORRY. I'M SORRY. I'M SORRY. I'M SORRY. I'M SORRY.
UMM... WHY'RE YOU TWO APOLOGIZING?

It's a tricky curse.

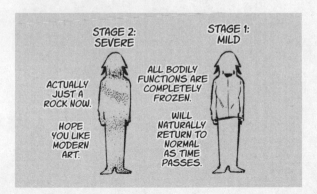

STAGE 2:
SEVERE

STAGE 1:
MILD

ACTUALLY
JUST A
ROCK NOW.

HOPE
YOU LIKE
MODERN
ART.

ALL BODILY
FUNCTIONS ARE
COMPLETELY
FROZEN.

WILL
NATURALLY
RETURN TO
NORMAL
AS TIME
PASSES.

It's Just **Not My Night!**

⮞ Tale of a Fallen Vampire Queen ⮜

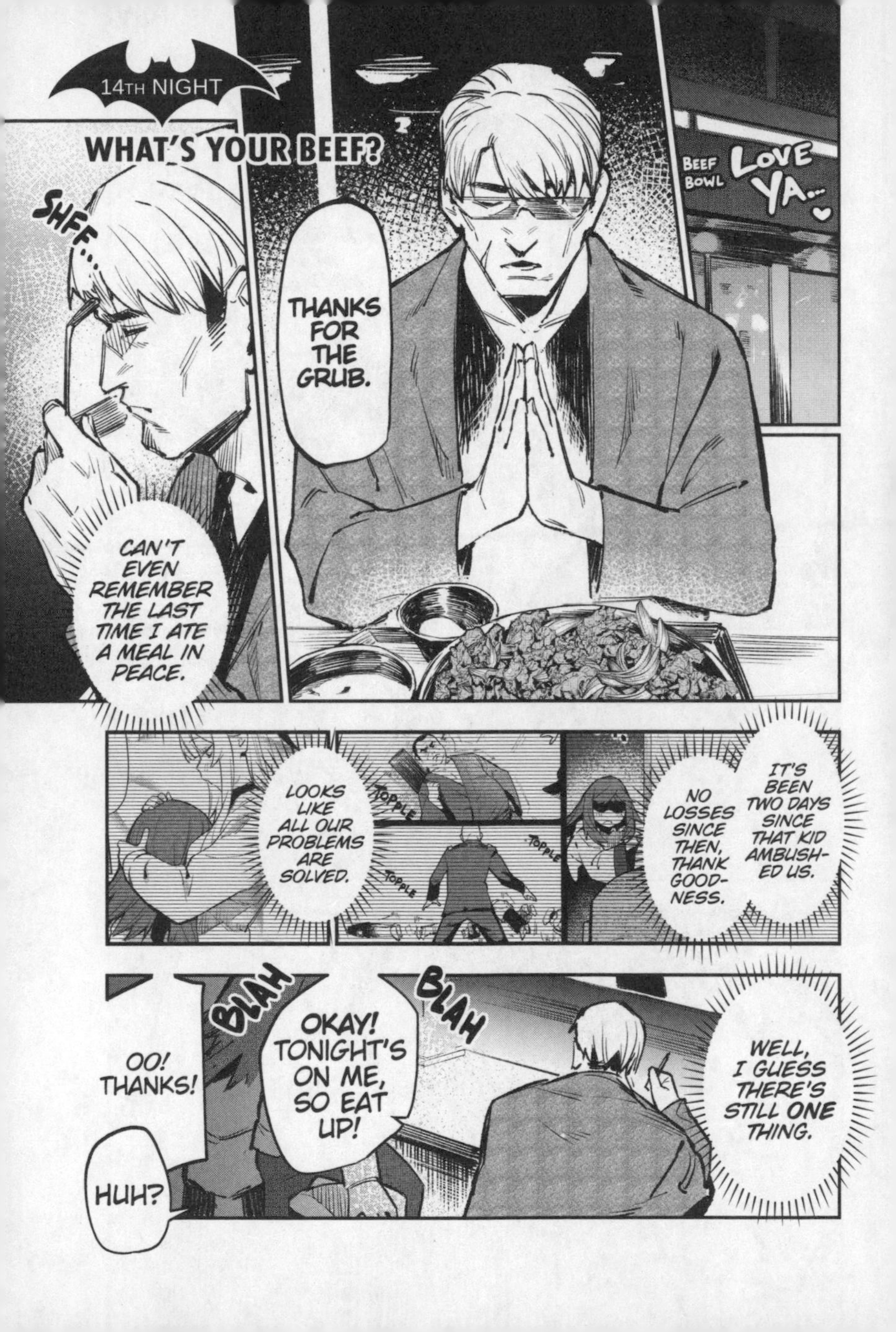
14TH NIGHT
WHAT'S YOUR BEEF?
BEEF BOWL
LOVE YA...
THANKS FOR THE GRUB.
SHFF...
CAN'T EVEN REMEMBER THE LAST TIME I ATE A MEAL IN PEACE.
IT'S BEEN TWO DAYS SINCE THAT KID AMBUSH-ED US.
NO LOSSES SINCE THEN, THANK GOOD-NESS.
TOPPLE
TOPPLE
LOOKS LIKE ALL OUR PROBLEMS ARE SOLVED.
TOPPLE
WELL, I GUESS THERE'S STILL ONE THING.
BLAH
BLAH
OKAY! TONIGHT'S ON ME, SO EAT UP!
OO! THANKS!
HUH?

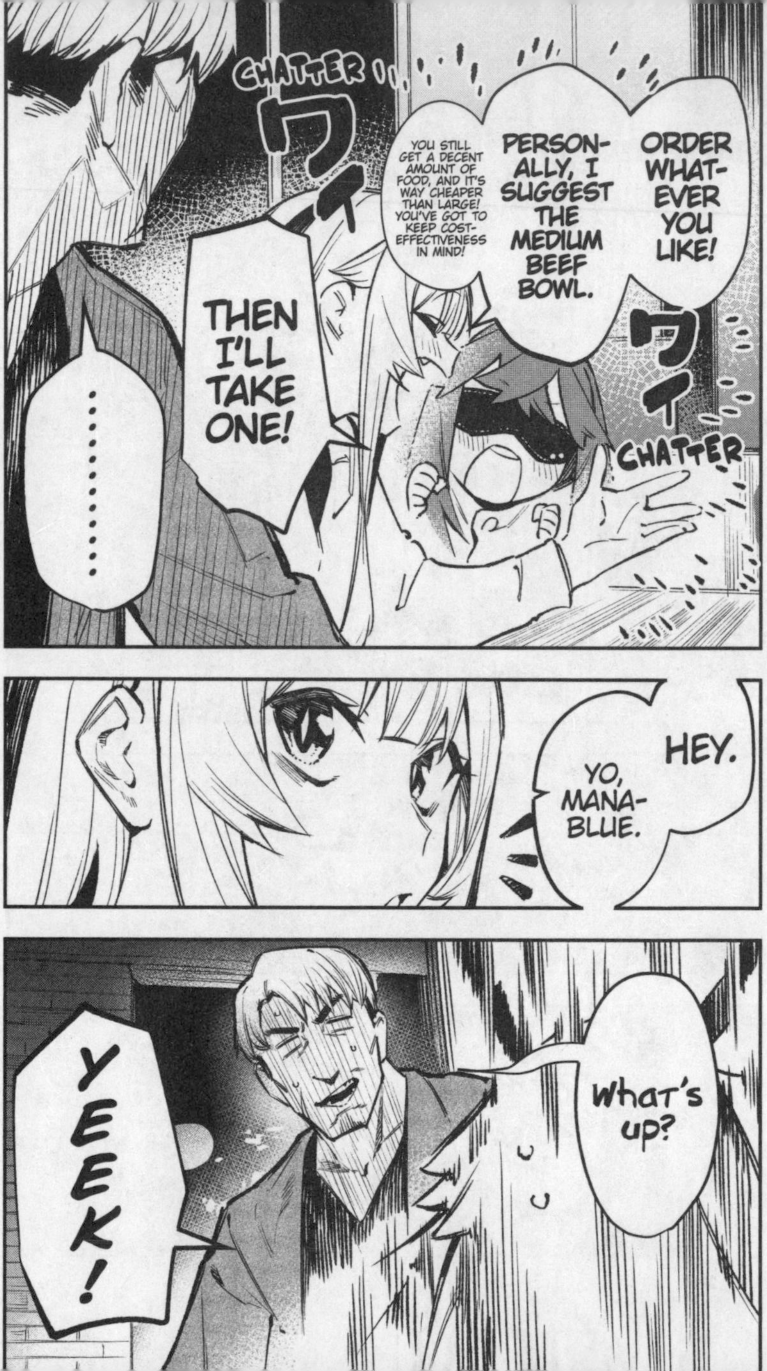

CHATTER
ワイ
ORDER WHATEVER YOU LIKE!
PERSONALLY, I SUGGEST THE MEDIUM BEEF BOWL.
YOU STILL GET A DECENT AMOUNT OF FOOD, AND IT'S WAY CHEAPER THAN LARGE! YOU'VE GOT TO KEEP COST-EFFECTIVENESS IN MIND!
ワイ
CHATTER
THEN I'LL TAKE ONE!
......
HEY.
YO, MANA-BLUE.
What's up?
YEEK!

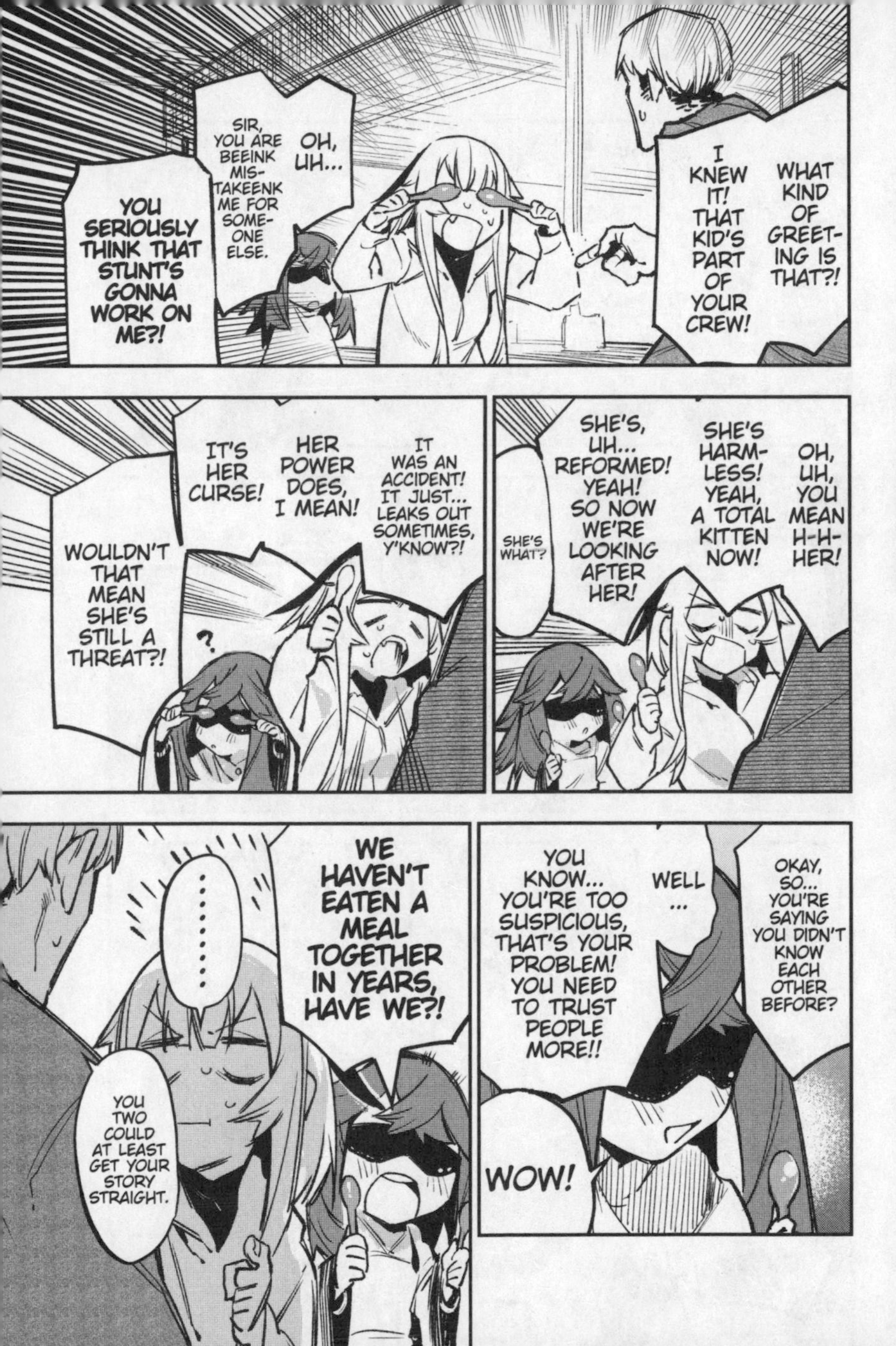
WHAT KIND OF GREETING IS THAT?!
I KNEW IT! THAT KID'S PART OF YOUR CREW!
OH, UH...
SIR, YOU ARE BEEINK MISTAKEENK ME FOR SOMEONE ELSE.
YOU SERIOUSLY THINK THAT STUNT'S GONNA WORK ON ME?!
OH, UH, YOU MEAN H-H-HER!
SHE'S HARMLESS! YEAH, A TOTAL KITTEN NOW!
SHE'S, UH... REFORMED! YEAH! SO NOW WE'RE LOOKING AFTER HER!
SHE'S WHAT?
IT WAS AN ACCIDENT! IT JUST... LEAKS OUT SOMETIMES, Y'KNOW?!
HER POWER DOES, I MEAN!
IT'S HER CURSE!
WOULDN'T THAT MEAN SHE'S STILL A THREAT?!
?
OKAY, SO... YOU'RE SAYING YOU DIDN'T KNOW EACH OTHER BEFORE?
WELL...
YOU KNOW... YOU'RE TOO SUSPICIOUS, THAT'S YOUR PROBLEM! YOU NEED TO TRUST PEOPLE MORE!!
WOW!
WE HAVEN'T EATEN A MEAL TOGETHER IN YEARS, HAVE WE?!
......
YOU TWO COULD AT LEAST GET YOUR STORY STRAIGHT.

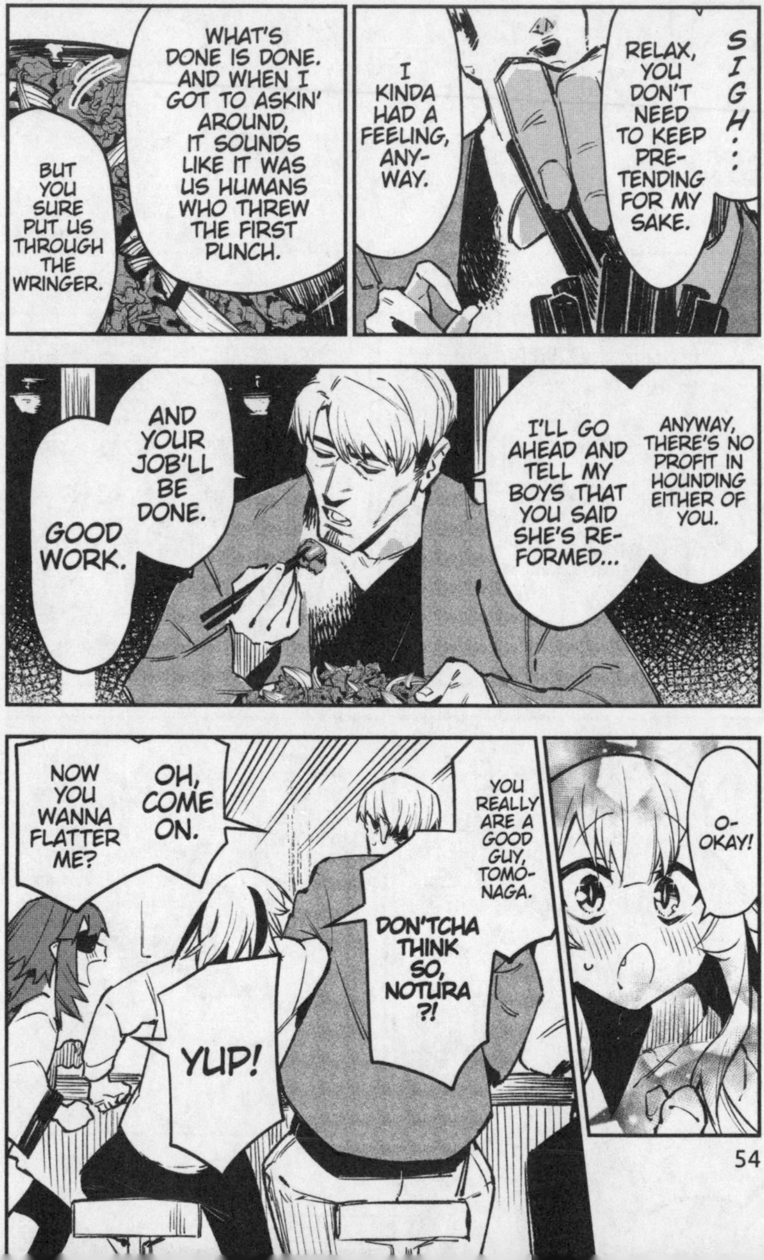
SIGH...
RELAX, YOU DON'T NEED TO KEEP PRETENDING FOR MY SAKE.
I KINDA HAD A FEELING, ANYWAY.
WHAT'S DONE IS DONE. AND WHEN I GOT TO ASKIN' AROUND, IT SOUNDS LIKE IT WAS US HUMANS WHO THREW THE FIRST PUNCH.
BUT YOU SURE PUT US THROUGH THE WRINGER.
ANYWAY, THERE'S NO PROFIT IN HOUNDING EITHER OF YOU.
I'LL GO AHEAD AND TELL MY BOYS THAT YOU SAID SHE'S REFORMED...
AND YOUR JOB'LL BE DONE.
GOOD WORK.
O-OKAY!
YOU REALLY ARE A GOOD GUY, TOMONAGA.
DON'TCHA THINK SO, NOTURA?!
YUP!
OH, COME ON.
NOW YOU WANNA FLATTER ME?

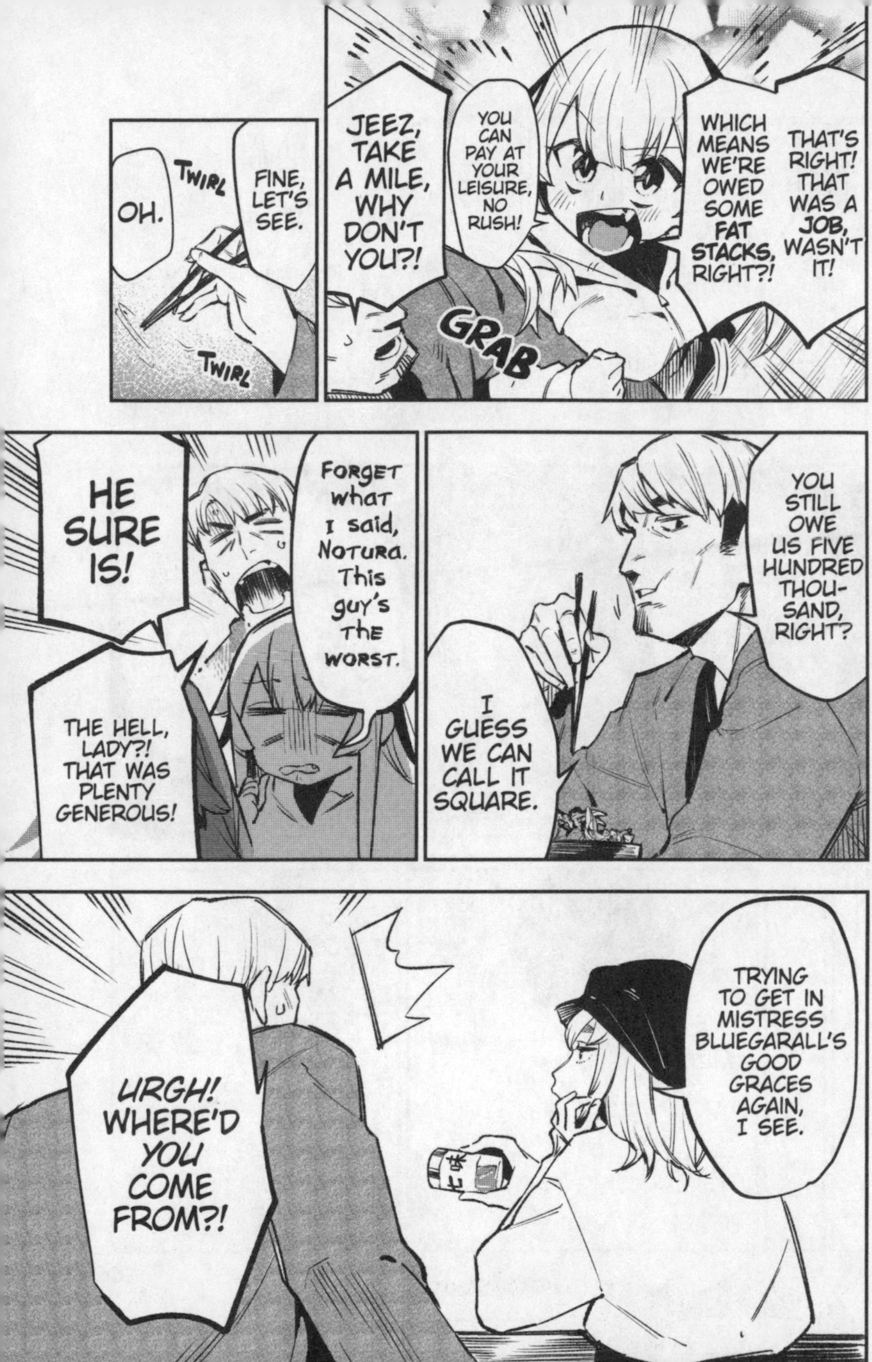
THAT'S RIGHT! THAT WAS A JOB, WASN'T IT!
WHICH MEANS WE'RE OWED SOME FAT STACKS, RIGHT?!
YOU CAN PAY AT YOUR LEISURE, NO RUSH!
JEEZ, TAKE A MILE, WHY DON'T YOU?!
GRAB
FINE, LET'S SEE.
TWIRL
OH.
TWIRL
YOU STILL OWE US FIVE HUNDRED THOUSAND, RIGHT?
I GUESS WE CAN CALL IT SQUARE.
Forget what I said, Notura. This guy's the worst.
HE SURE IS!
THE HELL, LADY?! THAT WAS PLENTY GENEROUS!
TRYING TO GET IN MISTRESS BLUEGARALL'S GOOD GRACES AGAIN, I SEE.
URGH! WHERE'D YOU COME FROM?!

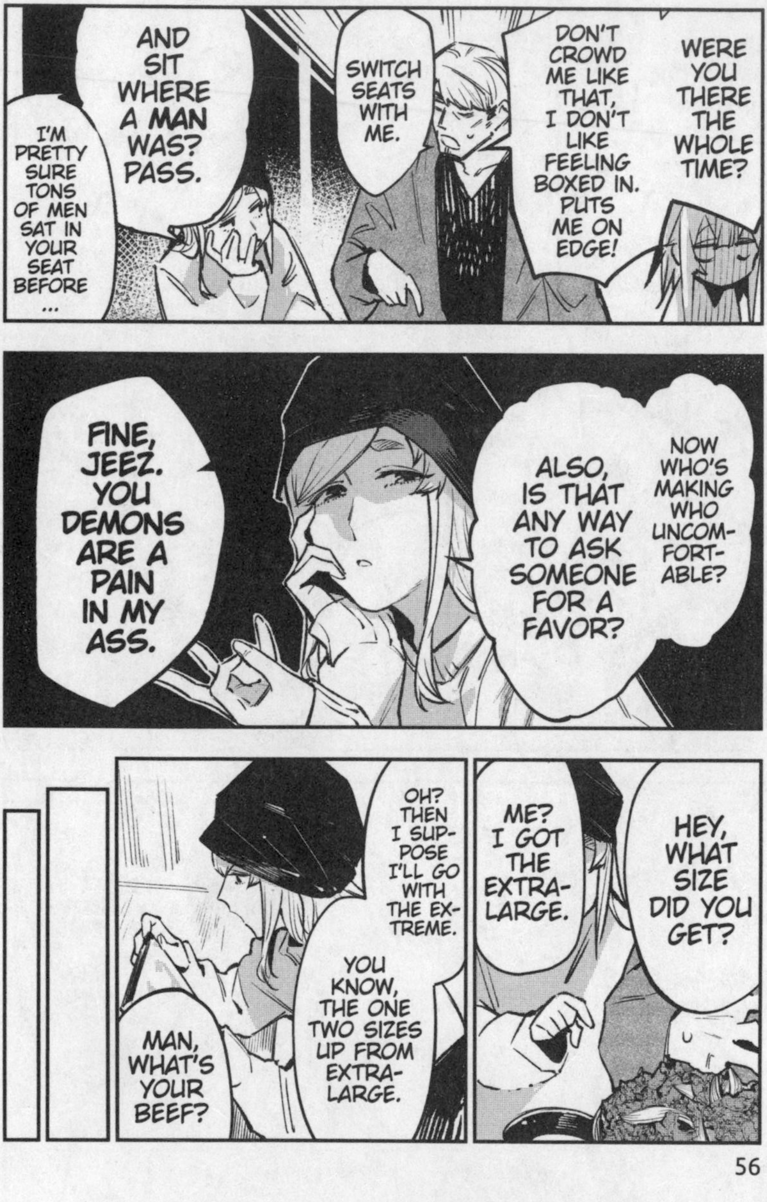
WERE YOU THERE THE WHOLE TIME?
DON'T CROWD ME LIKE THAT, I DON'T LIKE FEELING BOXED IN. PUTS ME ON EDGE!
SWITCH SEATS WITH ME.
AND SIT WHERE A MAN WAS? PASS.
I'M PRETTY SURE TONS OF MEN SAT IN YOUR SEAT BEFORE ...
NOW WHO'S MAKING WHO UNCOM-FORT-ABLE?
ALSO, IS THAT ANY WAY TO ASK SOMEONE FOR A FAVOR?
FINE, JEEZ. YOU DEMONS ARE A PAIN IN MY ASS.
HEY, WHAT SIZE DID YOU GET?
ME? I GOT THE EXTRA-LARGE.
OH? THEN I SUP-POSE I'LL GO WITH THE EX-TREME.
YOU KNOW, THE ONE TWO SIZES UP FROM EXTRA-LARGE.
MAN, WHAT'S YOUR BEEF?

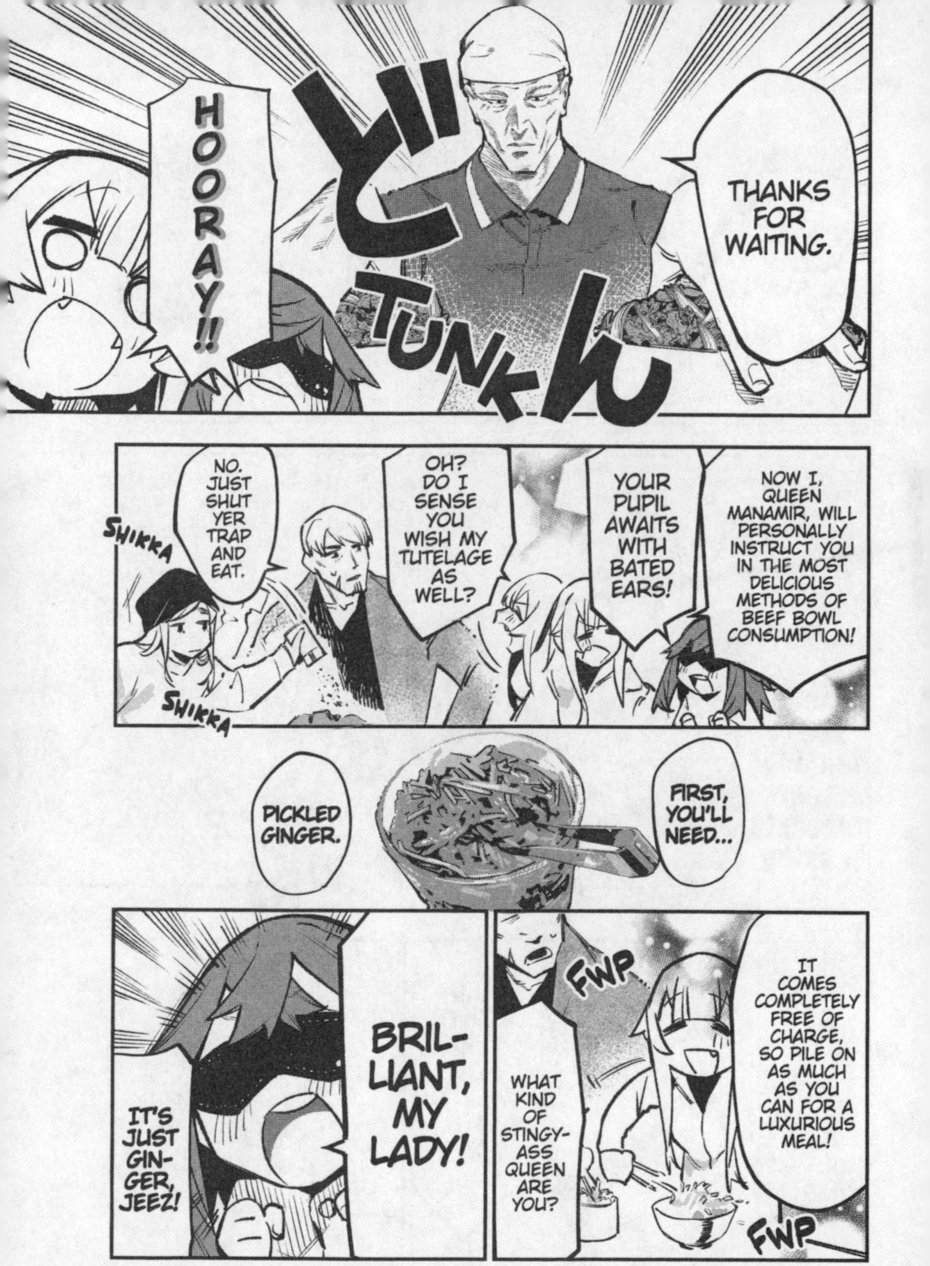
THANKS FOR WAITING.
TUNK
HOORAY!!
NOW I, QUEEN MANAMIR, WILL PERSONALLY INSTRUCT YOU IN THE MOST DELICIOUS METHODS OF BEEF BOWL CONSUMPTION!
YOUR PUPIL AWAITS WITH BATED EARS!
OH? DO I SENSE YOU WISH MY TUTELAGE AS WELL?
NO. JUST SHUT YER TRAP AND EAT.
SHIKKA
SHIKKA
FIRST, YOU'LL NEED...
PICKLED GINGER.
IT COMES COMPLETELY FREE OF CHARGE, SO PILE ON AS MUCH AS YOU CAN FOR A LUXURIOUS MEAL!
FWP
WHAT KIND OF STINGY-ASS QUEEN ARE YOU?
FWP
BRIL-LIANT, MY LADY!
IT'S JUST GIN-GER, JEEZ!

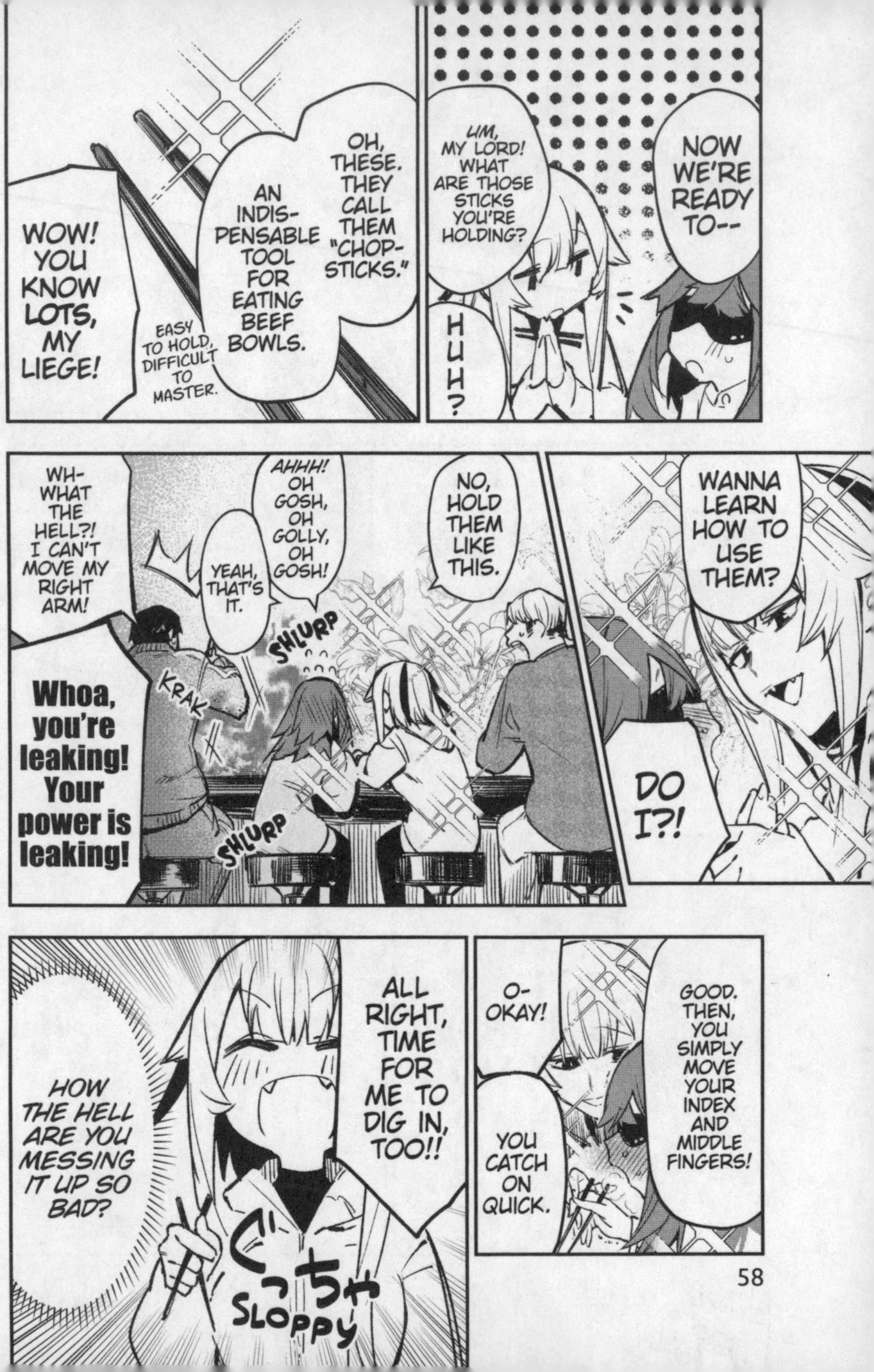
NOW WE'RE READY TO--
UM, MY LORD! WHAT ARE THOSE STICKS YOU'RE HOLDING?
HUH?
OH, THESE. THEY CALL THEM "CHOP-STICKS."
AN INDIS-PENSABLE TOOL FOR EATING BEEF BOWLS.
EASY TO HOLD, DIFFICULT TO MASTER.
WOW! YOU KNOW LOTS, MY LIEGE!
WANNA LEARN HOW TO USE THEM?
DO I?!
NO, HOLD THEM LIKE THIS.
AHHH! OH GOSH, OH GOLLY, OH GOSH!
YEAH, THAT'S IT.
SHLURP
SHLURP
WH-WHAT THE HELL?! I CAN'T MOVE MY RIGHT ARM!
KRAK
Whoa, you're leaking! Your power is leaking!
GOOD. THEN, YOU SIMPLY MOVE YOUR INDEX AND MIDDLE FINGERS!
O-OKAY!
YOU CATCH ON QUICK.
ALL RIGHT, TIME FOR ME TO DIG IN, TOO!!
HOW THE HELL ARE YOU MESSING IT UP SO BAD?
ぐっちゃ
SLOPPY

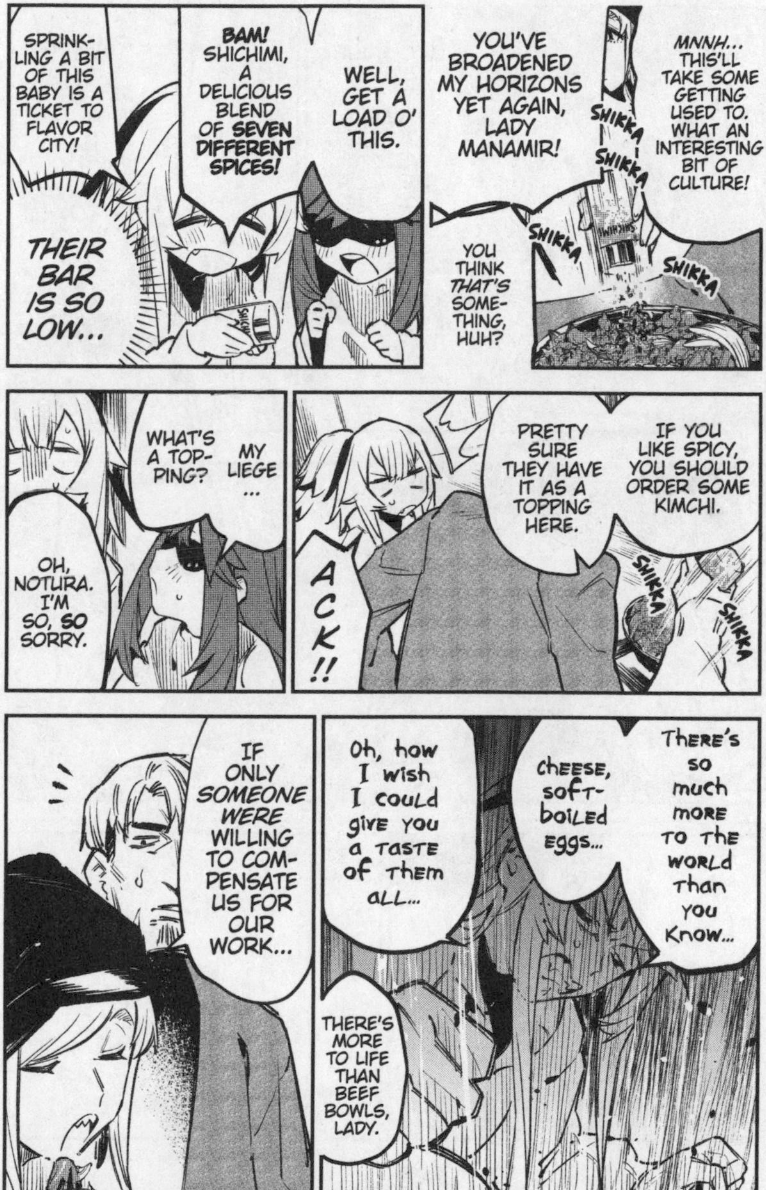
MNNH… THIS'LL TAKE SOME GETTING USED TO. WHAT AN INTERESTING BIT OF CULTURE!
SHIKKA SHIKKA
YOU'VE BROADENED MY HORIZONS YET AGAIN, LADY MANAMIR!
SHIKKA SHIKKA
YOU THINK THAT'S SOMETHING, HUH?
WELL, GET A LOAD O' THIS.
BAM! SHICHIMI, A DELICIOUS BLEND OF SEVEN DIFFERENT SPICES!
SPRINKLING A BIT OF THIS BABY IS A TICKET TO FLAVOR CITY!
THEIR BAR IS SO LOW…
IF YOU LIKE SPICY, YOU SHOULD ORDER SOME KIMCHI.
PRETTY SURE THEY HAVE IT AS A TOPPING HERE.
SHIKKA SHIKKA
ACK!!
MY LIEGE…
WHAT'S A TOP-PING?
OH, NOTURA. I'M SO, SO SORRY.
There's so much more to the world than you know…
Cheese, soft-boiled eggs…
Oh, how I wish I could give you a taste of them all…
THERE'S MORE TO LIFE THAN BEEF BOWLS, LADY.
IF ONLY SOMEONE WERE WILLING TO COMPENSATE US FOR OUR WORK…

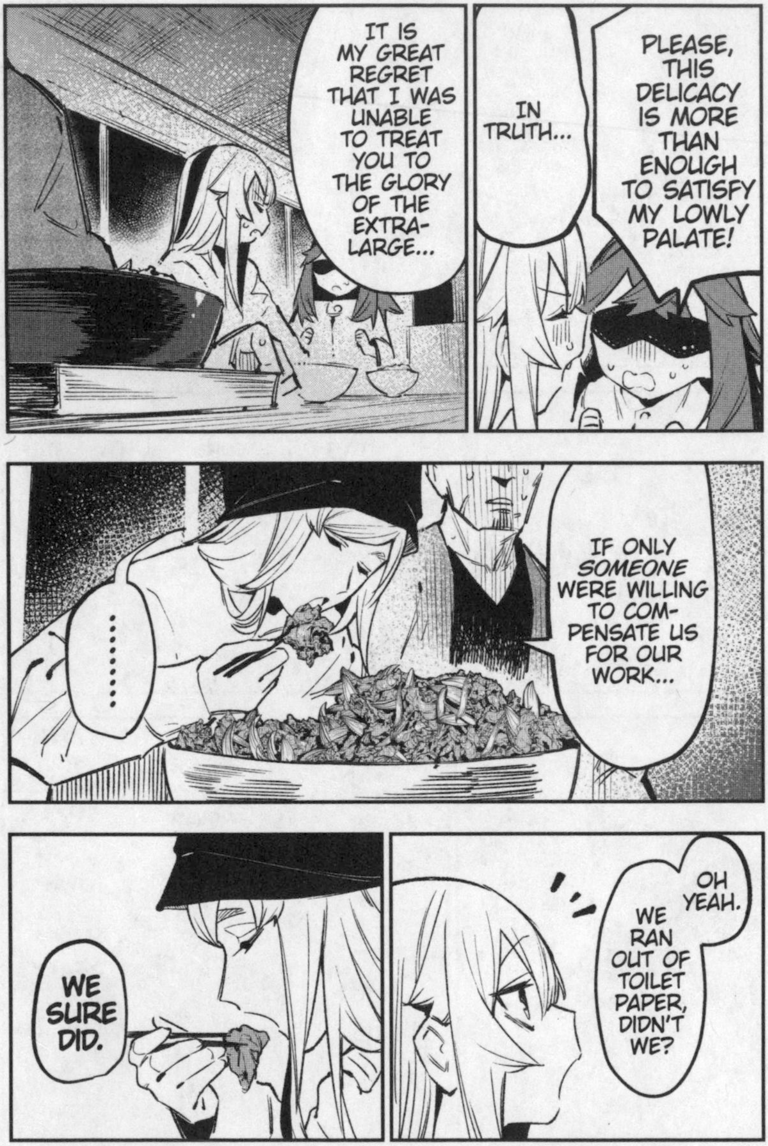
PLEASE, THIS DELICACY IS MORE THAN ENOUGH TO SATISFY MY LOWLY PALATE!
IN TRUTH...
IT IS MY GREAT REGRET THAT I WAS UNABLE TO TREAT YOU TO THE GLORY OF THE EXTRA-LARGE...
IF ONLY *SOMEONE* WERE WILLING TO COMPENSATE US FOR OUR WORK...
......
OH YEAH. WE RAN OUT OF TOILET PAPER, DIDN'T WE?
WE SURE DID.

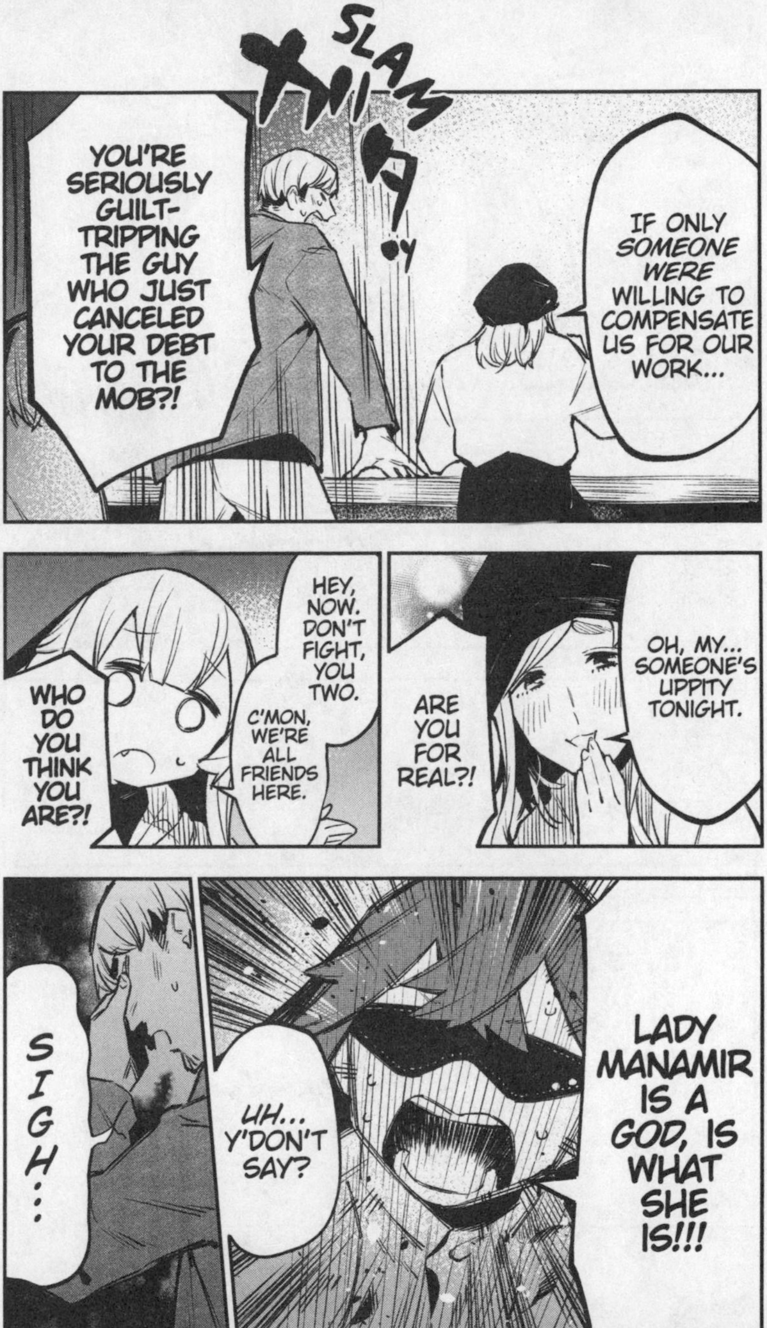
IF ONLY SOMEONE WERE WILLING TO COMPENSATE US FOR OUR WORK...
SLAM
YOU'RE SERIOUSLY GUILT-TRIPPING THE GUY WHO JUST CANCELED YOUR DEBT TO THE MOB?!
OH, MY... SOMEONE'S UPPITY TONIGHT.
ARE YOU FOR REAL?!
HEY, NOW. DON'T FIGHT, YOU TWO.
C'MON, WE'RE ALL FRIENDS HERE.
WHO DO YOU THINK YOU ARE?!
LADY MANAMIR IS A GOD, IS WHAT SHE IS!!!
UH... Y'DON'T SAY?
SIGH...

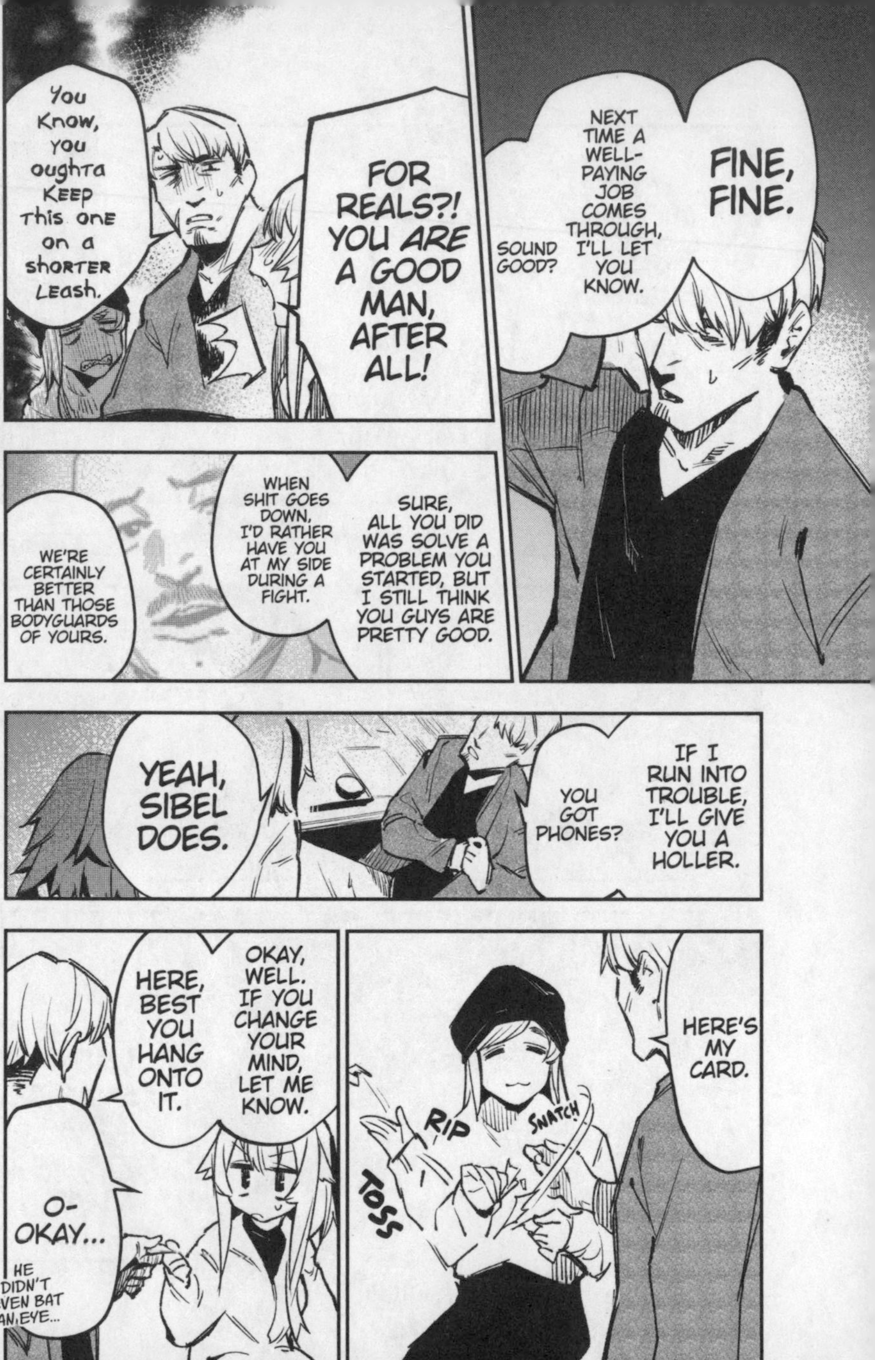
FINE, FINE.
NEXT TIME A WELL-PAYING JOB COMES THROUGH, I'LL LET YOU KNOW.
SOUND GOOD?
FOR REALS?! YOU ARE A GOOD MAN, AFTER ALL!
You Know, you oughta Keep this one on a shorter Leash.
SURE, ALL YOU DID WAS SOLVE A PROBLEM YOU STARTED, BUT I STILL THINK YOU GUYS ARE PRETTY GOOD.
WHEN SHIT GOES DOWN, I'D RATHER HAVE YOU AT MY SIDE DURING A FIGHT.
WE'RE CERTAINLY BETTER THAN THOSE BODYGUARDS OF YOURS.
IF I RUN INTO TROUBLE, I'LL GIVE YOU A HOLLER.
YOU GOT PHONES?
YEAH, SIBEL DOES.
HERE'S MY CARD.
SNATCH
RIP
TOSS
OKAY, WELL. IF YOU CHANGE YOUR MIND, LET ME KNOW.
HERE, BEST YOU HANG ONTO IT.
O-OKAY...
HE DIDN'T EVEN BAT AN EYE...

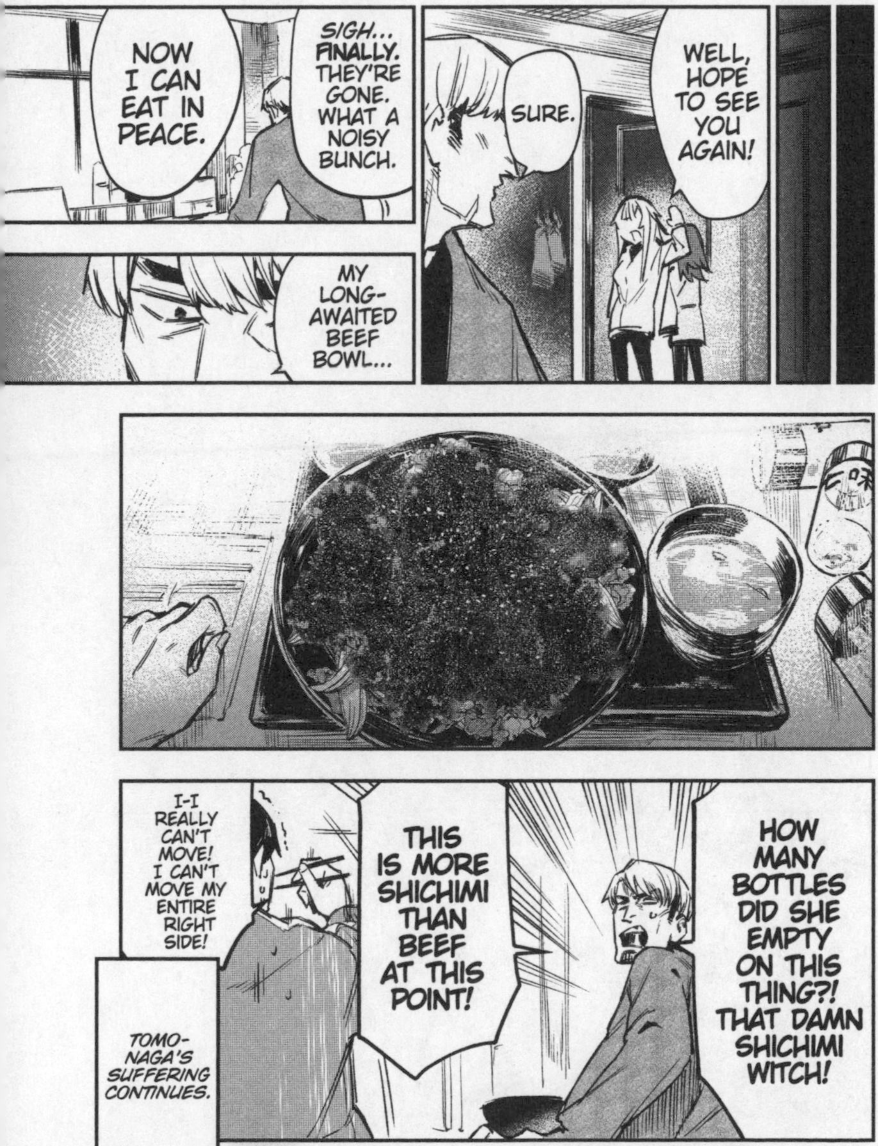
WELL, HOPE TO SEE YOU AGAIN!
SURE.
SIGH... FINALLY. THEY'RE GONE. WHAT A NOISY BUNCH.
NOW I CAN EAT IN PEACE.
MY LONG-AWAITED BEEF BOWL...
HOW MANY BOTTLES DID SHE EMPTY ON THIS THING?! THAT DAMN SHICHIMI WITCH!
THIS IS MORE SHICHIMI THAN BEEF AT THIS POINT!
I-I REALLY CAN'T MOVE! I CAN'T MOVE MY ENTIRE RIGHT SIDE!
TOMONAGA'S SUFFERING CONTINUES.

14TH NIGHT - **END**

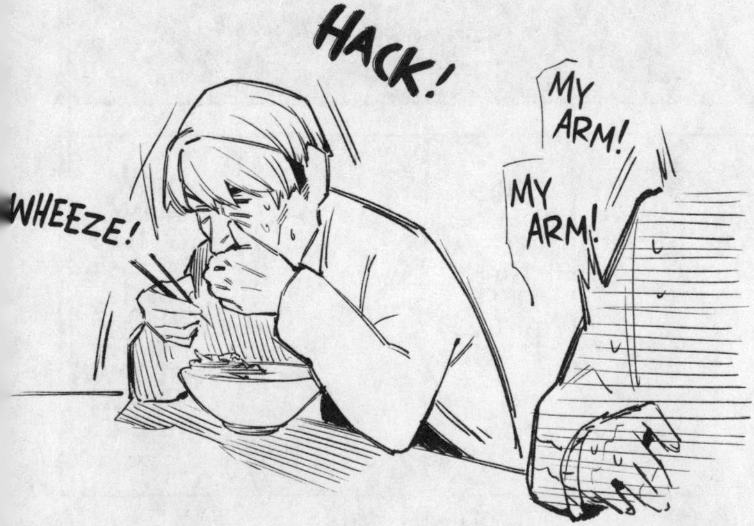
MY ARM!
HACK!
MY ARM!
WHEEZE!

15TH NIGHT
FISHIN' FER TROUBLE

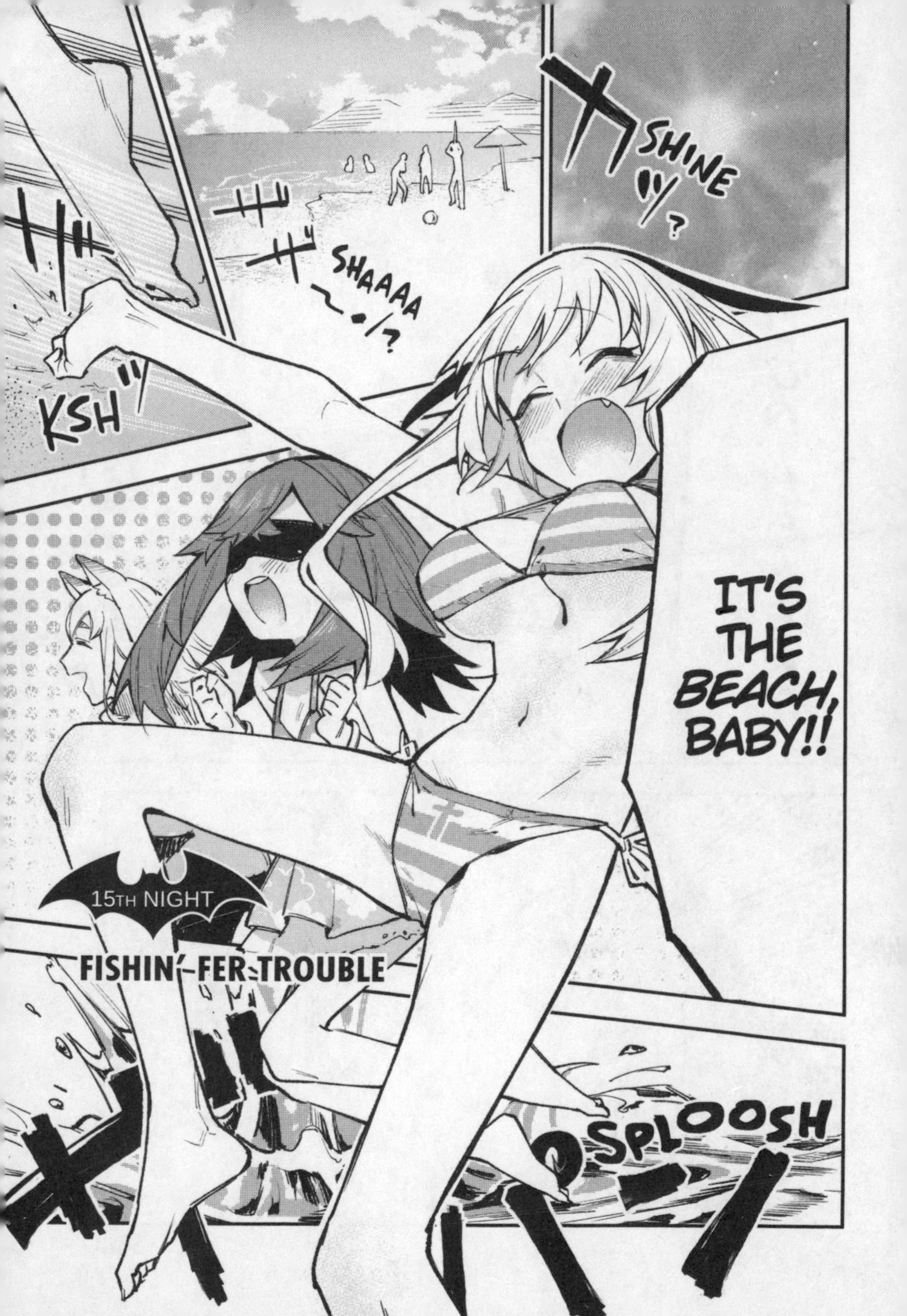
SHINE
SHAAAA
KSH
IT'S THE BEACH, BABY!!
15TH NIGHT
FISHIN' FER TROUBLE
SPLOOSH

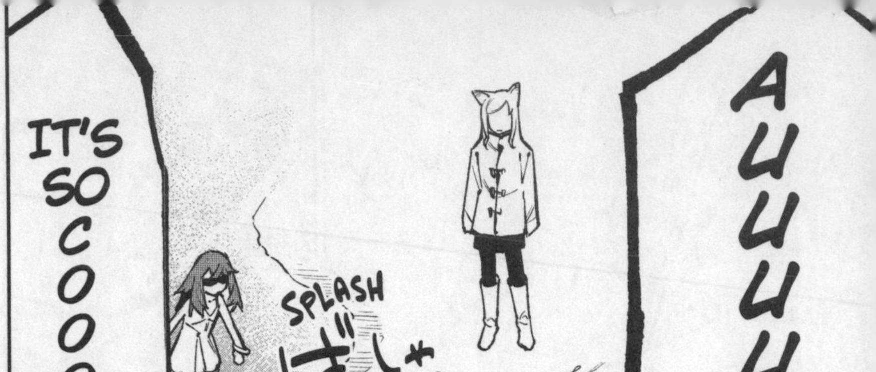
AUUUUUUGH!!
SPLASH
ばしゃ
ゴロゴロゴロ
ROLL ROLL ROLL ROLL
IT'S SO COOOOLLLLD!!
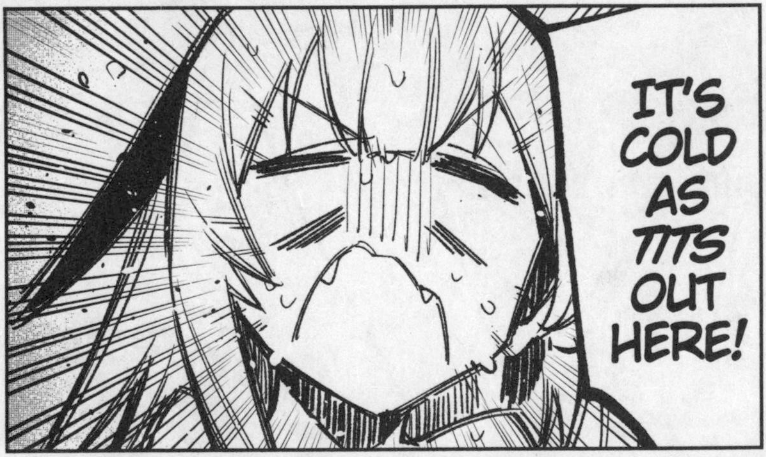
IT'S COLD AS TITS OUT HERE!

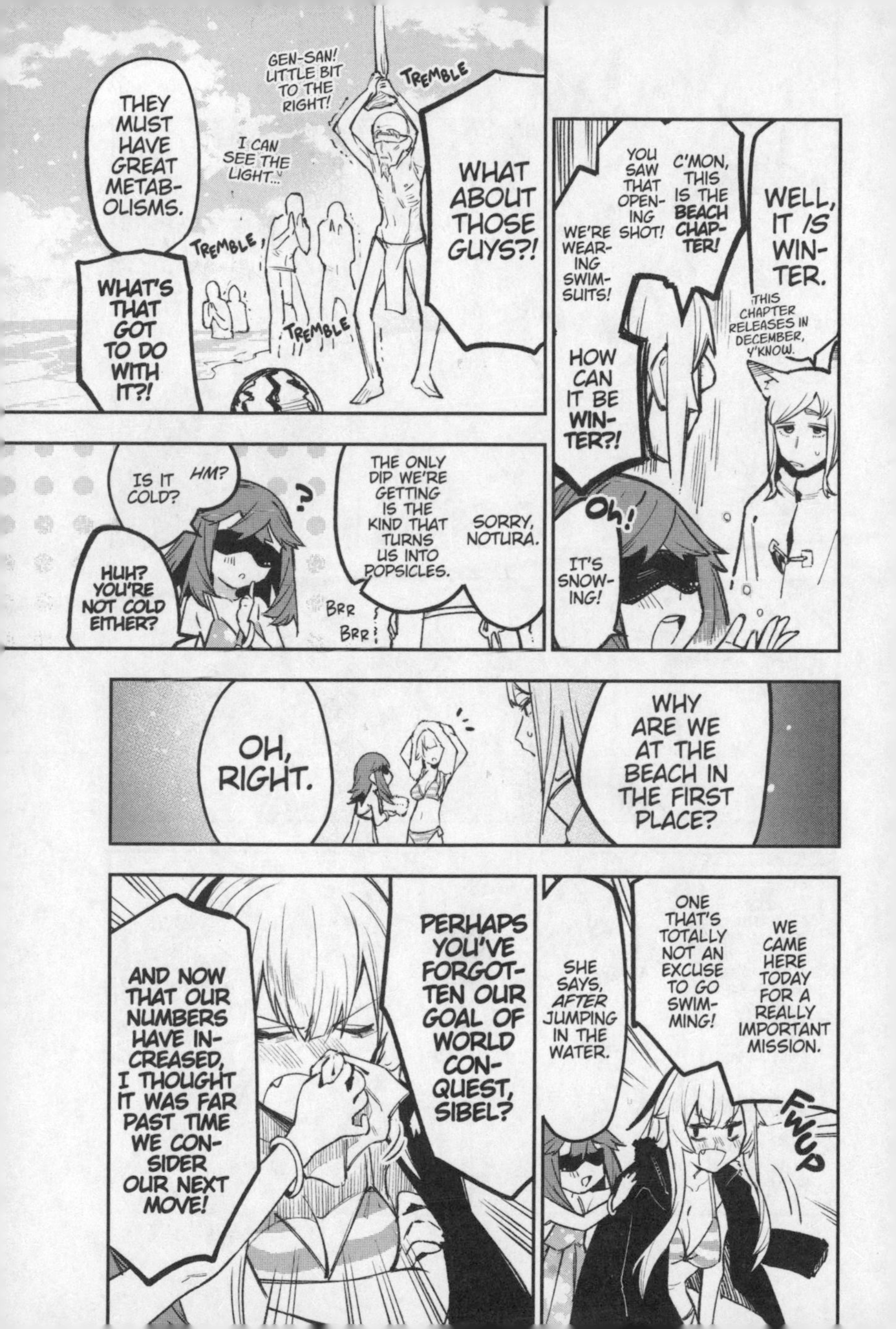

WELL, IT *IS* WINTER.
THIS CHAPTER RELEASES IN DECEMBER, Y'KNOW.
C'MON, THIS IS THE **BEACH CHAPTER!**
YOU SAW THAT OPENING SHOT!
WE'RE WEARING SWIMSUITS!
HOW CAN IT BE **WINTER?!**
OH!
IT'S SNOWING!
WHAT ABOUT THOSE GUYS?!
TREMBLE
GEN-SAN! LITTLE BIT TO THE RIGHT!
I CAN SEE THE LIGHT...
TREMBLE
TREMBLE
THEY MUST HAVE GREAT METABOLISMS.
WHAT'S THAT GOT TO DO WITH IT?!
SORRY, NOTURA.
THE ONLY DIP WE'RE GETTING IS THE KIND THAT TURNS US INTO POPSICLES.
BRR
BRR
?
HM?
IS IT COLD?
HUH? YOU'RE NOT COLD EITHER?
WHY ARE WE AT THE BEACH IN THE FIRST PLACE?
OH, RIGHT.
WE CAME HERE TODAY FOR A REALLY IMPORTANT MISSION.
ONE THAT'S TOTALLY NOT AN EXCUSE TO GO SWIMMING!
SHE SAYS, *AFTER* JUMPING IN THE WATER.
FWUP
PERHAPS YOU'VE FORGOTTEN OUR GOAL OF WORLD CONQUEST, SIBEL?
AND NOW THAT OUR NUMBERS HAVE INCREASED, I THOUGHT IT WAS FAR PAST TIME WE CONSIDER OUR NEXT MOVE!

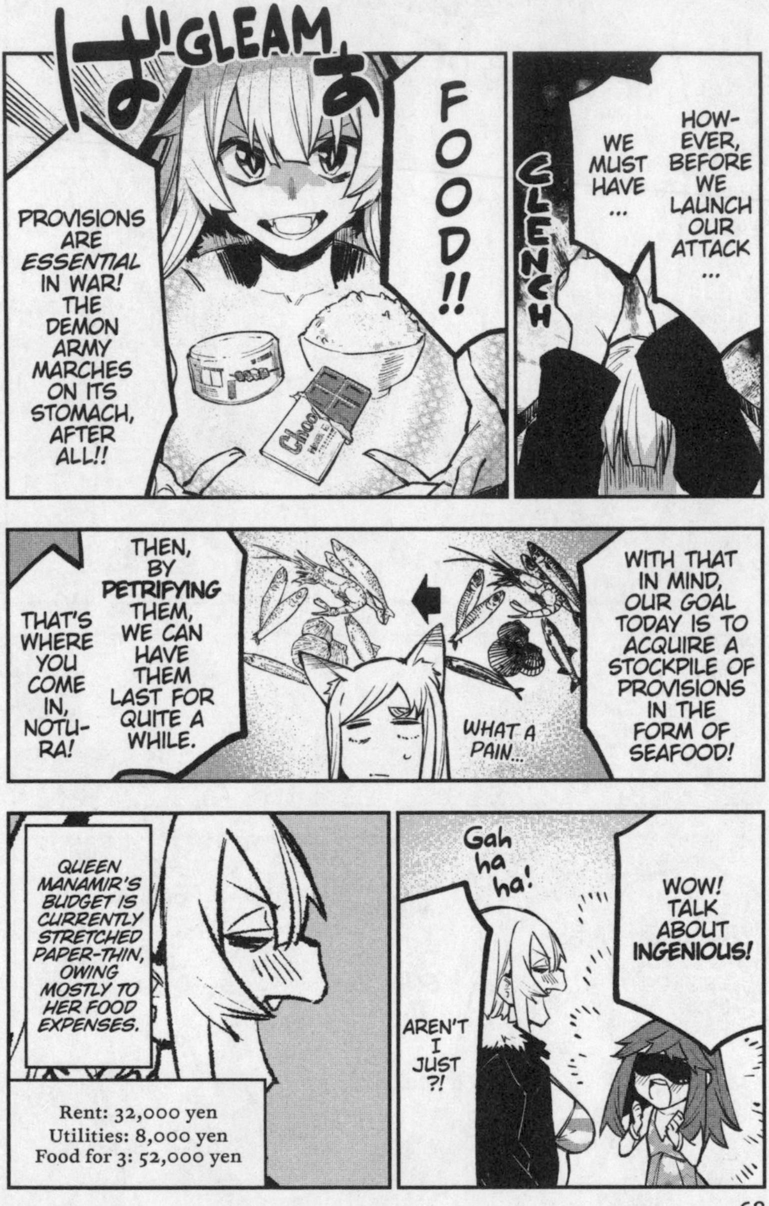
HOW-EVER, BEFORE WE LAUNCH OUR ATTACK...
WE MUST HAVE...
CLENCH
ぱ GLEAM あ
FOOD!!
PROVISIONS ARE ESSENTIAL IN WAR! THE DEMON ARMY MARCHES ON ITS STOMACH, AFTER ALL!!
WITH THAT IN MIND, OUR GOAL TODAY IS TO ACQUIRE A STOCKPILE OF PROVISIONS IN THE FORM OF SEAFOOD!
WHAT A PAIN...
THEN, BY PETRIFYING THEM, WE CAN HAVE THEM LAST FOR QUITE A WHILE.
THAT'S WHERE YOU COME IN, NOTU-RA!
WOW! TALK ABOUT INGENIOUS!
Gah ha ha!
AREN'T I JUST ?!
QUEEN MANAMIR'S BUDGET IS CURRENTLY STRETCHED PAPER-THIN, OWING MOSTLY TO HER FOOD EXPENSES.
Rent: 32,000 yen
Utilities: 8,000 yen
Food for 3: 52,000 yen

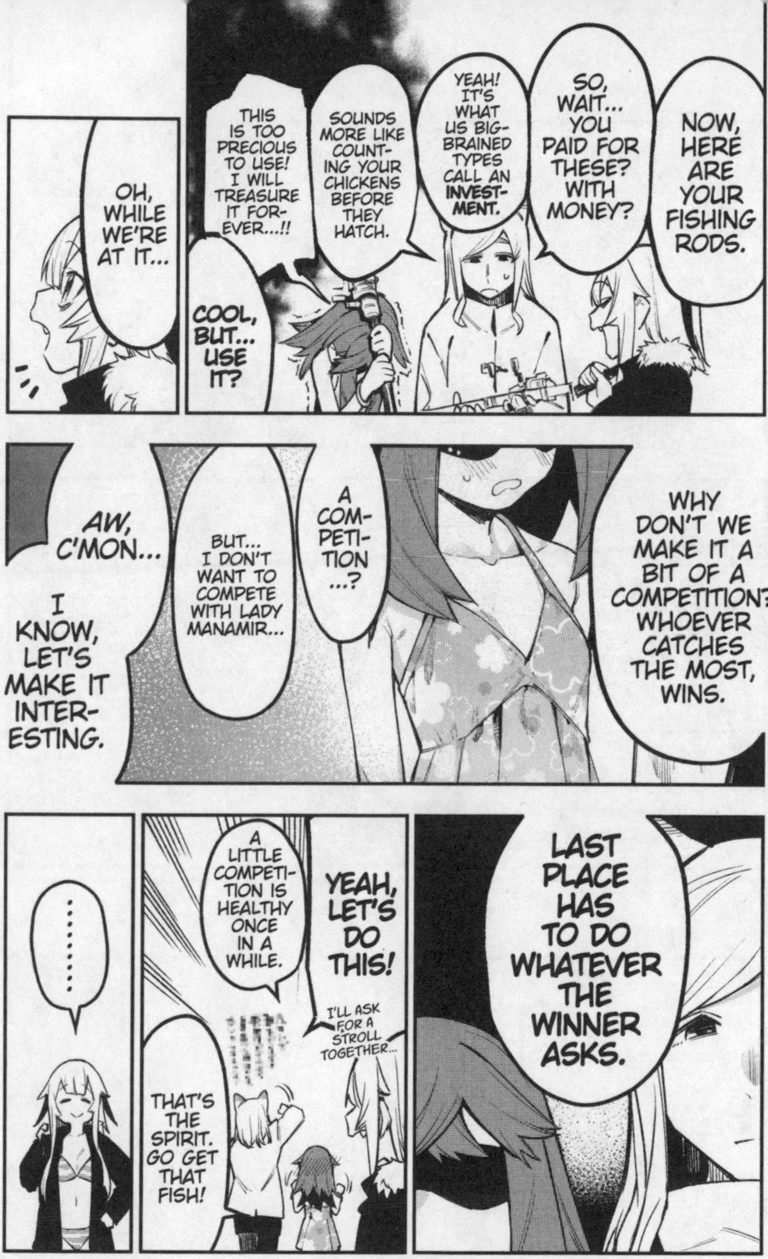
NOW, HERE ARE YOUR FISHING RODS.
SO, WAIT... YOU PAID FOR THESE? WITH MONEY?
YEAH! IT'S WHAT US BIG-BRAINED TYPES CALL AN INVESTMENT.
SOUNDS MORE LIKE COUNTING YOUR CHICKENS BEFORE THEY HATCH.
THIS IS TOO PRECIOUS TO USE! I WILL TREASURE IT FOREVER...!!
COOL, BUT... USE IT?
OH, WHILE WE'RE AT IT...
WHY DON'T WE MAKE IT A BIT OF A COMPETITION? WHOEVER CATCHES THE MOST, WINS.
A COMPETITION...?
BUT... I DON'T WANT TO COMPETE WITH LADY MANAMIR...
AW, C'MON...
I KNOW, LET'S MAKE IT INTERESTING.
LAST PLACE HAS TO DO WHATEVER THE WINNER ASKS.
YEAH, LET'S DO THIS!
A LITTLE COMPETITION IS HEALTHY ONCE IN A WHILE.
I'LL ASK FOR A STROLL TOGETHER...
THAT'S THE SPIRIT. GO GET THAT FISH!
......

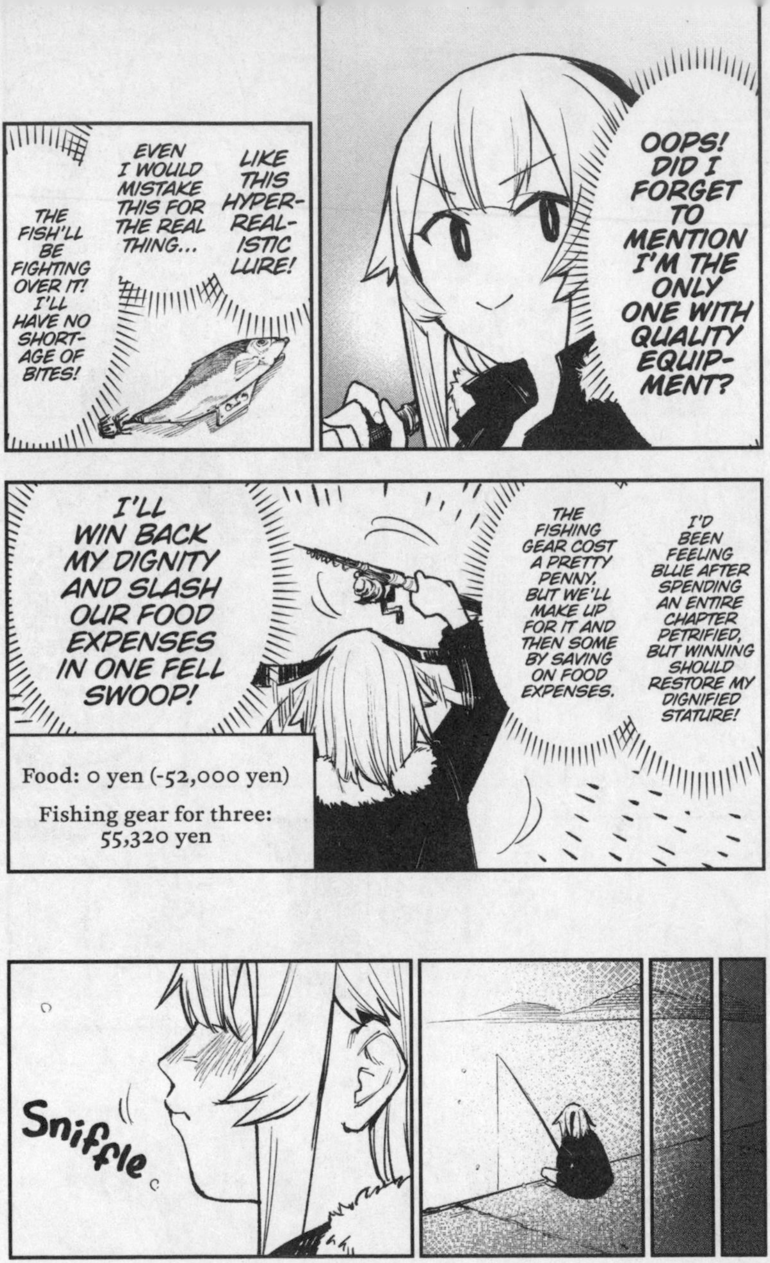
OOPS! DID I FORGET TO MENTION I'M THE ONLY ONE WITH QUALITY EQUIP-MENT?
LIKE THIS HYPER-REAL-ISTIC LURE!
EVEN I WOULD MISTAKE THIS FOR THE REAL THING...
THE FISH'LL BE FIGHTING OVER IT! I'LL HAVE NO SHORT-AGE OF BITES!
I'D BEEN FEELING BLUE AFTER SPENDING AN ENTIRE CHAPTER PETRIFIED, BUT WINNING SHOULD RESTORE MY DIGNIFIED STATURE!
THE FISHING GEAR COST A PRETTY PENNY, BUT WE'LL MAKE UP FOR IT AND THEN SOME BY SAVING ON FOOD EXPENSES.
I'LL WIN BACK MY DIGNITY AND SLASH OUR FOOD EXPENSES IN ONE FELL SWOOP!
Food: 0 yen (-52,000 yen)
Fishing gear for three: 55,320 yen
Sniffle

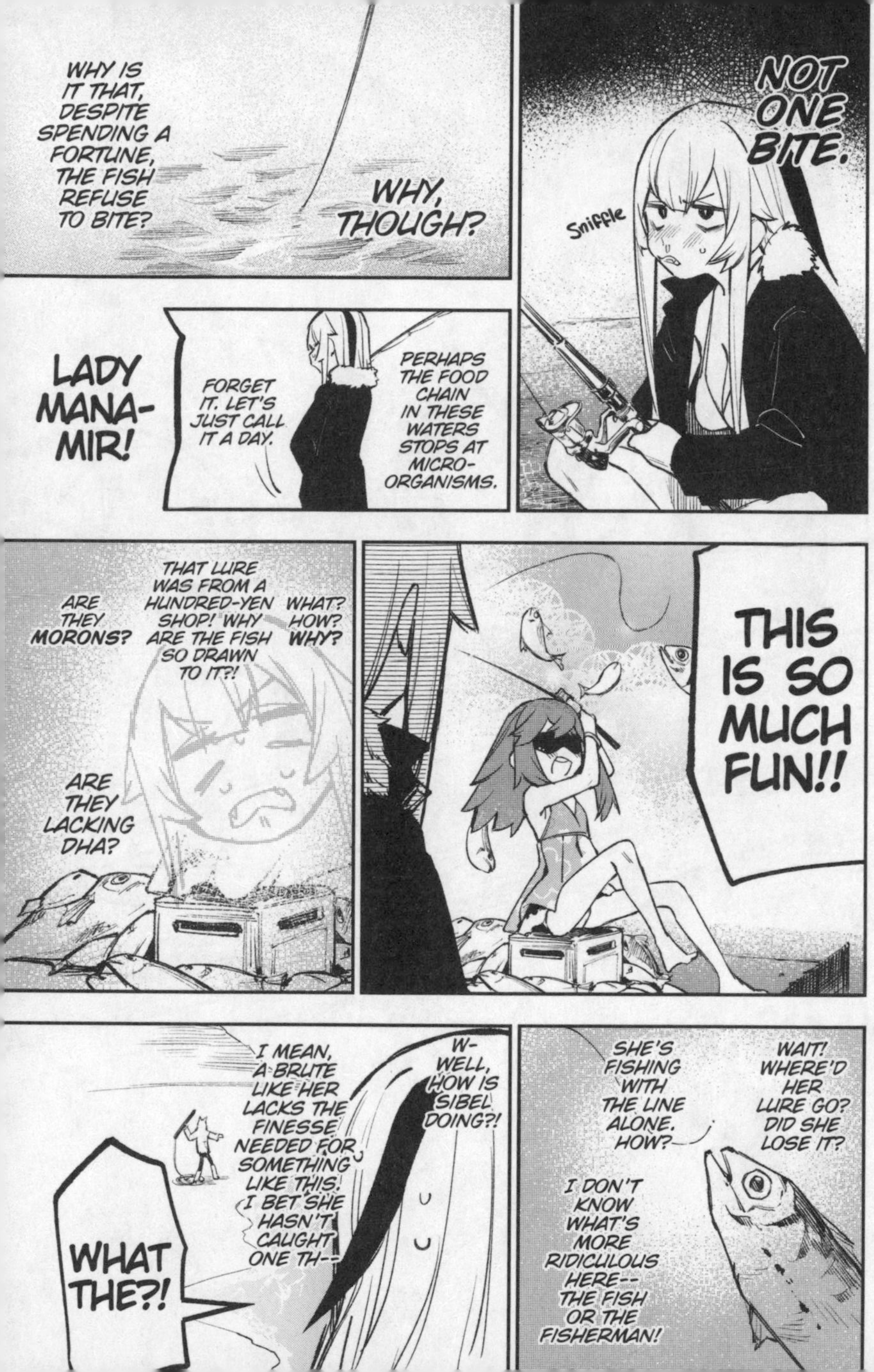
NOT ONE BITE.
Sniffle
WHY IS IT THAT, DESPITE SPENDING A FORTUNE, THE FISH REFUSE TO BITE?
WHY, THOUGH?
PERHAPS THE FOOD CHAIN IN THESE WATERS STOPS AT MICRO-ORGANISMS.
FORGET IT. LET'S JUST CALL IT A DAY.
LADY MANA-MIR!
THIS IS SO MUCH FUN!!
WHAT? HOW? WHY?
THAT LURE WAS FROM A HUNDRED-YEN SHOP! WHY ARE THE FISH SO DRAWN TO IT?!
ARE THEY MORONS?
ARE THEY LACKING DHA?
WAIT! WHERE'D HER LURE GO? DID SHE LOSE IT?
SHE'S FISHING WITH THE LINE ALONE. HOW?
I DON'T KNOW WHAT'S MORE RIDICULOUS HERE-- THE FISH OR THE FISHERMAN!
W-WELL, HOW IS SIBEL DOING?!
I MEAN, A BRUTE LIKE HER LACKS THE FINESSE NEEDED FOR SOMETHING LIKE THIS. I BET SHE HASN'T CAUGHT ONE TH--
WHAT THE?!

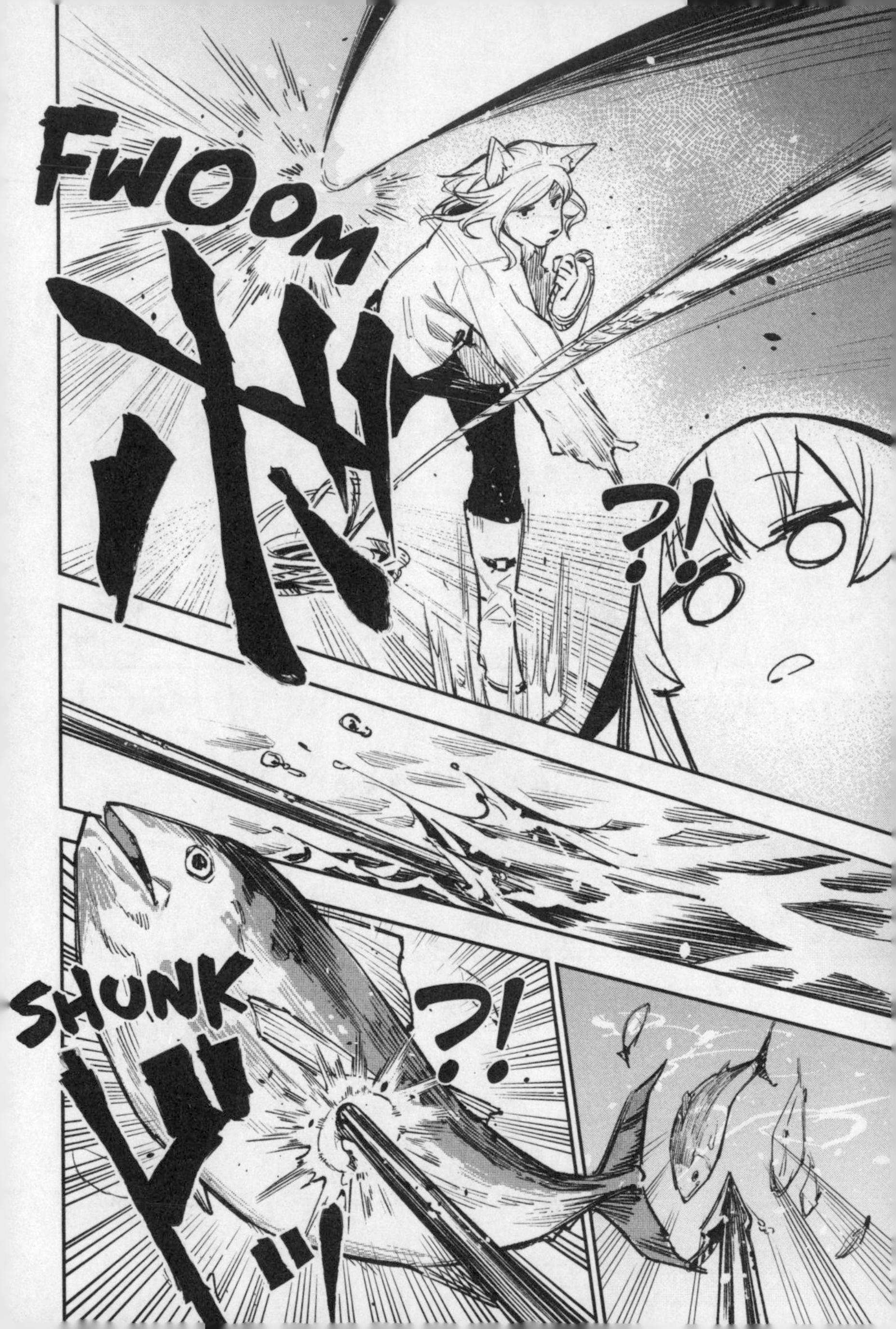
FWOOM
?!
SHUNK
?!

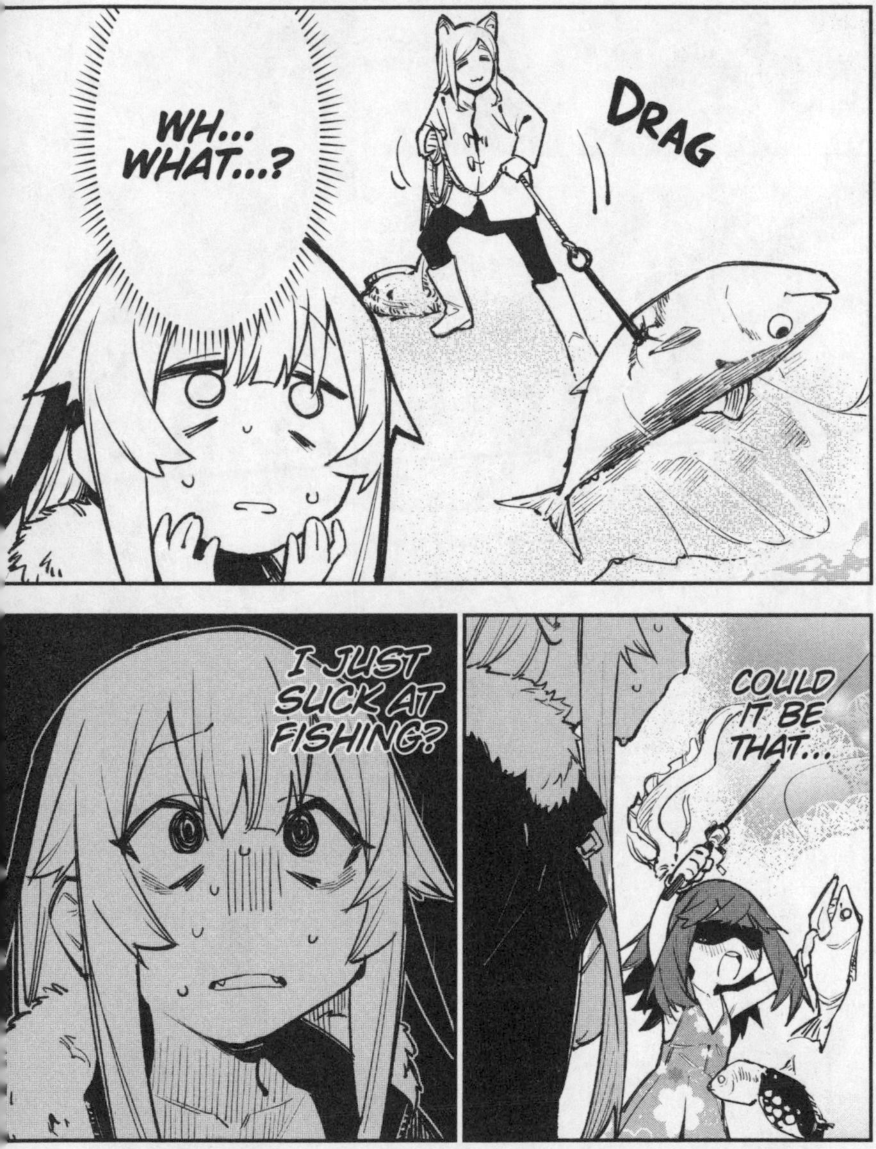
DRAG
WH... WHAT...?
COULD IT BE THAT...
I JUST SUCK AT FISHING?

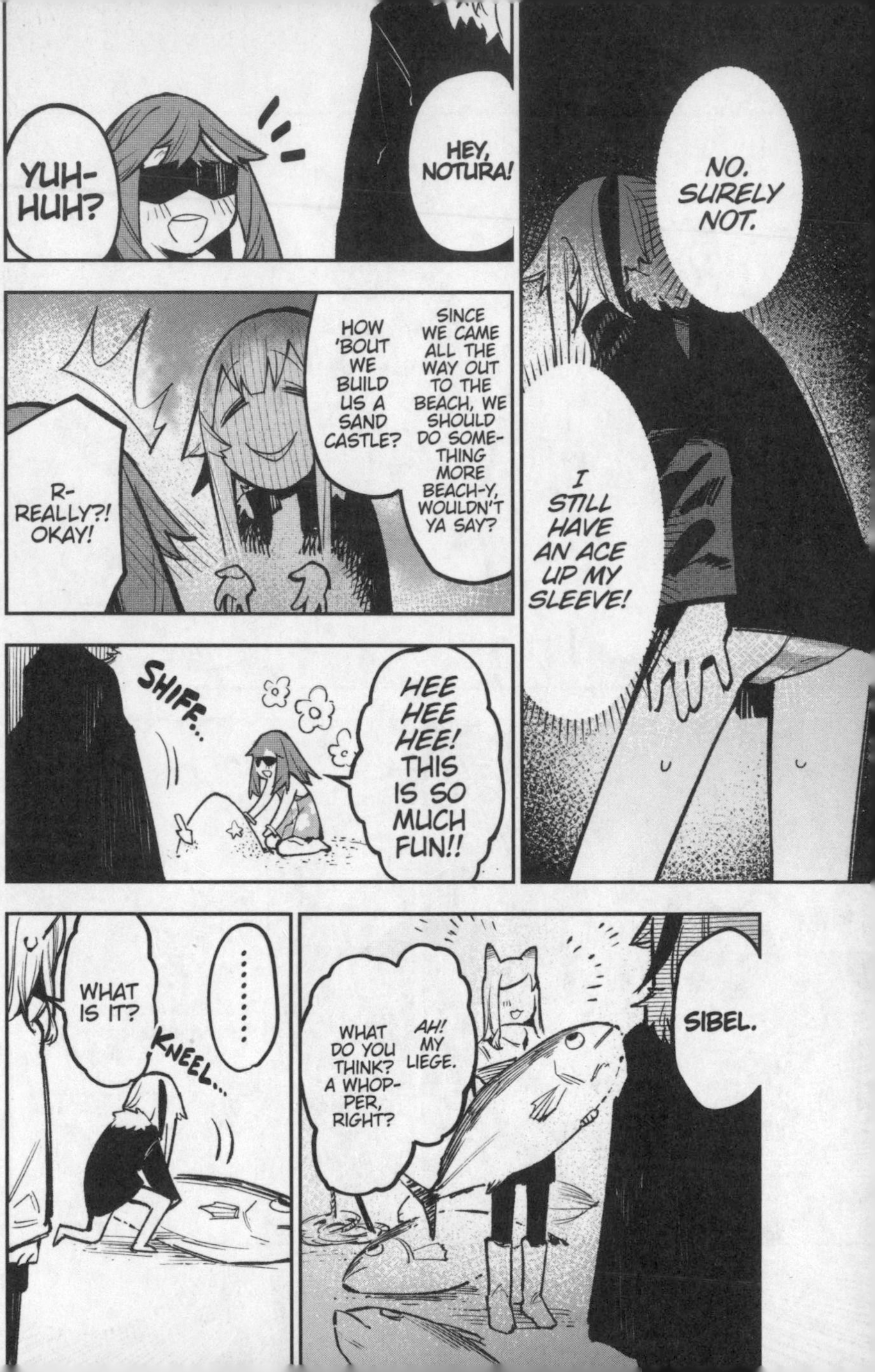
NO. SURELY NOT.
I STILL HAVE AN ACE UP MY SLEEVE!
HEY, NOTURA!
YUH-HUH?
SINCE WE CAME ALL THE WAY OUT TO THE BEACH, WE SHOULD DO SOMETHING MORE BEACH-Y, WOULDN'T YA SAY?
HOW 'BOUT WE BUILD US A SAND CASTLE?
R-REALLY?! OKAY!
HEE HEE HEE! THIS IS SO MUCH FUN!!
SHIFF...
SIBEL.
AH! MY LIEGE.
WHAT DO YOU THINK? A WHOPPER, RIGHT?
......
WHAT IS IT?
KNEEL...

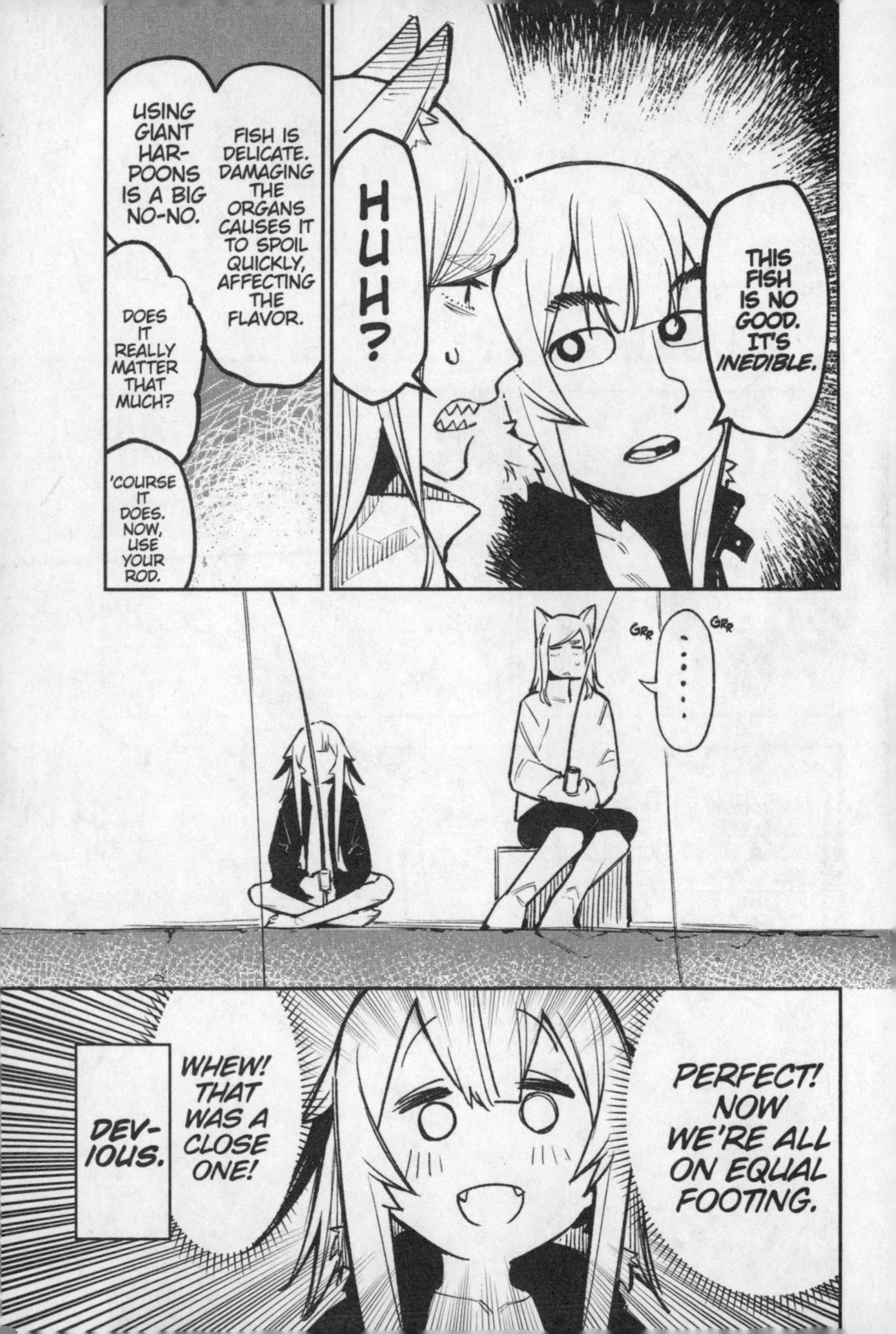
THIS FISH IS NO GOOD. IT'S *INEDIBLE.*
HUH?
FISH IS DELICATE. DAMAGING THE ORGANS CAUSES IT TO SPOIL QUICKLY, AFFECTING THE FLAVOR.
USING GIANT HAR-POONS IS A BIG NO-NO.
DOES IT REALLY MATTER THAT MUCH?
'COURSE IT DOES. NOW, USE YOUR ROD.
GRR
GRR
......
PERFECT! NOW WE'RE ALL ON EQUAL FOOTING.
WHEW! THAT WAS A CLOSE ONE!
DEV-IOUS.

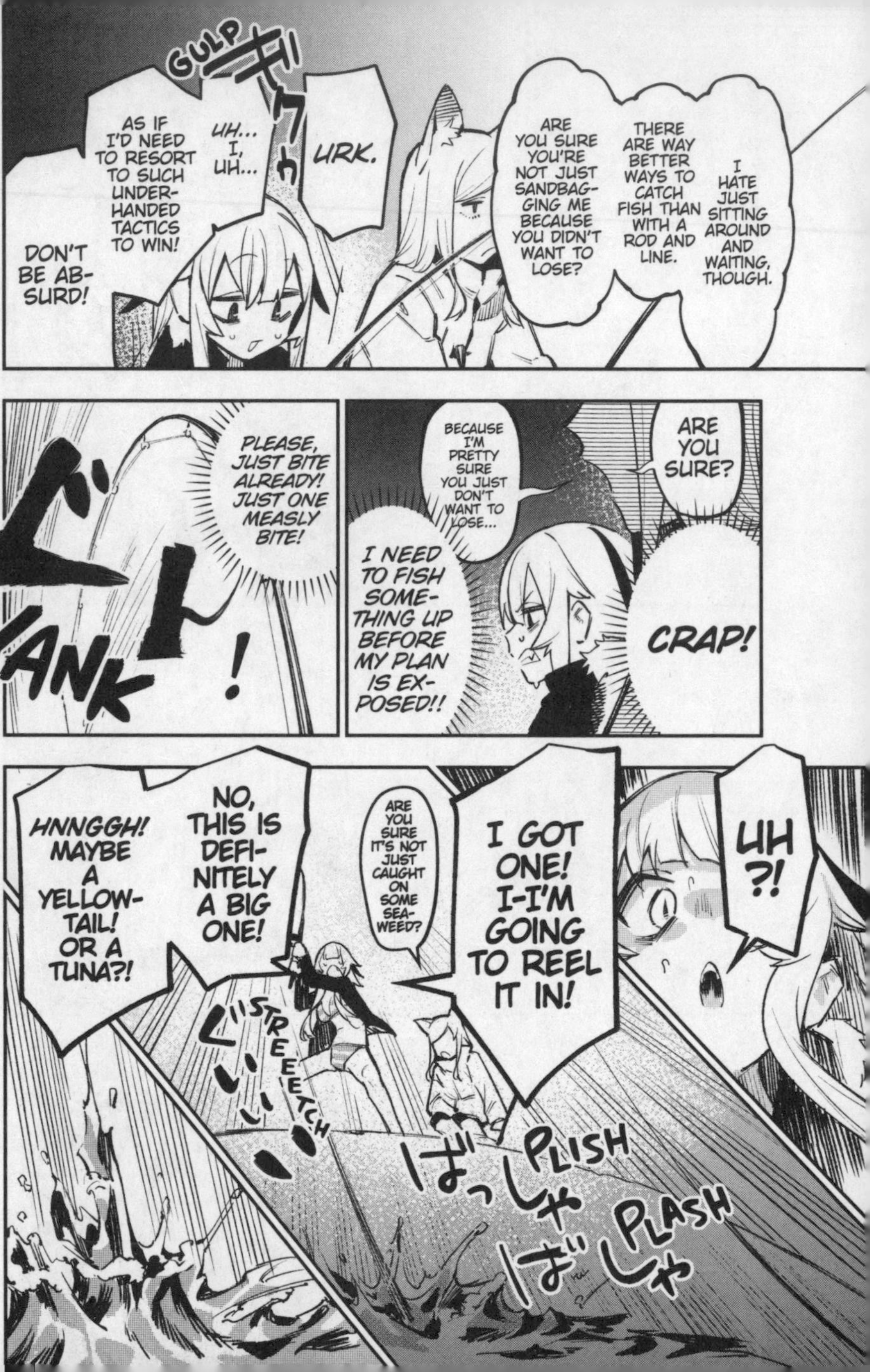
I HATE JUST SITTING AROUND AND WAITING, THOUGH.
THERE ARE WAY BETTER WAYS TO CATCH FISH THAN WITH A ROD AND LINE.
ARE YOU SURE YOU'RE NOT JUST SANDBAGGING ME BECAUSE YOU DIDN'T WANT TO LOSE?
GULP
URK.
UH... I, UH...
AS IF I'D NEED TO RESORT TO SUCH UNDERHANDED TACTICS TO WIN!
DON'T BE ABSURD!
ARE YOU SURE?
BECAUSE I'M PRETTY SURE YOU JUST DON'T WANT TO LOSE...
CRAP!
I NEED TO FISH SOMETHING UP BEFORE MY PLAN IS EXPOSED!!
PLEASE, JUST BITE ALREADY! JUST ONE MEASLY BITE!
YANK
!
UH ?!
I GOT ONE! I-I'M GOING TO REEL IT IN!
ARE YOU SURE IT'S NOT JUST CAUGHT ON SOME SEAWEED?
NO, THIS IS DEFINITELY A BIG ONE!
HNNGGH! MAYBE A YELLOWTAIL! OR A TUNA?!
STREEEETCH
PLISH
PLASH

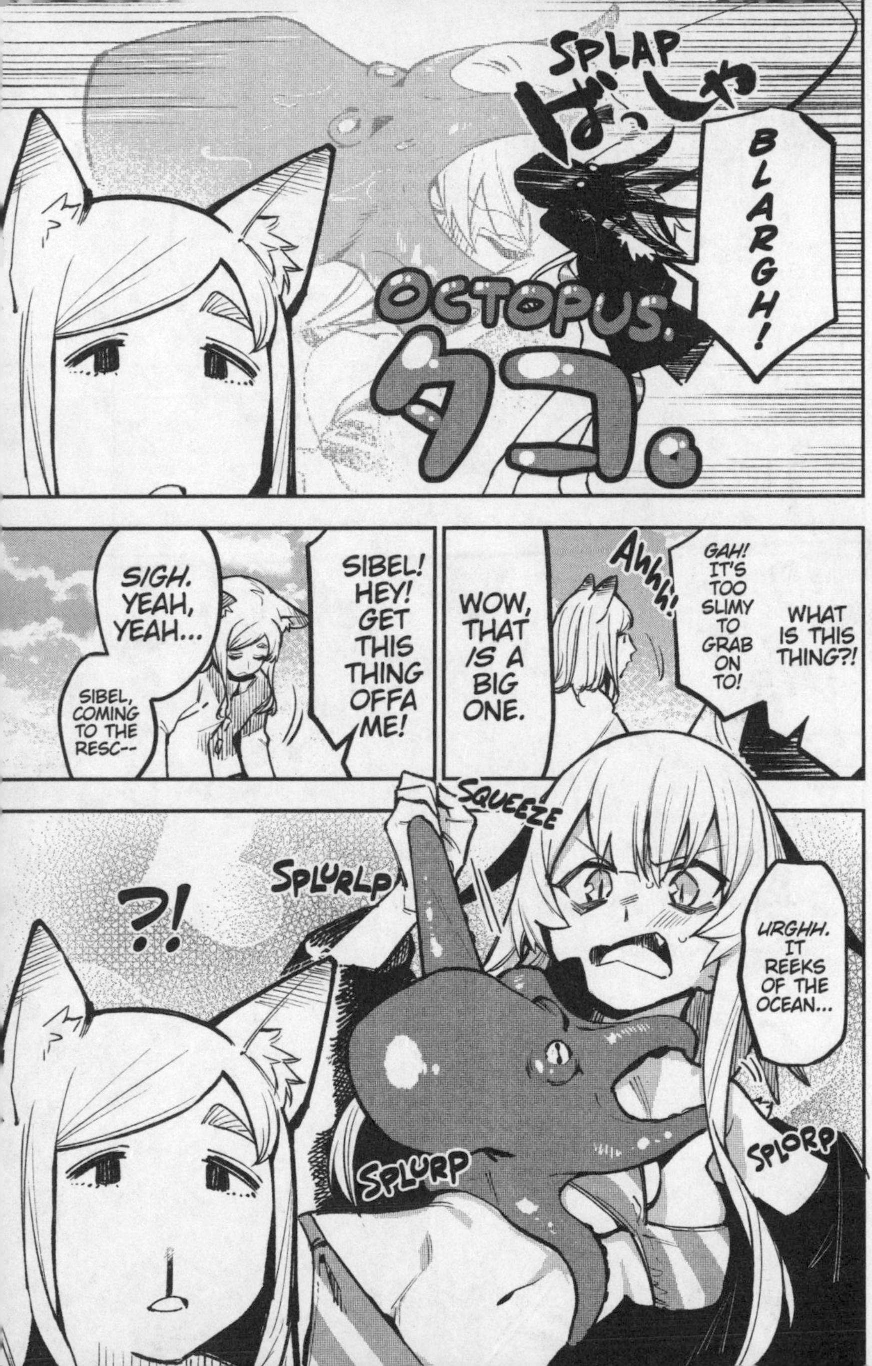
SPLAP
ばっしゃ
BLARGH!
OCTOPUS.
タコ。
WHAT IS THIS THING?!
GAH! IT'S TOO SLIMY TO GRAB ON TO!
Ahhh!
WOW, THAT IS A BIG ONE.
SIBEL! HEY! GET THIS THING OFFA ME!
SIGH. YEAH, YEAH...
SIBEL, COMING TO THE RESC--
SQUEEZE
URGHH. IT REEKS OF THE OCEAN...
SPLURLP
?!
SPLORP
SPLURP

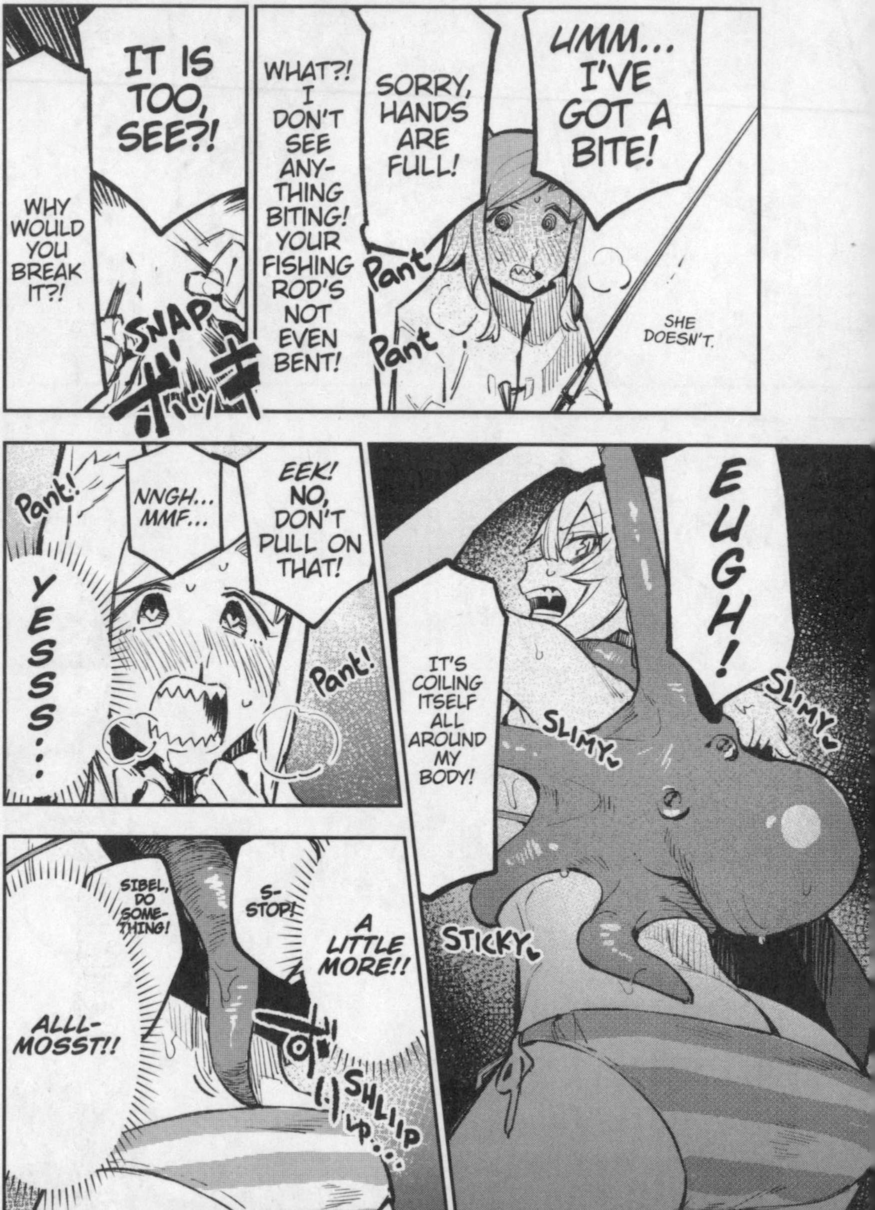
UMM... I'VE GOT A BITE!
SORRY, HANDS ARE FULL!
Pant
Pant
WHAT?! I DON'T SEE ANY-THING BITING! YOUR FISHING ROD'S NOT EVEN BENT!
SHE DOESN'T.
IT IS TOO, SEE?!
WHY WOULD YOU BREAK IT?!
SNAP
EUGH!
IT'S COILING ITSELF ALL AROUND MY BODY!
SLIMY
SLIMY
STICKY
EEK! NO, DON'T PULL ON THAT!
NNGH... MMF...
Pant!
YESSS...
Pant!
A LITTLE MORE!!
S-STOP!
SIBEL, DO SOME-THING!
ALLL-MOSST!!
SHLIIP
up...

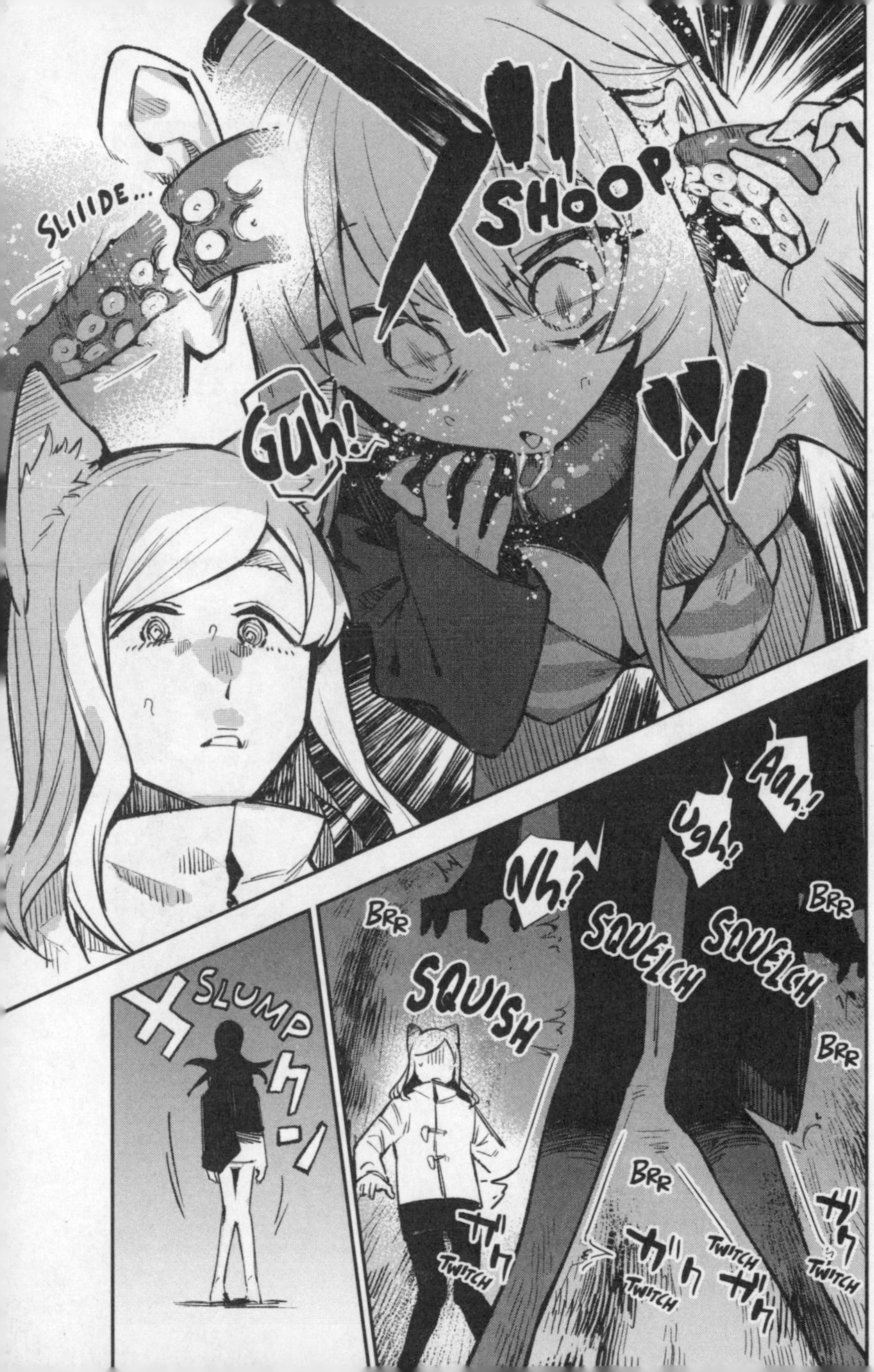
SHOOP
SLIIIDE...
GUH!
AAH!
UGH!
NH!
BRR
SQUELCH
SQUELCH
BRR
SQUISH
BRR
BRR
TWITCH
TWITCH
TWITCH
TWITCH
SLUMP

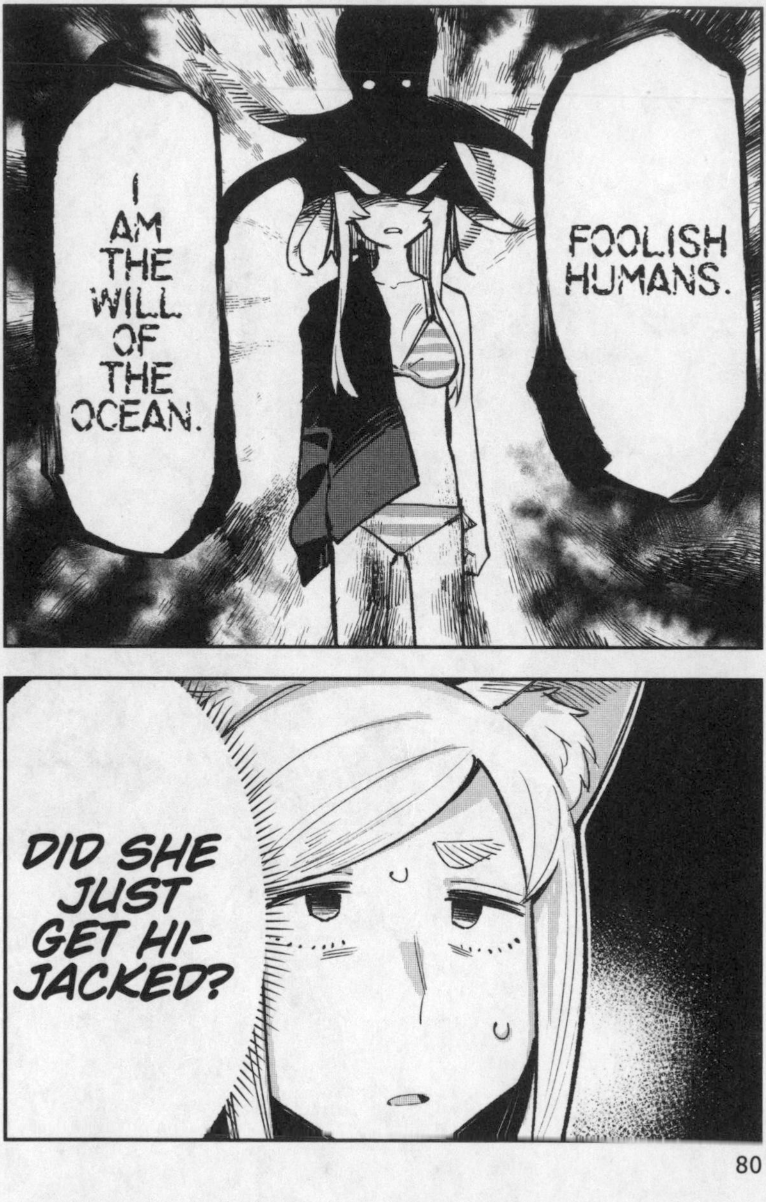
FOOLISH HUMANS.
I AM THE WILL OF THE OCEAN.
DID SHE JUST GET HI-JACKED?

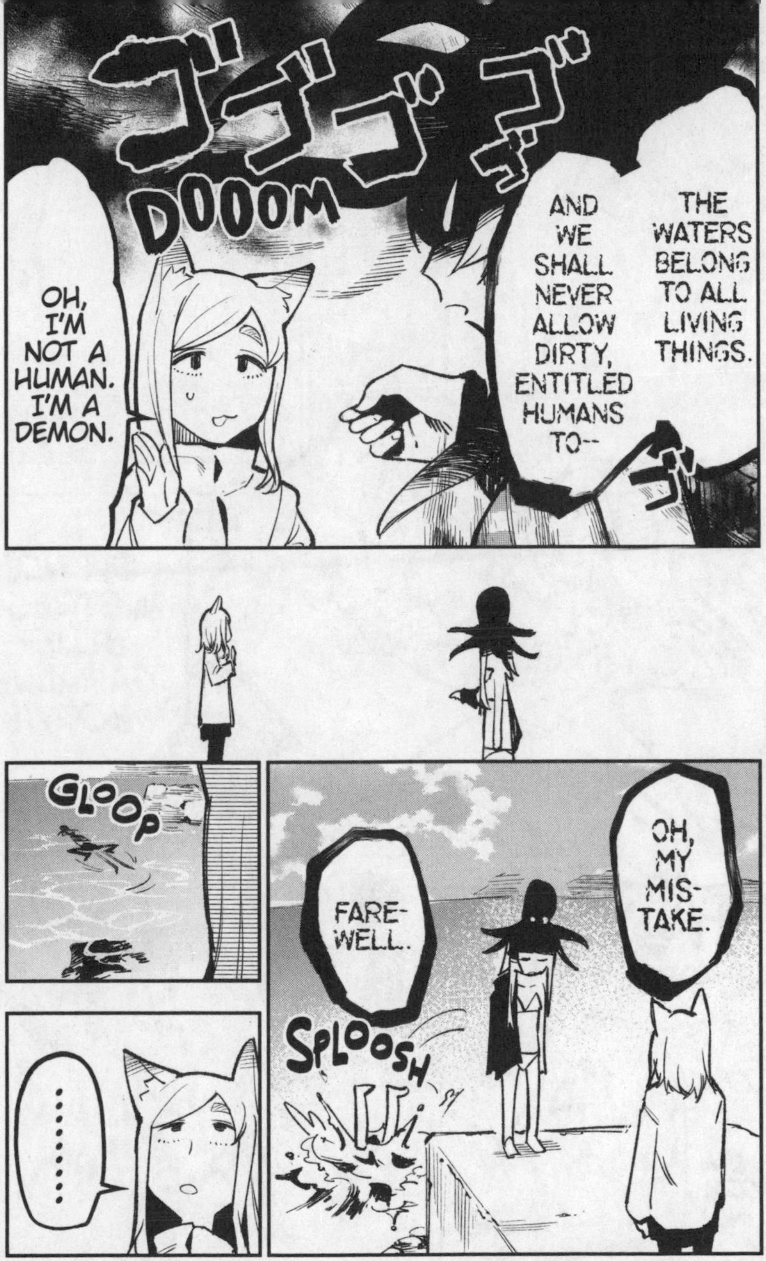
ゴゴゴゴ
DOOOM
THE WATERS BELONG TO ALL LIVING THINGS.
AND WE SHALL NEVER ALLOW DIRTY, ENTITLED HUMANS TO--
OH, I'M NOT A HUMAN. I'M A DEMON.
OH, MY MIS-TAKE.
FARE-WELL.
SPLOOSH
GLOOP
....

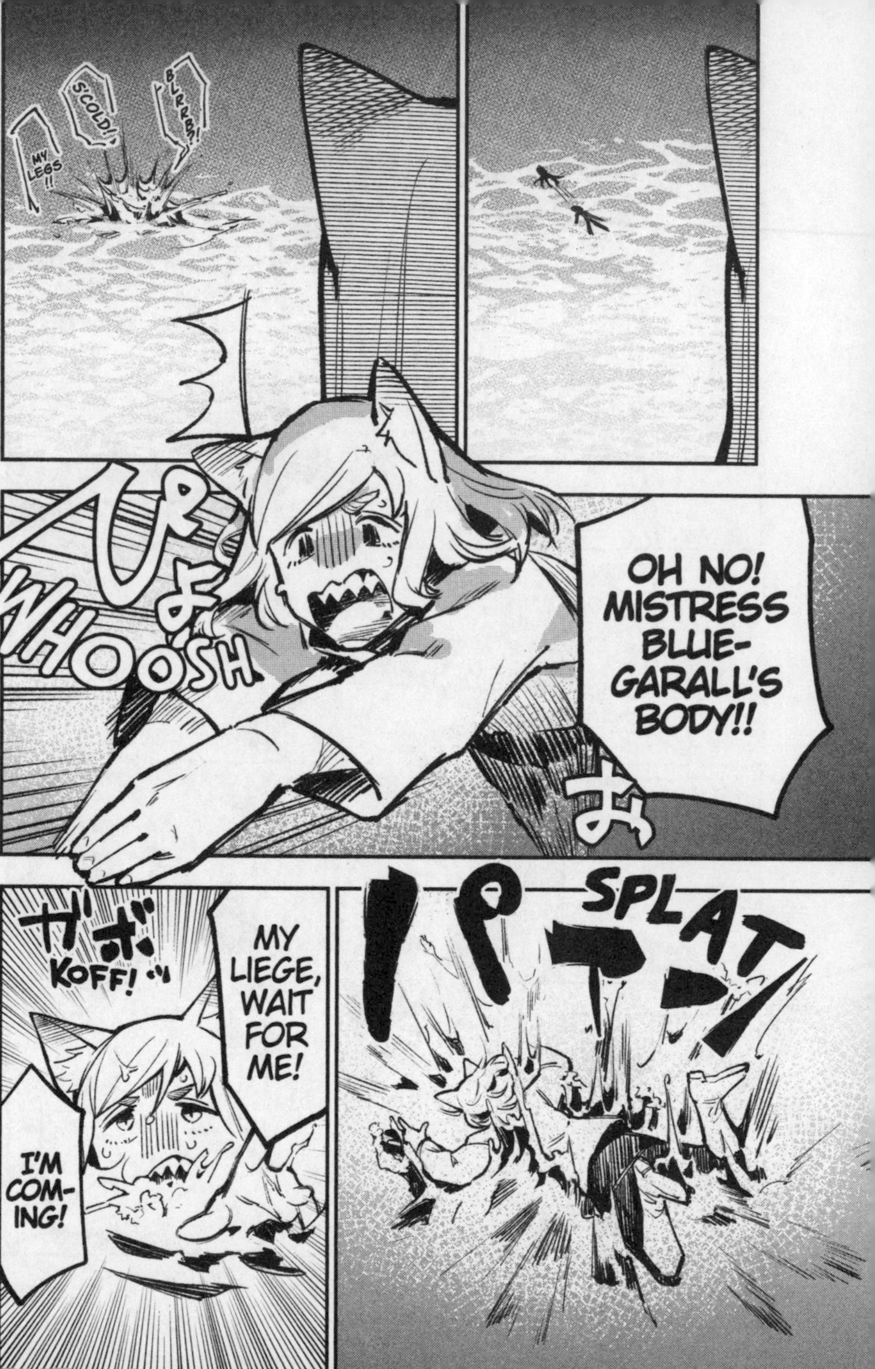
BLRRB?!
S'COLD!
MY LEGS!!
OH NO! MISTRESS BLUE-GARALL'S BODY!!
ぴょ
WHOOSH
お
パァーン
SPLAT
MY LIEGE, WAIT FOR ME!
ガボ
KOFF!
I'M COMING!

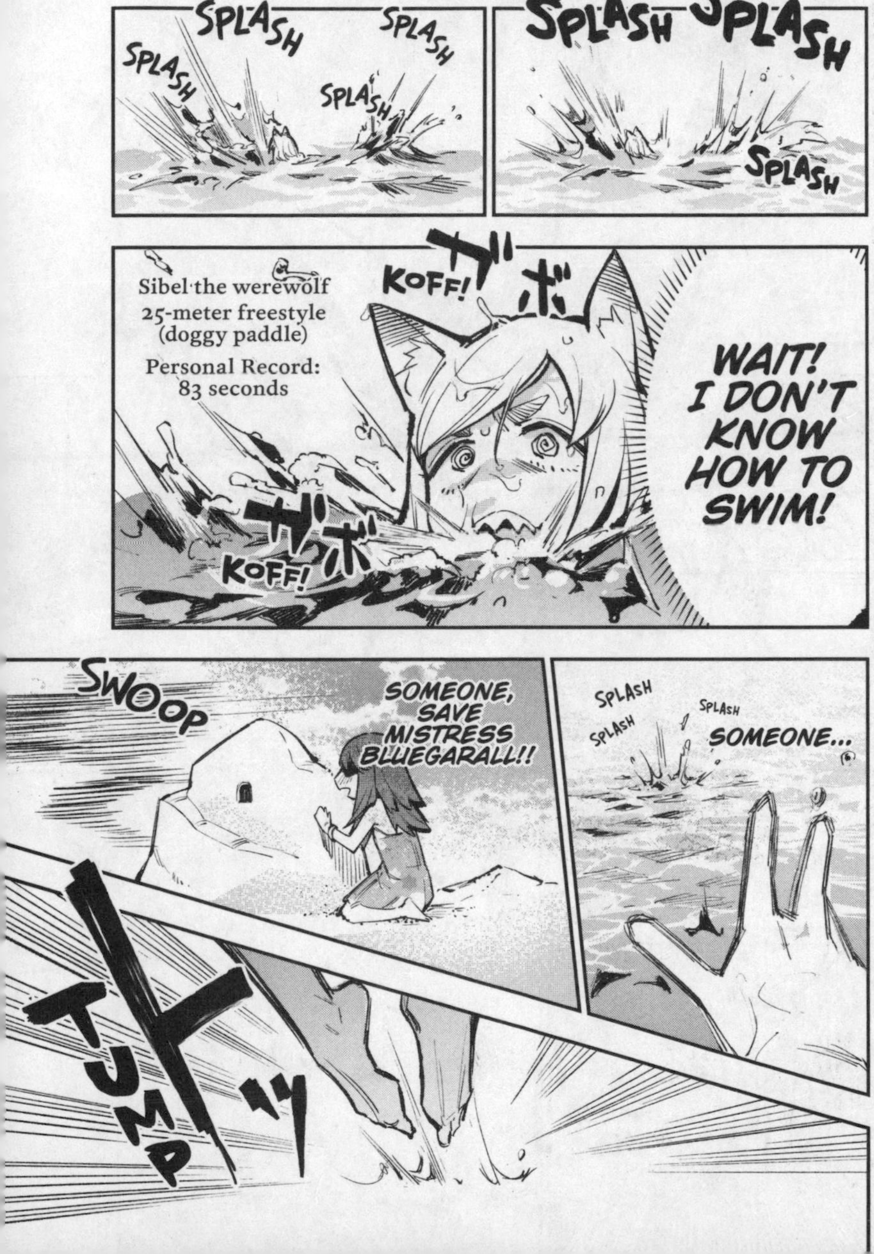
SPLASH
SPLASH
SPLASH
SPLASH
SPLASH
SPLASH
SPLASH
WAIT! I DON'T KNOW HOW TO SWIM!
ガボ
KOFF!
Sibel the werewolf
25-meter freestyle
(doggy paddle)
Personal Record:
83 seconds
ガボ
KOFF!
SPLASH
SPLASH
SPLASH
SOMEONE...
SOMEONE, SAVE MISTRESS BLUEGARALL!!
SWOOP
JUMP

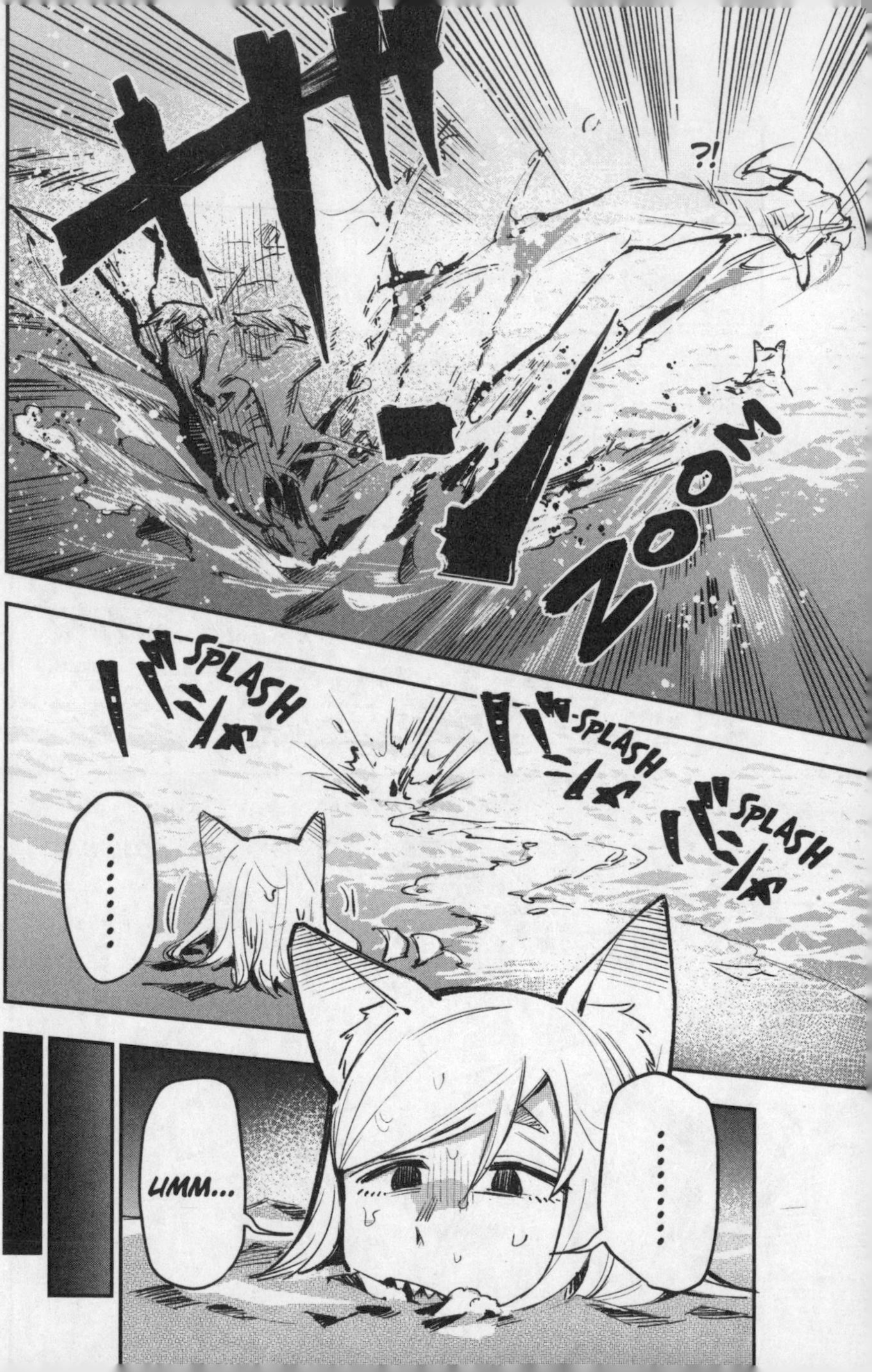
?!
ZOOM
SPLASH
SPLASH
SPLASH
....
....
UMM...

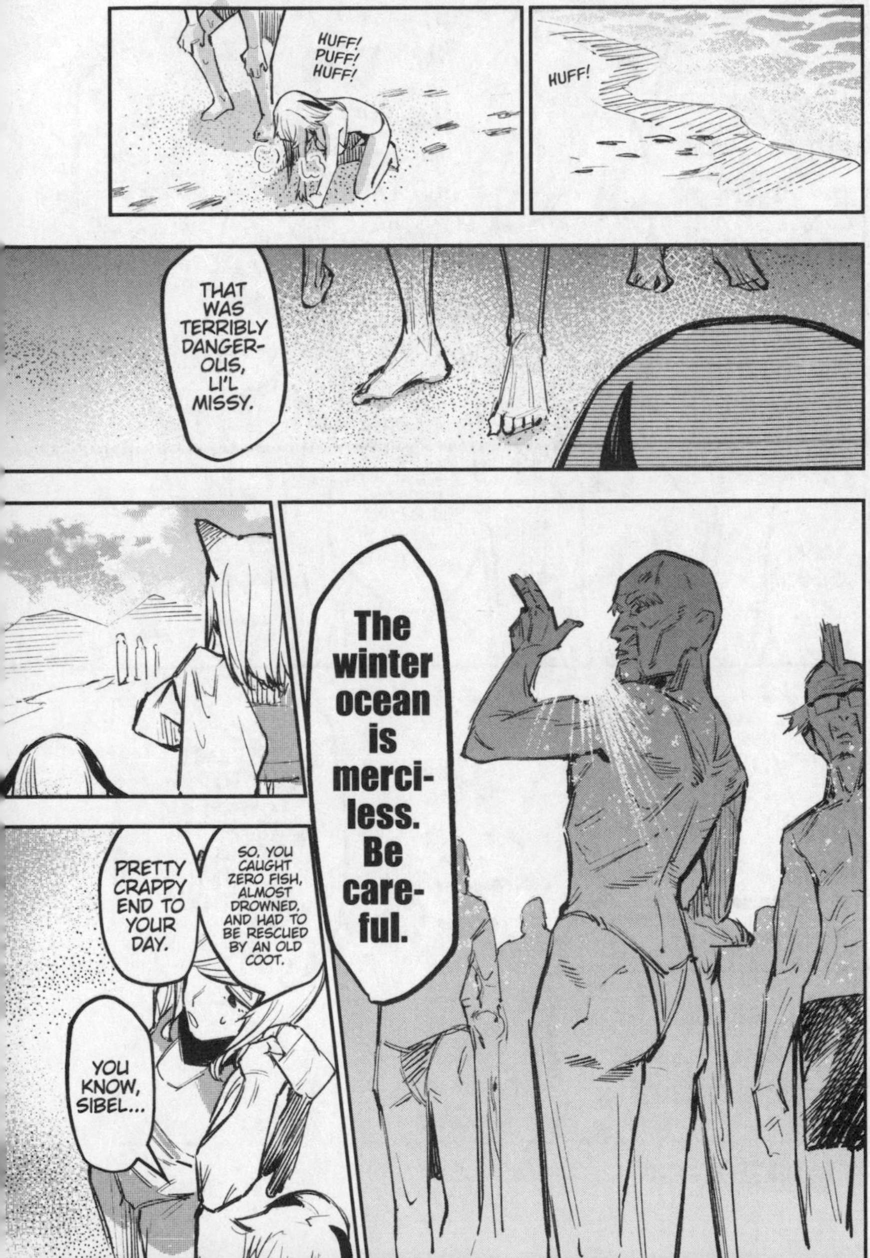
HUFF!
HUFF! PUFF! HUFF!
THAT WAS TERRIBLY DANGER-OUS, LI'L MISSY.
The winter ocean is merci-less. Be care-ful.
SO, YOU CAUGHT ZERO FISH, ALMOST DROWNED, AND HAD TO BE RESCUED BY AN OLD COOT.
PRETTY CRAPPY END TO YOUR DAY.
YOU KNOW, SIBEL...

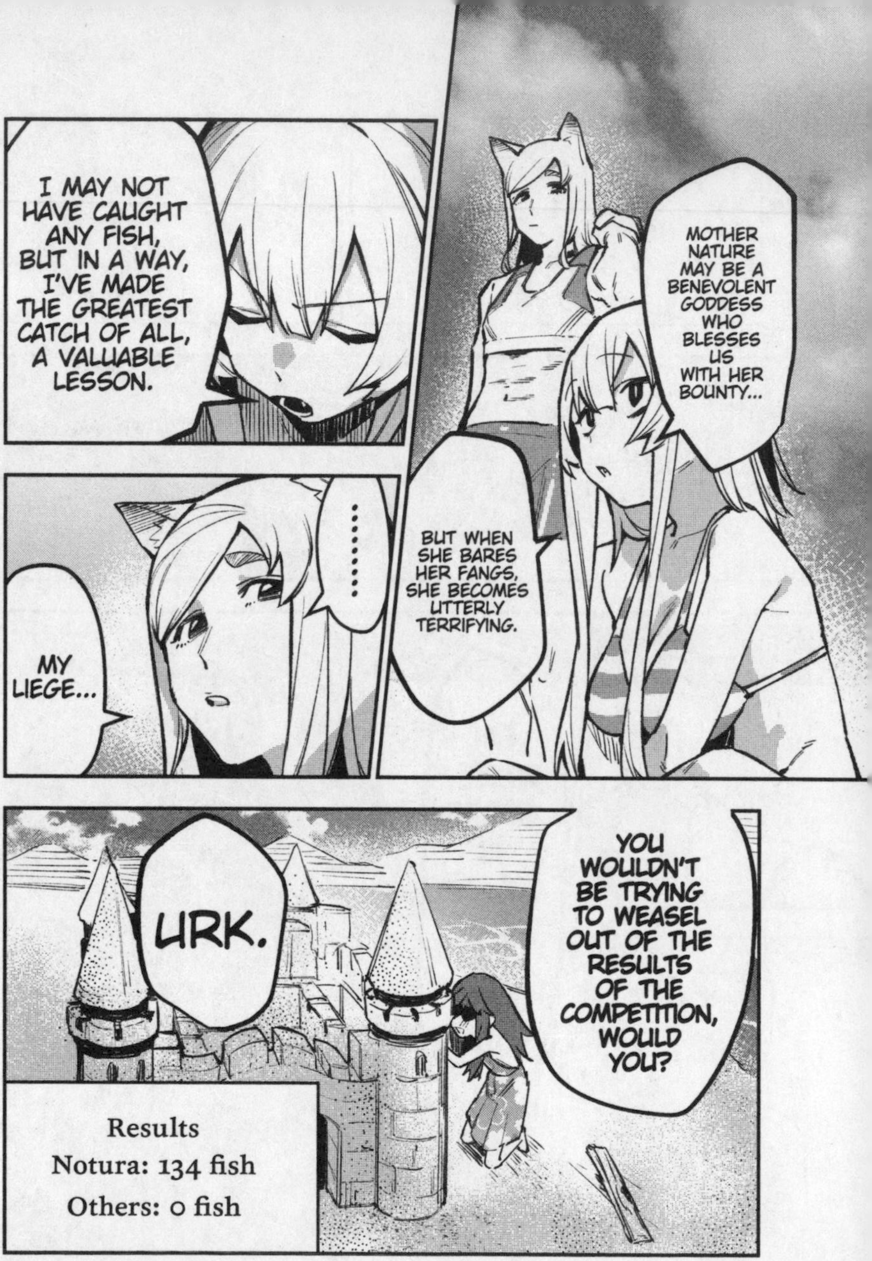
MOTHER NATURE MAY BE A BENEVOLENT GODDESS WHO BLESSES US WITH HER BOUNTY...
BUT WHEN SHE BARES HER FANGS, SHE BECOMES UTTERLY TERRIFYING.
I MAY NOT HAVE CAUGHT ANY FISH, BUT IN A WAY, I'VE MADE THE GREATEST CATCH OF ALL, A VALUABLE LESSON.
......
MY LIEGE...
YOU WOULDN'T BE TRYING TO WEASEL OUT OF THE RESULTS OF THE COMPETITION, WOULD YOU?
URK.
Results
Notura: 134 fish
Others: 0 fish

15TH NIGHT - END

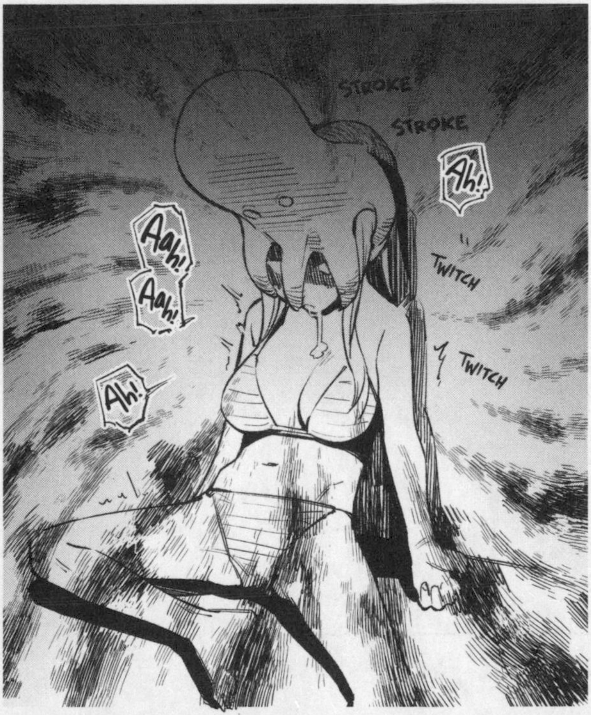
STROKE
STROKE
Ah!
TWITCH
TWITCH
Aah!
Aah!
Ah!

It's Just
Not My Night!
Tale of a Fallen Vampire Queen

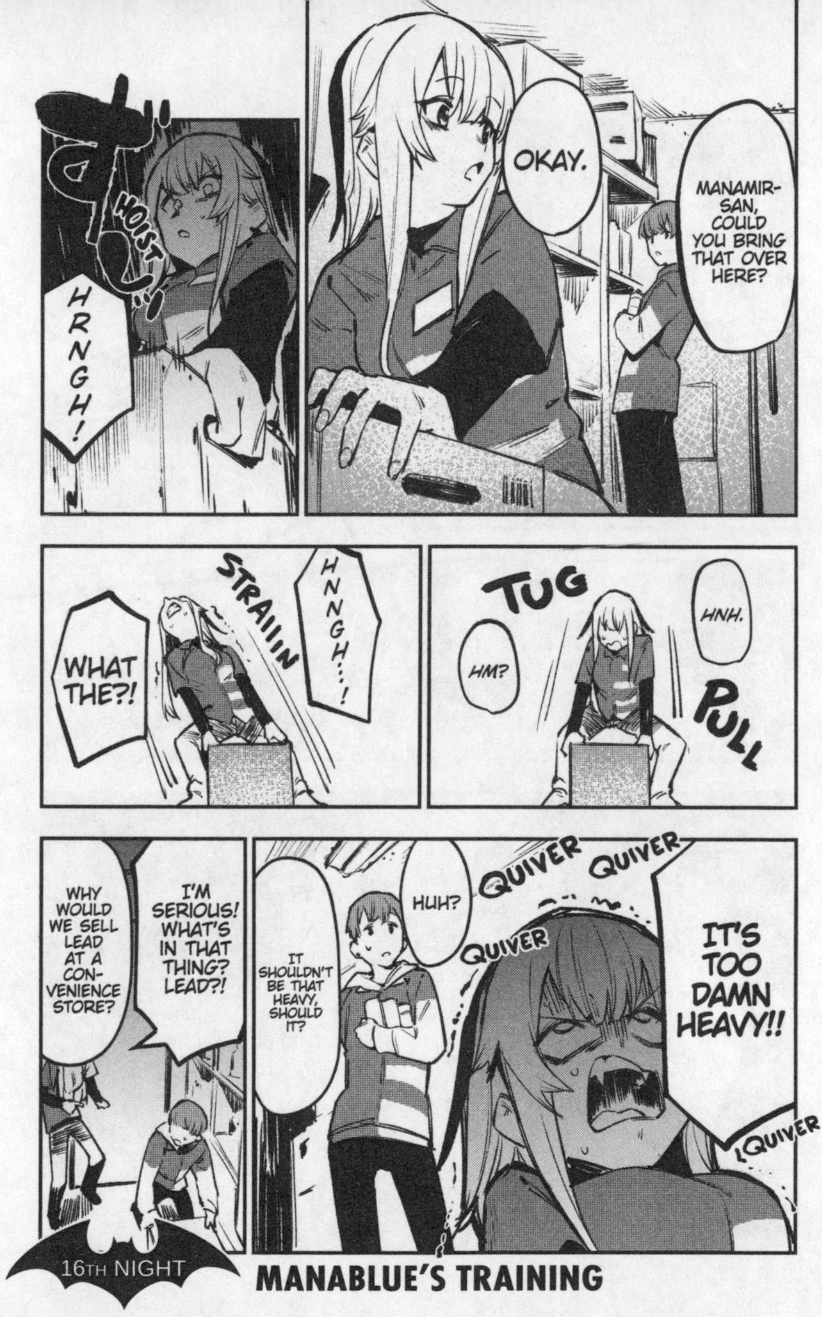
MANAMIR-SAN, COULD YOU BRING THAT OVER HERE?
OKAY.
HOIST
HRNGH!
HNH.
TUG
HM?
PULL
HNNGH...!
STRAIIIN
WHAT THE?!
QUIVER
QUIVER
IT'S TOO DAMN HEAVY!!
HUH?
QUIVER
IT SHOULDN'T BE THAT HEAVY, SHOULD IT?
QUIVER
I'M SERIOUS! WHAT'S IN THAT THING? LEAD?!
WHY WOULD WE SELL LEAD AT A CON-VENIENCE STORE?

16TH NIGHT

MANABLUE'S TRAINING

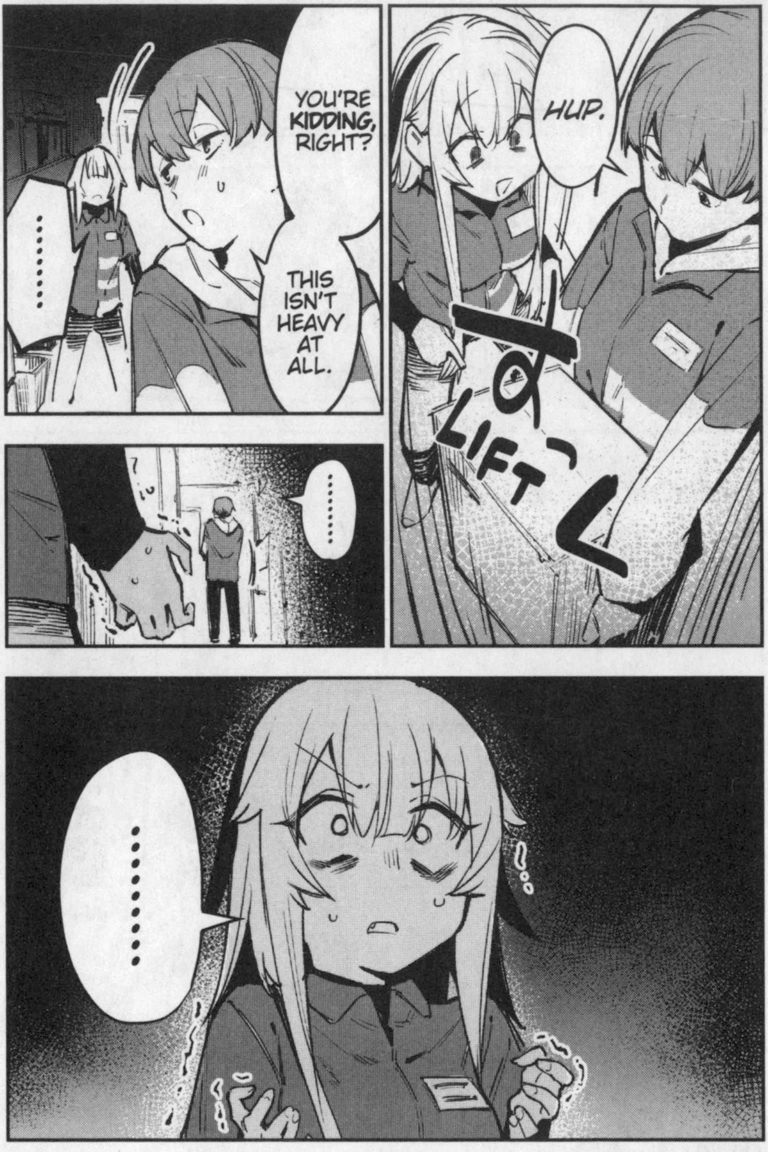
HUP.
LIFT
YOU'RE KIDDING, RIGHT?
THIS ISN'T HEAVY AT ALL.
......
......
....

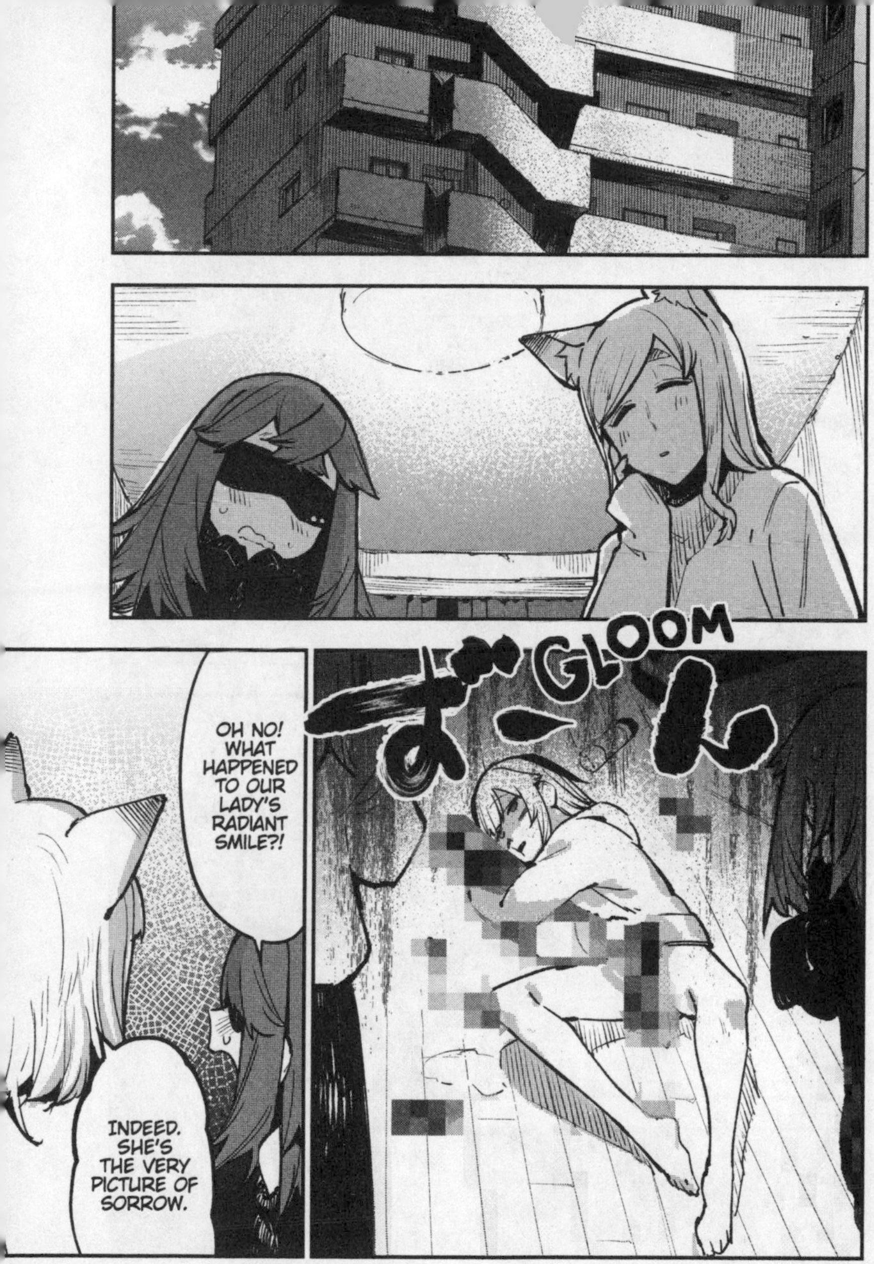
ずーん
GLOOM
OH NO! WHAT HAPPENED TO OUR LADY'S RADIANT SMILE?!
INDEED. SHE'S THE VERY PICTURE OF SORROW.

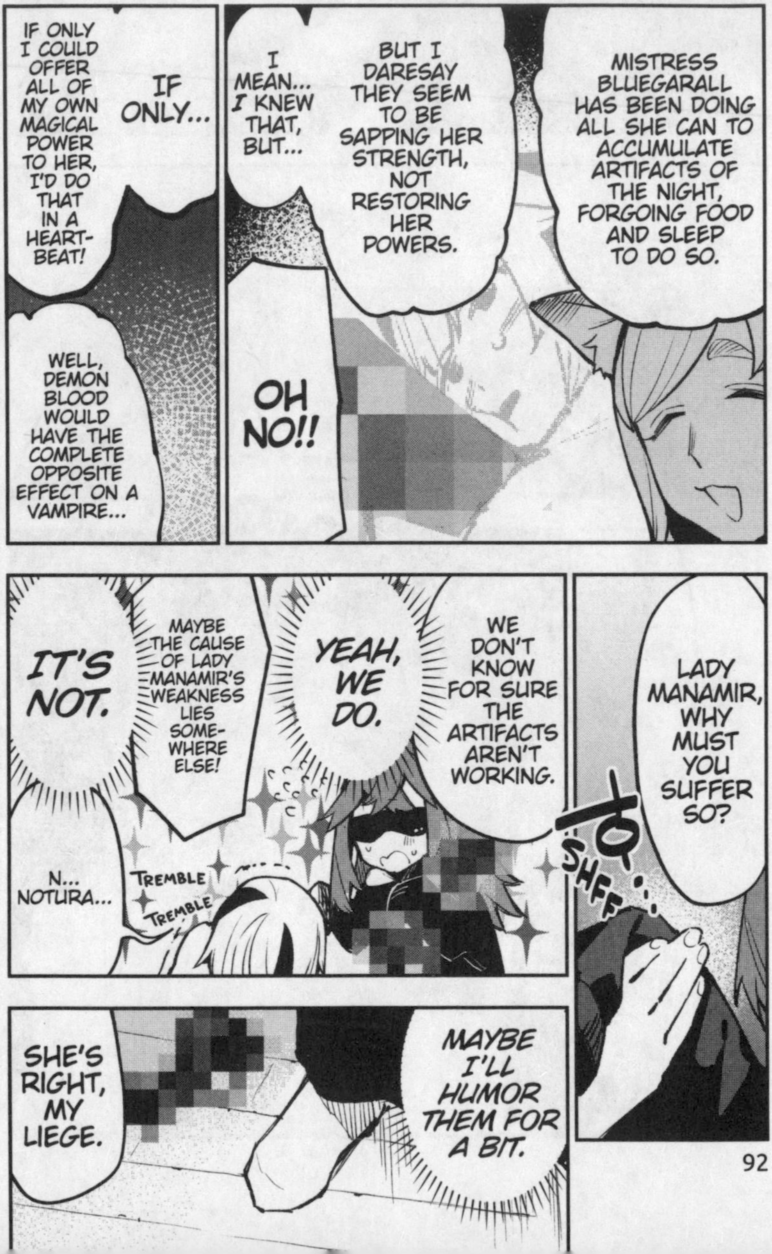
MISTRESS BLUEGARALL HAS BEEN DOING ALL SHE CAN TO ACCUMULATE ARTIFACTS OF THE NIGHT, FORGOING FOOD AND SLEEP TO DO SO.
BUT I DARESAY THEY SEEM TO BE SAPPING HER STRENGTH, NOT RESTORING HER POWERS.
I MEAN... I KNEW THAT, BUT...
OH NO!!
IF ONLY...
IF ONLY I COULD OFFER ALL OF MY OWN MAGICAL POWER TO HER, I'D DO THAT IN A HEART-BEAT!
WELL, DEMON BLOOD WOULD HAVE THE COMPLETE OPPOSITE EFFECT ON A VAMPIRE...
LADY MANAMIR, WHY MUST YOU SUFFER SO?
SHFF
WE DON'T KNOW FOR SURE THE ARTIFACTS AREN'T WORKING.
YEAH, WE DO.
MAYBE THE CAUSE OF LADY MANAMIR'S WEAKNESS LIES SOME-WHERE ELSE!
IT'S NOT.
N... NOTURA...
TREMBLE
TREMBLE
MAYBE I'LL HUMOR THEM FOR A BIT.
SHE'S RIGHT, MY LIEGE.

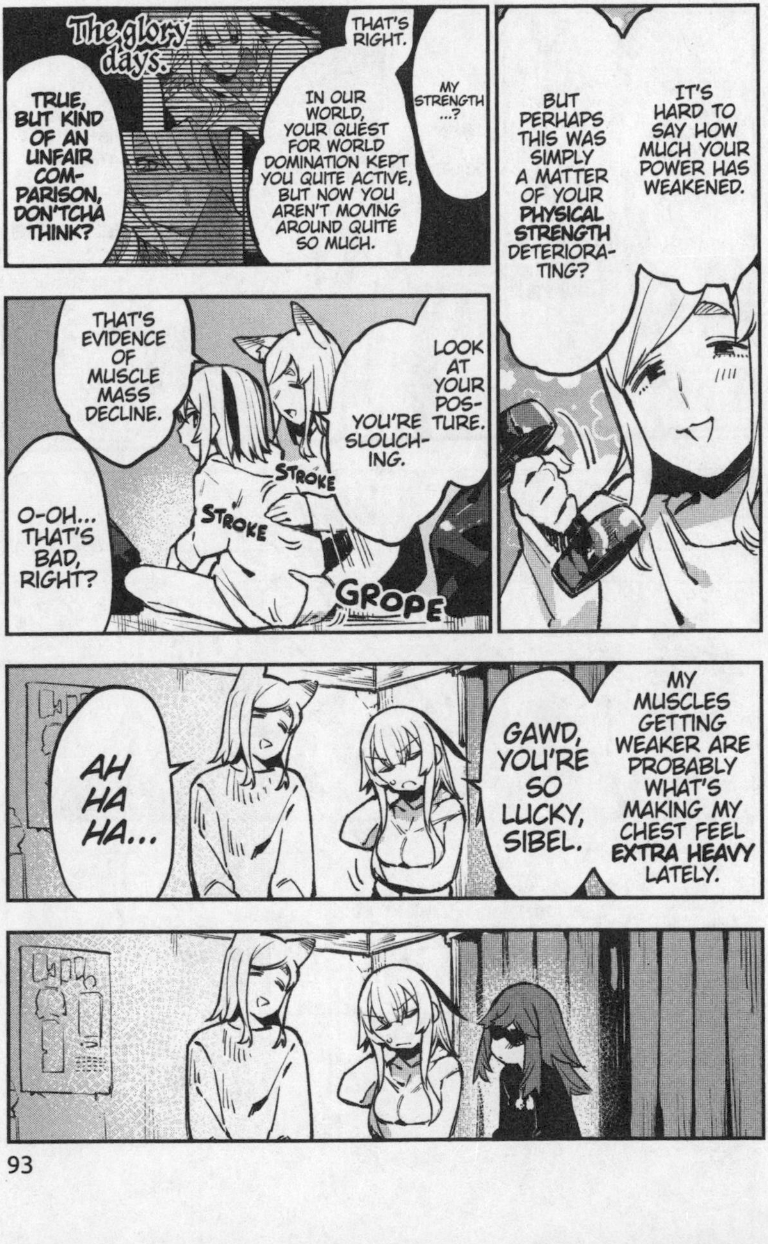

IT'S HARD TO SAY HOW MUCH YOUR POWER HAS WEAKENED.
BUT PERHAPS THIS WAS SIMPLY A MATTER OF YOUR PHYSICAL STRENGTH DETERIORATING?
MY STRENGTH ...?
THAT'S RIGHT.
IN OUR WORLD, YOUR QUEST FOR WORLD DOMINATION KEPT YOU QUITE ACTIVE, BUT NOW YOU AREN'T MOVING AROUND QUITE SO MUCH.
TRUE, BUT KIND OF AN UNFAIR COMPARISON, DON'TCHA THINK?
The glory days.
LOOK AT YOUR POSTURE.
YOU'RE SLOUCHING.
STROKE
STROKE
THAT'S EVIDENCE OF MUSCLE MASS DECLINE.
O-OH... THAT'S BAD, RIGHT?
GROPE
MY MUSCLES GETTING WEAKER ARE PROBABLY WHAT'S MAKING MY CHEST FEEL EXTRA HEAVY LATELY.
GAWD, YOU'RE SO LUCKY, SIBEL.
AH HA HA...

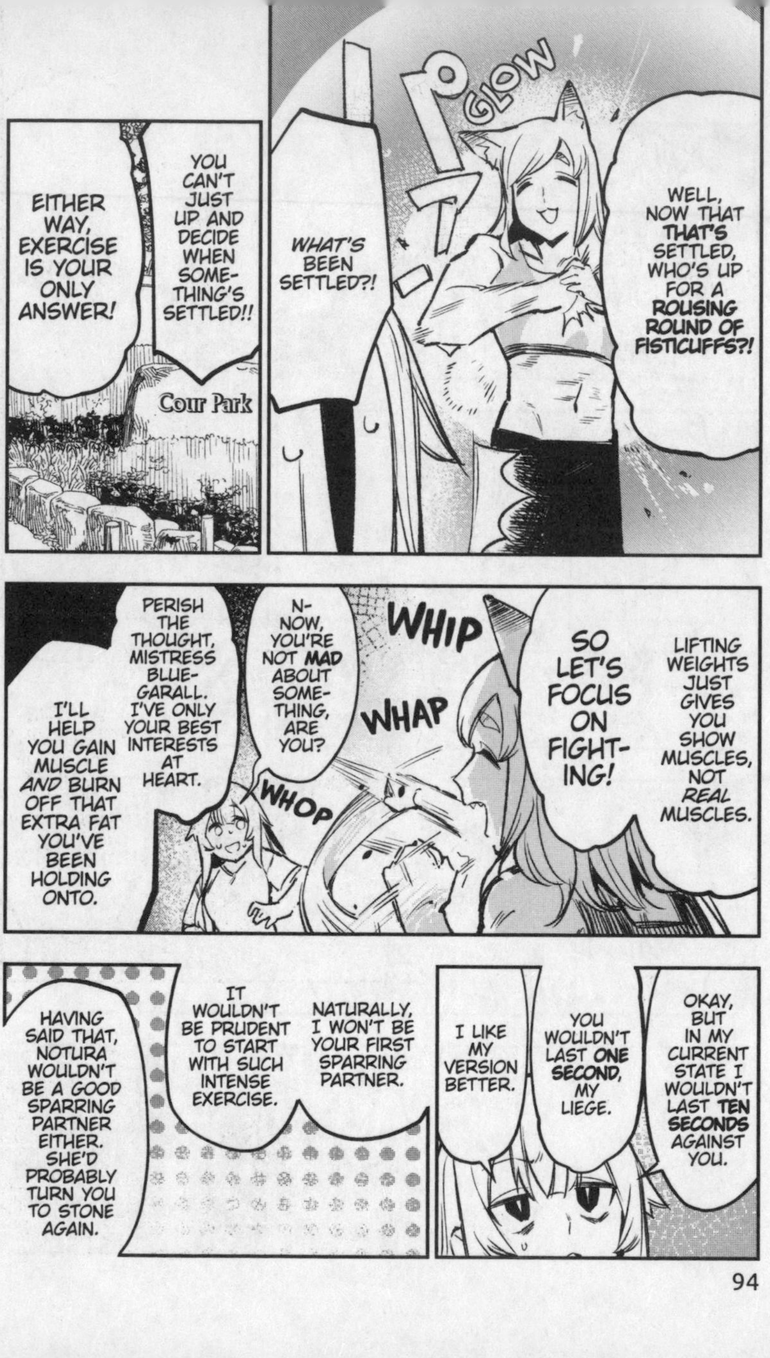
GLOW
WELL, NOW THAT THAT'S SETTLED, WHO'S UP FOR A ROUSING ROUND OF FISTICUFFS?!
WHAT'S BEEN SETTLED?!
YOU CAN'T JUST UP AND DECIDE WHEN SOMETHING'S SETTLED!!
EITHER WAY, EXERCISE IS YOUR ONLY ANSWER!
Cour Park
LIFTING WEIGHTS JUST GIVES YOU SHOW MUSCLES, NOT REAL MUSCLES.
SO LET'S FOCUS ON FIGHTING!
WHIP
WHAP
N-NOW, YOU'RE NOT MAD ABOUT SOMETHING, ARE YOU?
WHOP
PERISH THE THOUGHT, MISTRESS BLUEGARALL. I'VE ONLY YOUR BEST INTERESTS AT HEART.
I'LL HELP YOU GAIN MUSCLE AND BURN OFF THAT EXTRA FAT YOU'VE BEEN HOLDING ONTO.
OKAY, BUT IN MY CURRENT STATE I WOULDN'T LAST TEN SECONDS AGAINST YOU.
YOU WOULDN'T LAST ONE SECOND, MY LIEGE.
I LIKE MY VERSION BETTER.
NATURALLY, I WON'T BE YOUR FIRST SPARRING PARTNER.
IT WOULDN'T BE PRUDENT TO START WITH SUCH INTENSE EXERCISE.
HAVING SAID THAT, NOTURA WOULDN'T BE A GOOD SPARRING PARTNER EITHER. SHE'D PROBABLY TURN YOU TO STONE AGAIN.

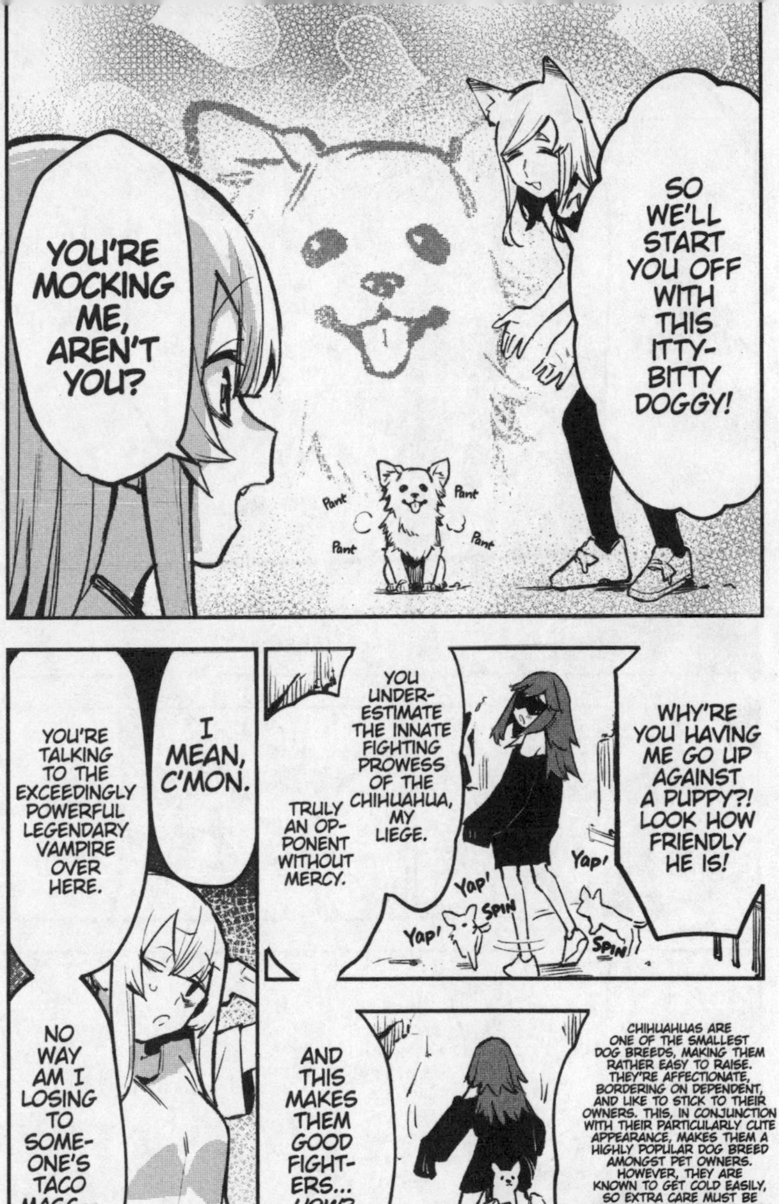
SO WE'LL START YOU OFF WITH THIS ITTY-BITTY DOGGY!
YOU'RE MOCKING ME, AREN'T YOU?
Pant
Pant
Pant
Pant
WHY'RE YOU HAVING ME GO UP AGAINST A PUPPY?! LOOK HOW FRIENDLY HE IS!
Yap!
Yap!
Yap!
SPIN
SPIN
YOU UNDER-ESTIMATE THE INNATE FIGHTING PROWESS OF THE CHIHUAHUA, MY LIEGE.
TRULY AN OP-PONENT WITHOUT MERCY.
CHIHUAHUAS ARE ONE OF THE SMALLEST DOG BREEDS, MAKING THEM RATHER EASY TO RAISE. THEY'RE AFFECTIONATE, BORDERING ON DEPENDENT, AND LIKE TO STICK TO THEIR OWNERS. THIS, IN CONJUNCTION WITH THEIR PARTICULARLY CUTE APPEARANCE, MAKES THEM A HIGHLY POPULAR DOG BREED AMONGST PET OWNERS. HOWEVER, THEY ARE KNOWN TO GET COLD EASILY, SO EXTRA CARE MUST BE TAKEN TO ENSURE THAT THEY ARE KEPT WARM WHEN THE WEATHER STARTS GETTING CHILLY.
AND THIS MAKES THEM GOOD FIGHT-ERS... *HOW?*
I MEAN, C'MON.
YOU'RE TALKING TO THE EXCEEDINGLY POWERFUL LEGENDARY VAMPIRE OVER HERE.
NO WAY AM I LOSING TO SOME-ONE'S TACO MASC--

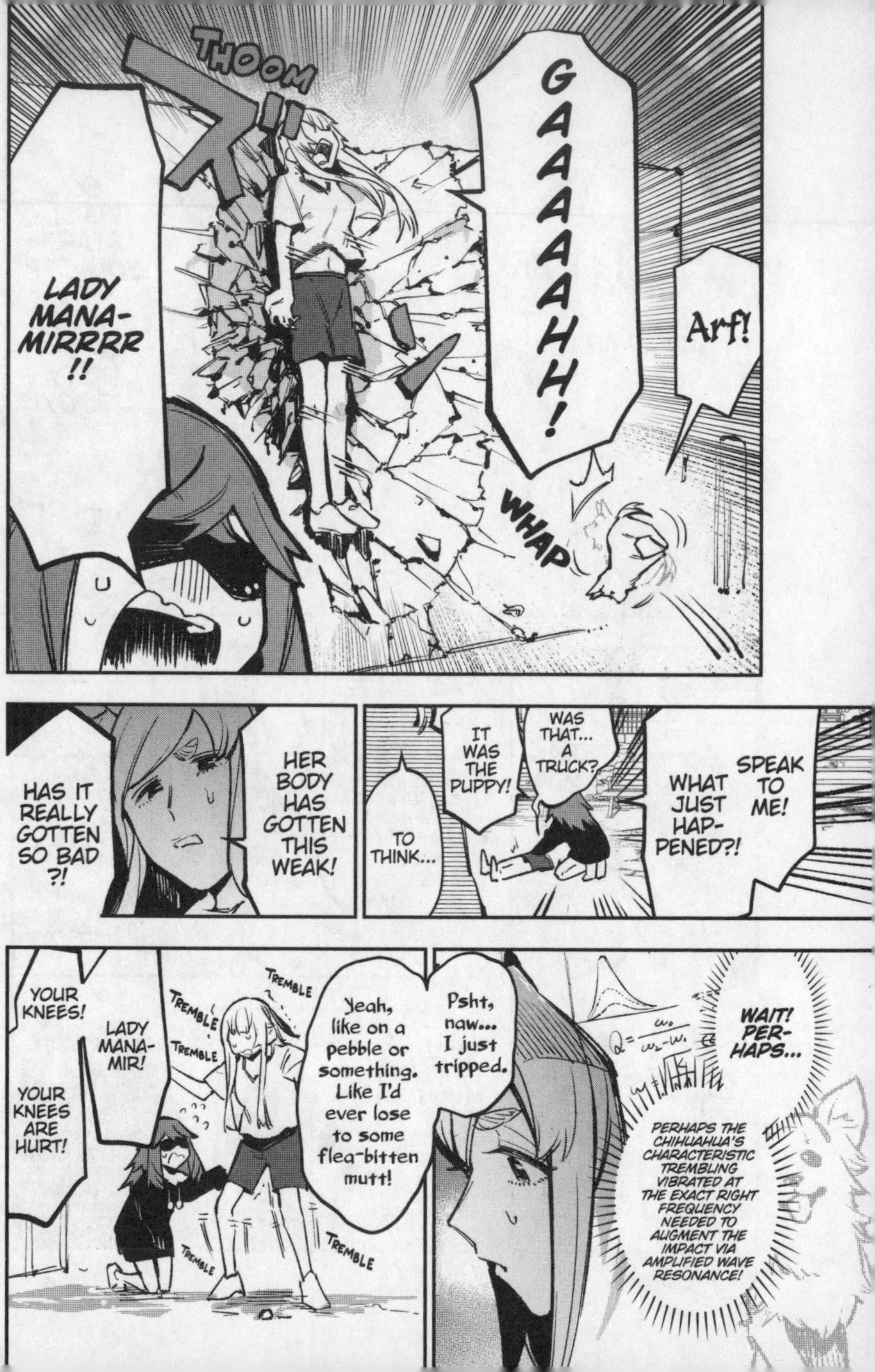

Arf!
GAAAAAAH!
THOOM
WHAP
LADY MANA-MIRRRR !!
SPEAK TO ME!
WHAT JUST HAP-PENED?!
WAS THAT... A TRUCK?
IT WAS THE PUPPY!
TO THINK...
HER BODY HAS GOTTEN THIS WEAK!
HAS IT REALLY GOTTEN SO BAD ?!
WAIT! PER-HAPS...
PERHAPS THE CHIHUAHUA'S CHARACTERISTIC TREMBLING VIBRATED AT THE EXACT RIGHT FREQUENCY NEEDED TO AUGMENT THE IMPACT VIA AMPLIFIED WAVE RESONANCE!
Psht, naw... I just tripped.
Yeah, like on a pebble or something. Like I'd ever lose to some flea-bitten mutt!
TREMBLE
TREMBLE
TREMBLE
TREMBLE
TREMBLE
YOUR KNEES!
LADY MANA-MIR!
YOUR KNEES ARE HURT!

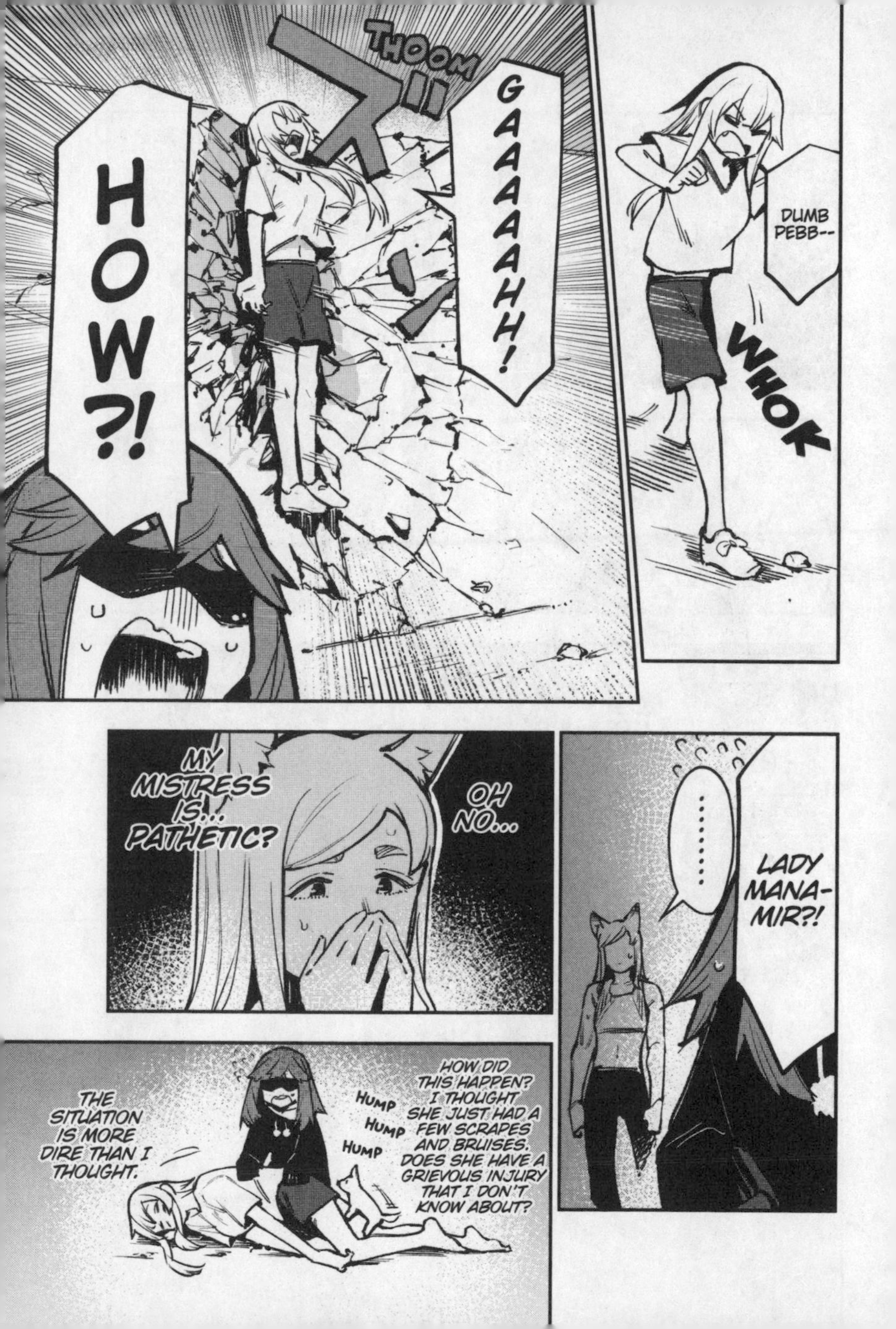
DUMB PEBB--
WHOK
THOOM
GAAAAAAHH!
HOW?!
......
LADY MANAMIR?!
OH NO...
MY MISTRESS IS... PATHETIC?
HOW DID THIS HAPPEN? I THOUGHT SHE JUST HAD A FEW SCRAPES AND BRUISES. DOES SHE HAVE A GRIEVOUS INJURY THAT I DON'T KNOW ABOUT?
HUMP
HUMP
HUMP
THE SITUATION IS MORE DIRE THAN I THOUGHT.

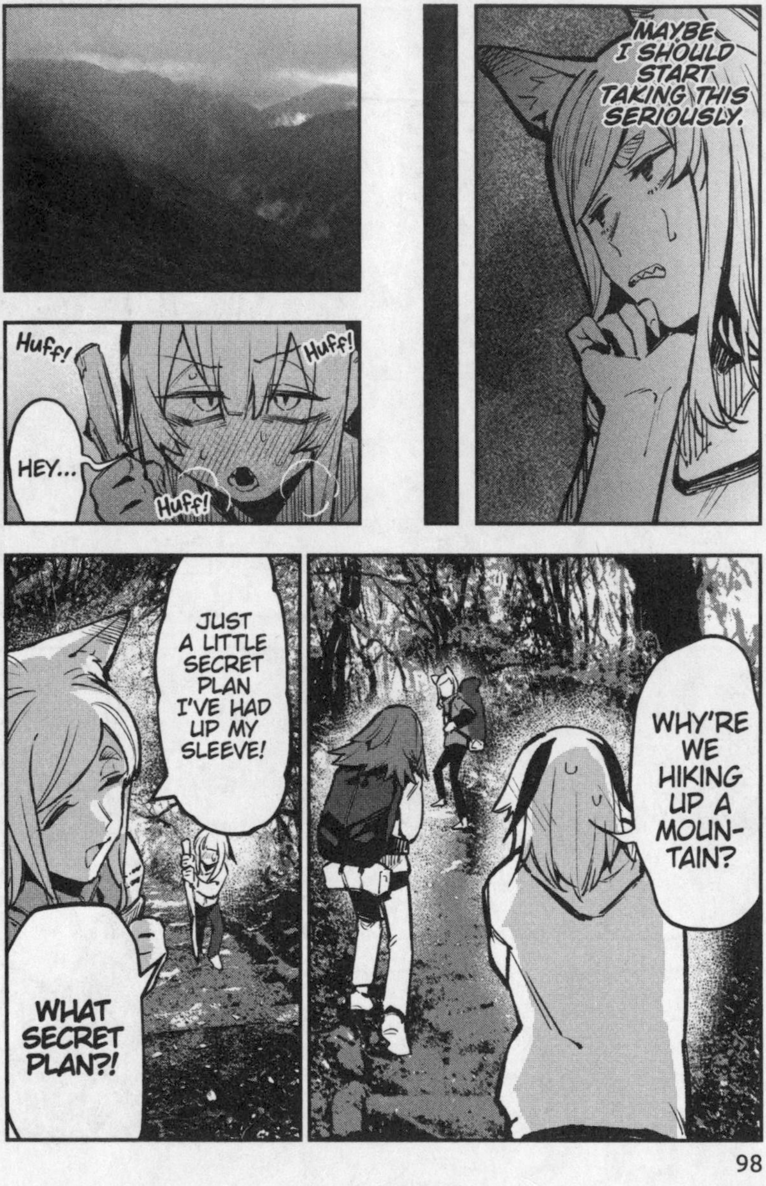
MAYBE I SHOULD START TAKING THIS SERIOUSLY.
Huff!
Huff!
HEY...
Huff!
WHY'RE WE HIKING UP A MOUN-TAIN?
JUST A LITTLE SECRET PLAN I'VE HAD UP MY SLEEVE!
WHAT SECRET PLAN?!

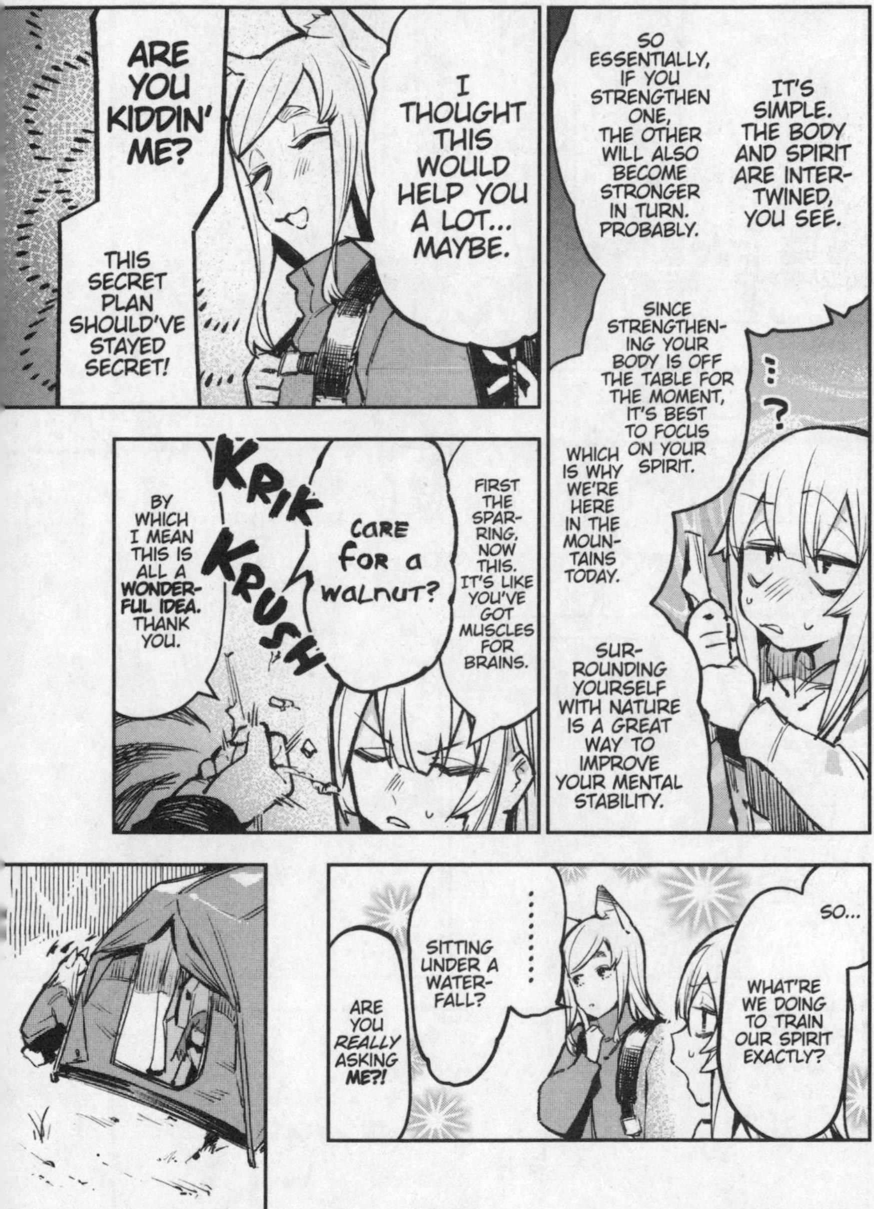
IT'S SIMPLE. THE BODY AND SPIRIT ARE INTER-TWINED, YOU SEE.
SO ESSENTIALLY, IF YOU STRENGTHEN ONE, THE OTHER WILL ALSO BECOME STRONGER IN TURN. PROBABLY.
...?
SINCE STRENGTHEN-ING YOUR BODY IS OFF THE TABLE FOR THE MOMENT, IT'S BEST TO FOCUS ON YOUR SPIRIT.
WHICH IS WHY WE'RE HERE IN THE MOUN-TAINS TODAY.
SUR-ROUNDING YOURSELF WITH NATURE IS A GREAT WAY TO IMPROVE YOUR MENTAL STABILITY.
I THOUGHT THIS WOULD HELP YOU A LOT... MAYBE.
ARE YOU KIDDIN' ME?
THIS SECRET PLAN SHOULD'VE STAYED SECRET!
FIRST THE SPAR-RING, NOW THIS. IT'S LIKE YOU'VE GOT MUSCLES FOR BRAINS.
Care for a walnut?
KRIK KRUSH
BY WHICH I MEAN THIS IS ALL A **WONDER-FUL IDEA.** THANK YOU.
SO...
WHAT'RE WE DOING TO TRAIN OUR SPIRIT EXACTLY?
......
SITTING UNDER A WATER-FALL?
ARE YOU *REALLY* ASKING **ME?!**

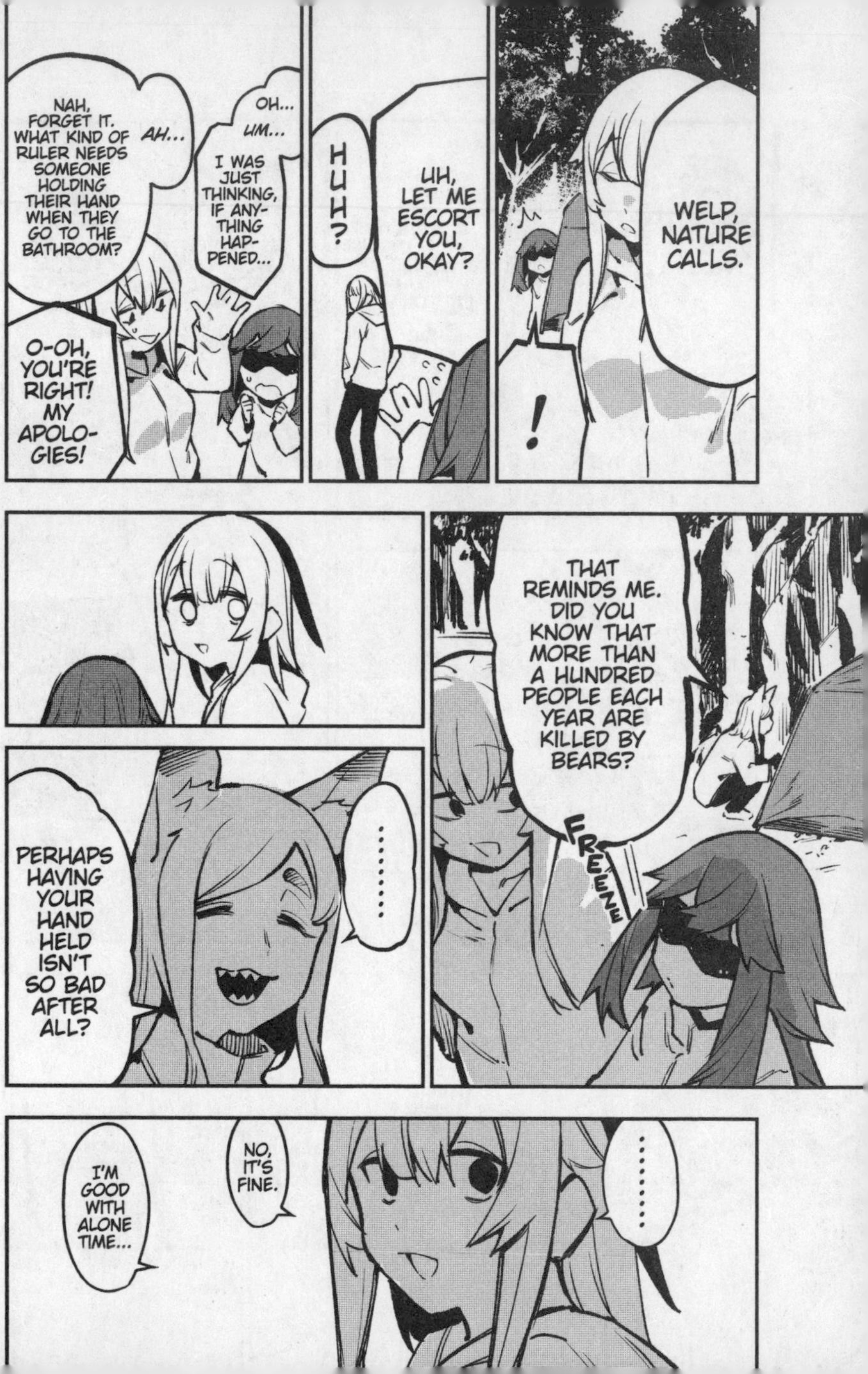
WELP, NATURE CALLS.
!
UH, LET ME ESCORT YOU, OKAY?
HUH?
OH... UM...
I WAS JUST THINKING, IF ANY-THING HAP-PENED...
AH...
NAH, FORGET IT. WHAT KIND OF RULER NEEDS SOMEONE HOLDING THEIR HAND WHEN THEY GO TO THE BATHROOM?
O-OH, YOU'RE RIGHT! MY APOLO-GIES!
THAT REMINDS ME. DID YOU KNOW THAT MORE THAN A HUNDRED PEOPLE EACH YEAR ARE KILLED BY BEARS?
FREEZE
......
PERHAPS HAVING YOUR HAND HELD ISN'T SO BAD AFTER ALL?
......
NO, IT'S FINE.
I'M GOOD WITH ALONE TIME...

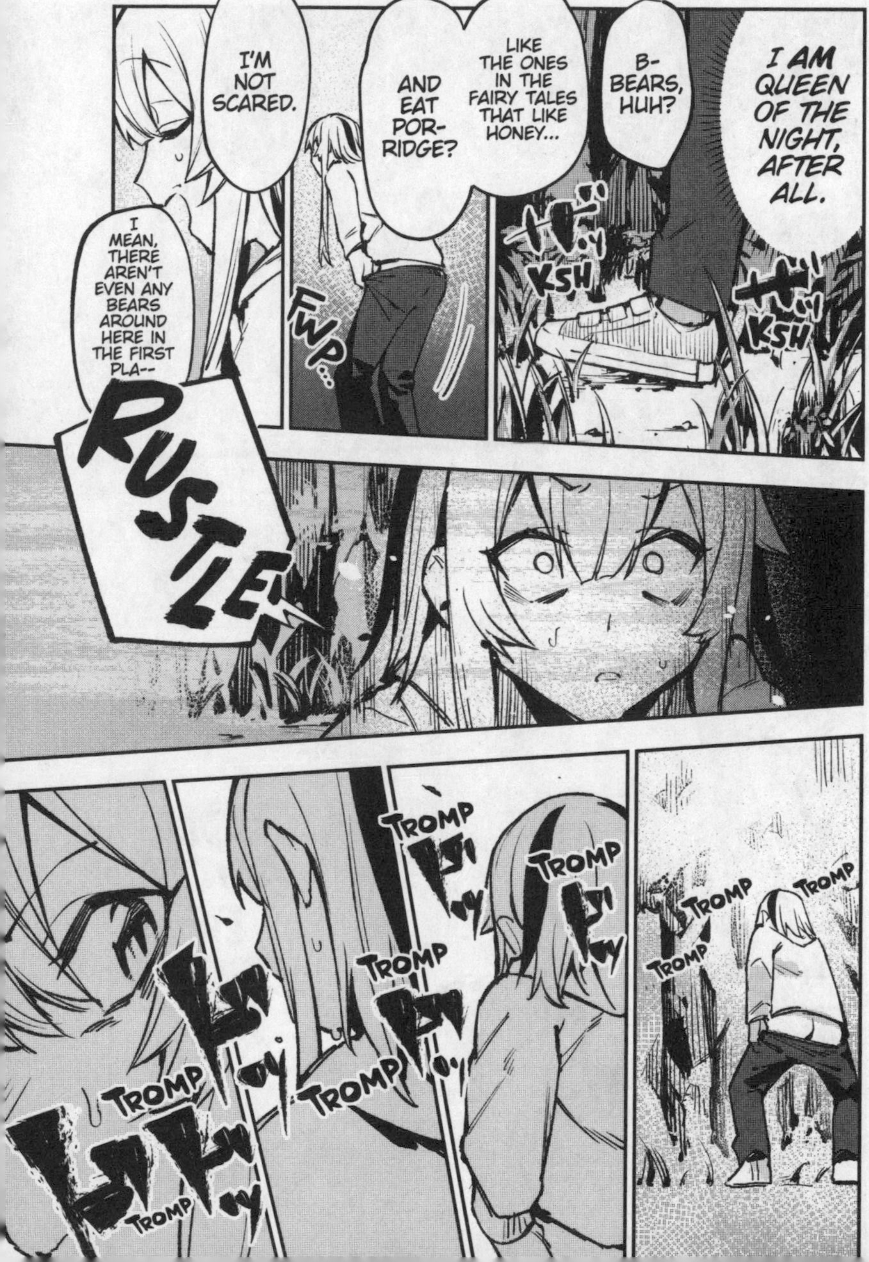
I AM QUEEN OF THE NIGHT, AFTER ALL.
B-BEARS, HUH?
KSH
KSH
LIKE THE ONES IN THE FAIRY TALES THAT LIKE HONEY...
AND EAT PORRIDGE?
FWP...
I'M NOT SCARED.
I MEAN, THERE AREN'T EVEN ANY BEARS AROUND HERE IN THE FIRST PLA--
RUSTLE
TROMP
TROMP
TROMP
TROMP
TROMP
TROMP
TROMP
TROMP
TROMP
TROMP

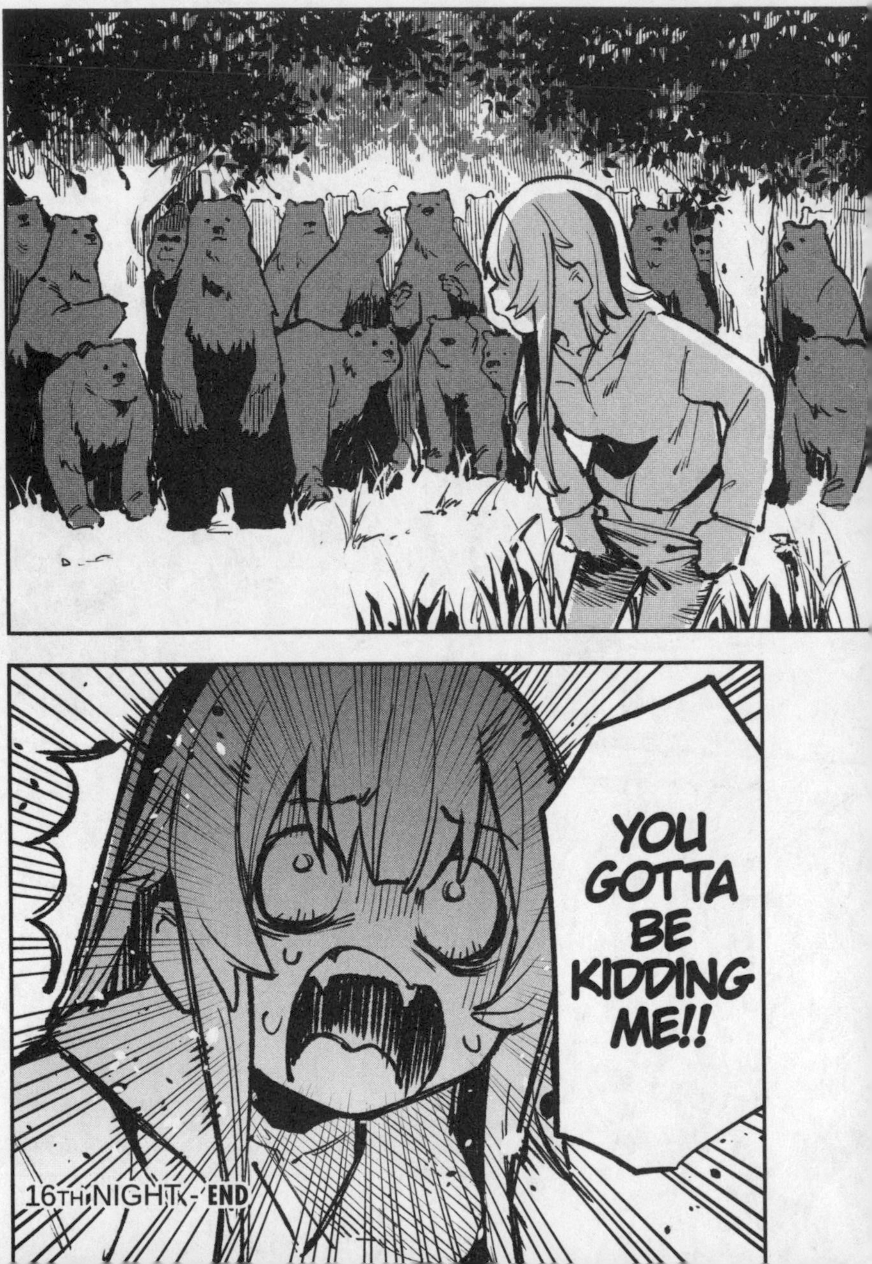
YOU GOTTA BE KIDDING ME!!
16TH NIGHT - END

Sidelong glances
are hot.

It's Just Not My Night!

Tale of a Fallen Vampire Queen

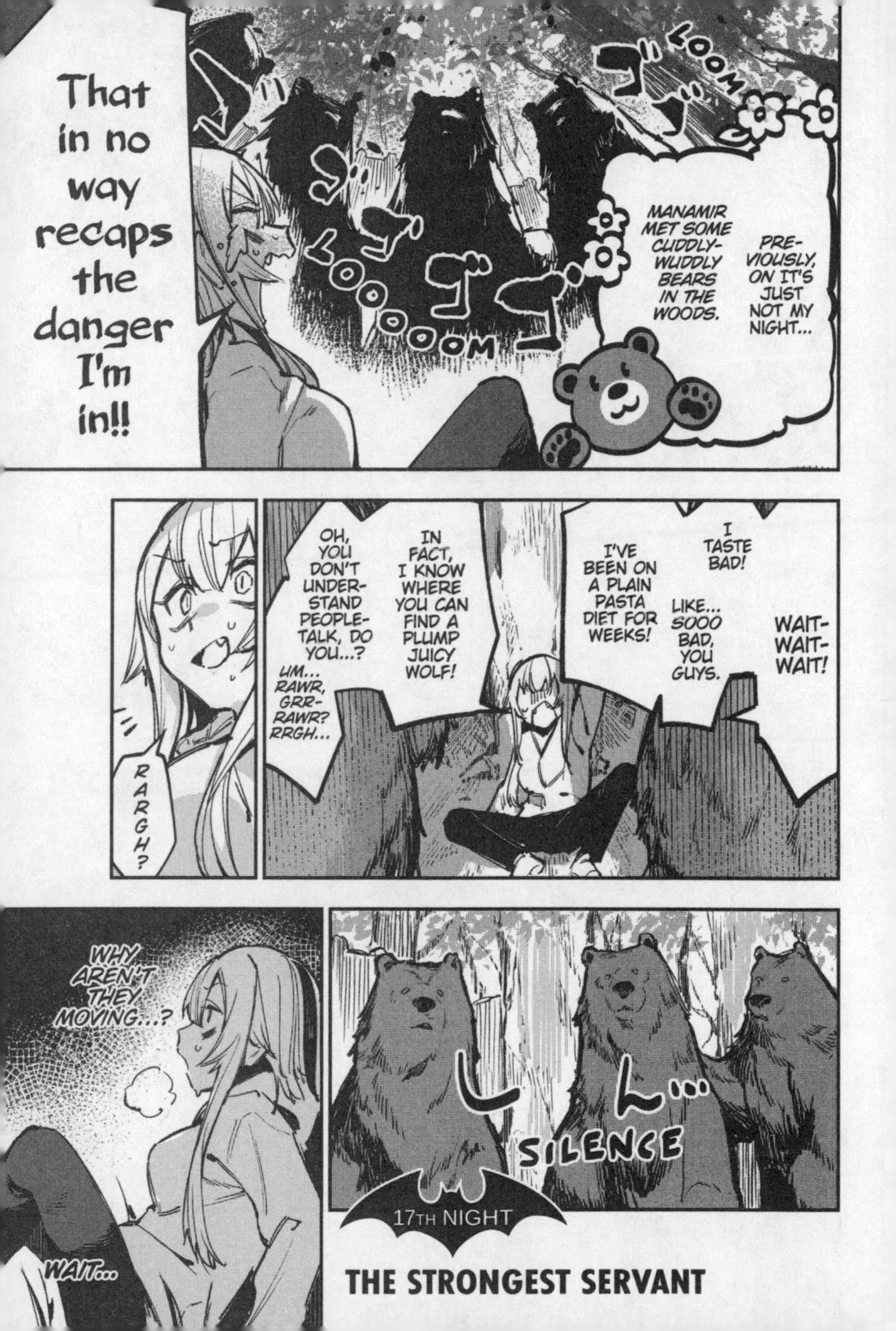
PREVIOUSLY, ON IT'S JUST NOT MY NIGHT...
MANAMIR MET SOME CUDDLY-WUDDLY BEARS IN THE WOODS.
LOOOM
LOOOOOOM
That in no way recaps the danger I'm in!!
WAIT-WAIT-WAIT!
I TASTE BAD!
LIKE... SOOO BAD, YOU GUYS.
I'VE BEEN ON A PLAIN PASTA DIET FOR WEEKS!
IN FACT, I KNOW WHERE YOU CAN FIND A PLUMP JUICY WOLF!
OH, YOU DON'T UNDER-STAND PEOPLE-TALK, DO YOU...?
UM... RAWR, GRR-RAWR? RRGH...
RARGH?
SILENCE
17TH NIGHT
THE STRONGEST SERVANT
WHY AREN'T THEY MOVING...?
WAIT...

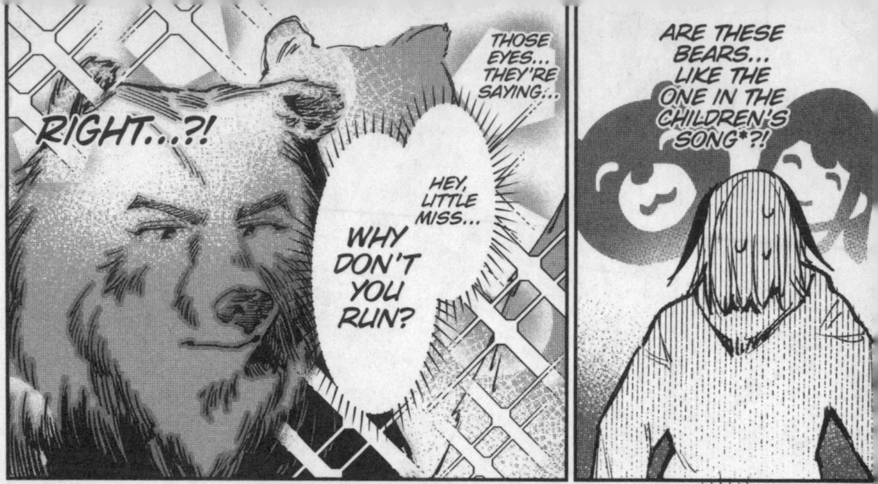
ARE THESE BEARS... LIKE THE ONE IN THE CHILDREN'S SONG*?!
THOSE EYES... THEY'RE SAYING...
HEY, LITTLE MISS... WHY DON'T YOU RUN?
RIGHT...?!

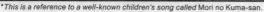

*This is a reference to a well-known children's song called Mori no Kuma-san.

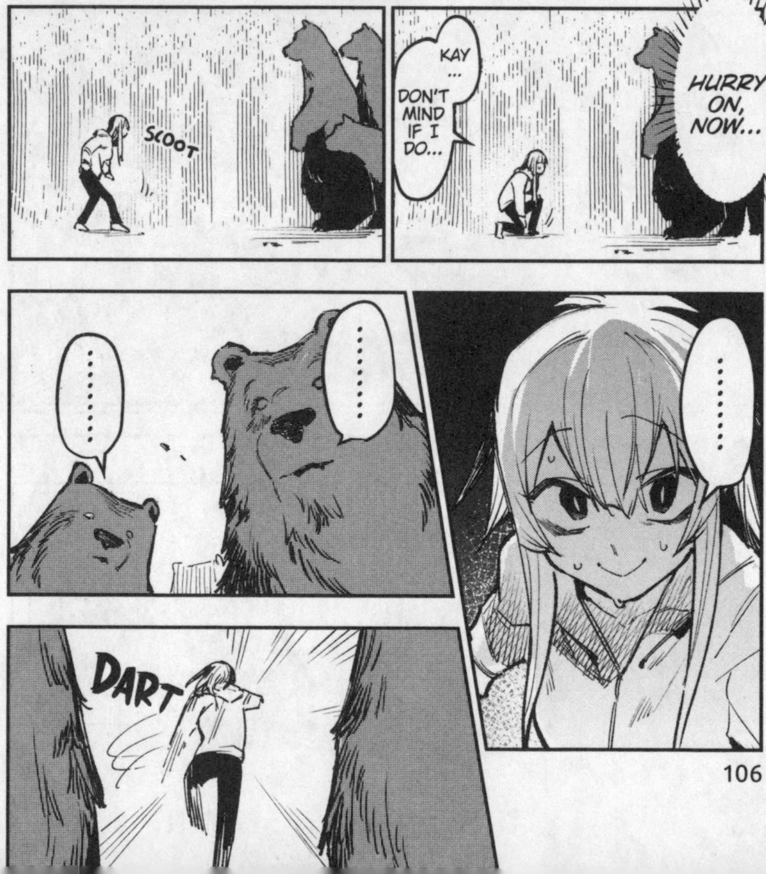
HURRY ON, NOW...
KAY... DON'T MIND IF I DO...
SCOOT
......
......
......
DART

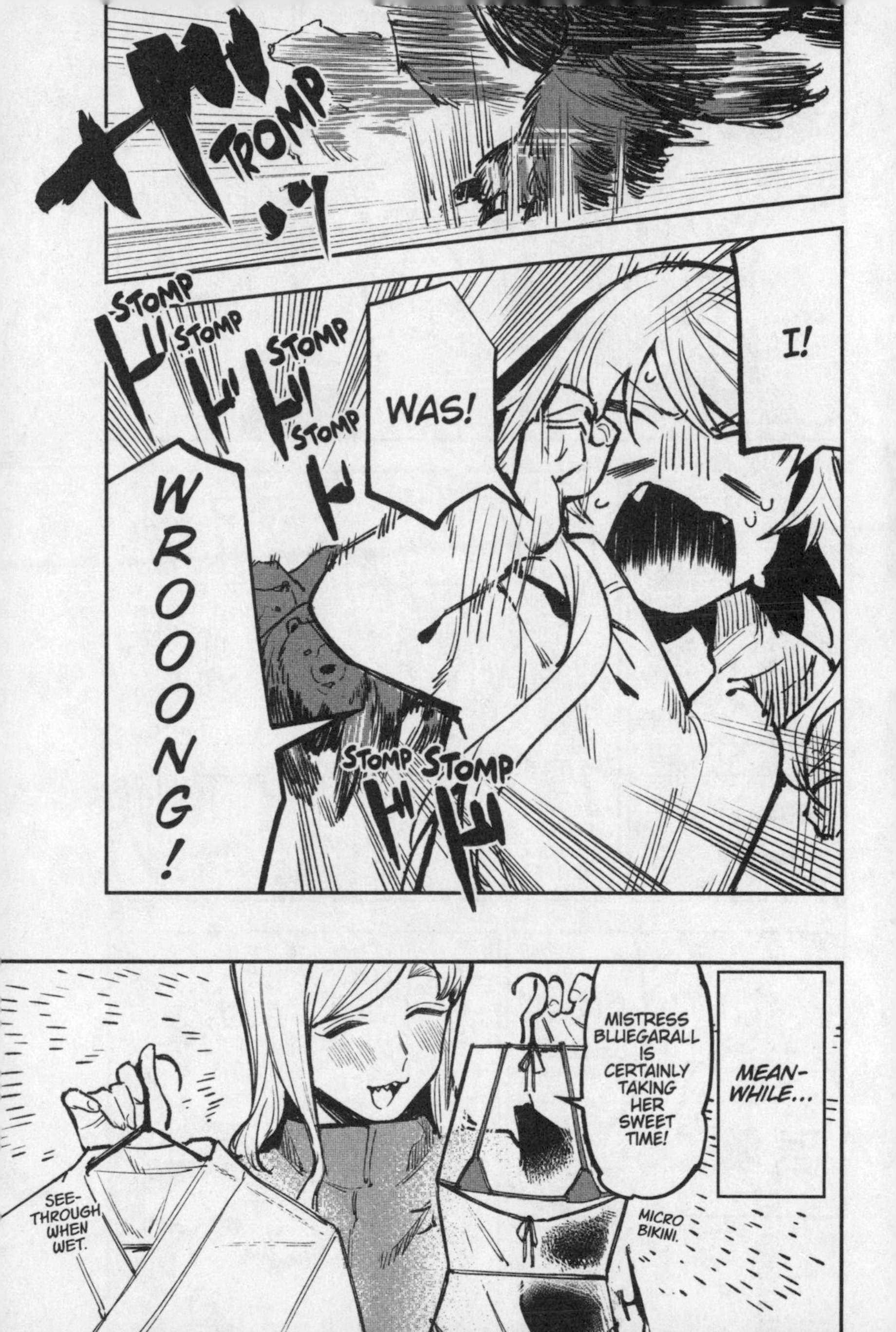
TROMP
I!
WAS!
WROOOONG!
STOMP
STOMP
STOMP
STOMP
STOMP STOMP
MEAN-WHILE...
MISTRESS BLUEGARALL IS CERTAINLY TAKING HER SWEET TIME!
MICRO BIKINI.
SEE-THROUGH WHEN WET.

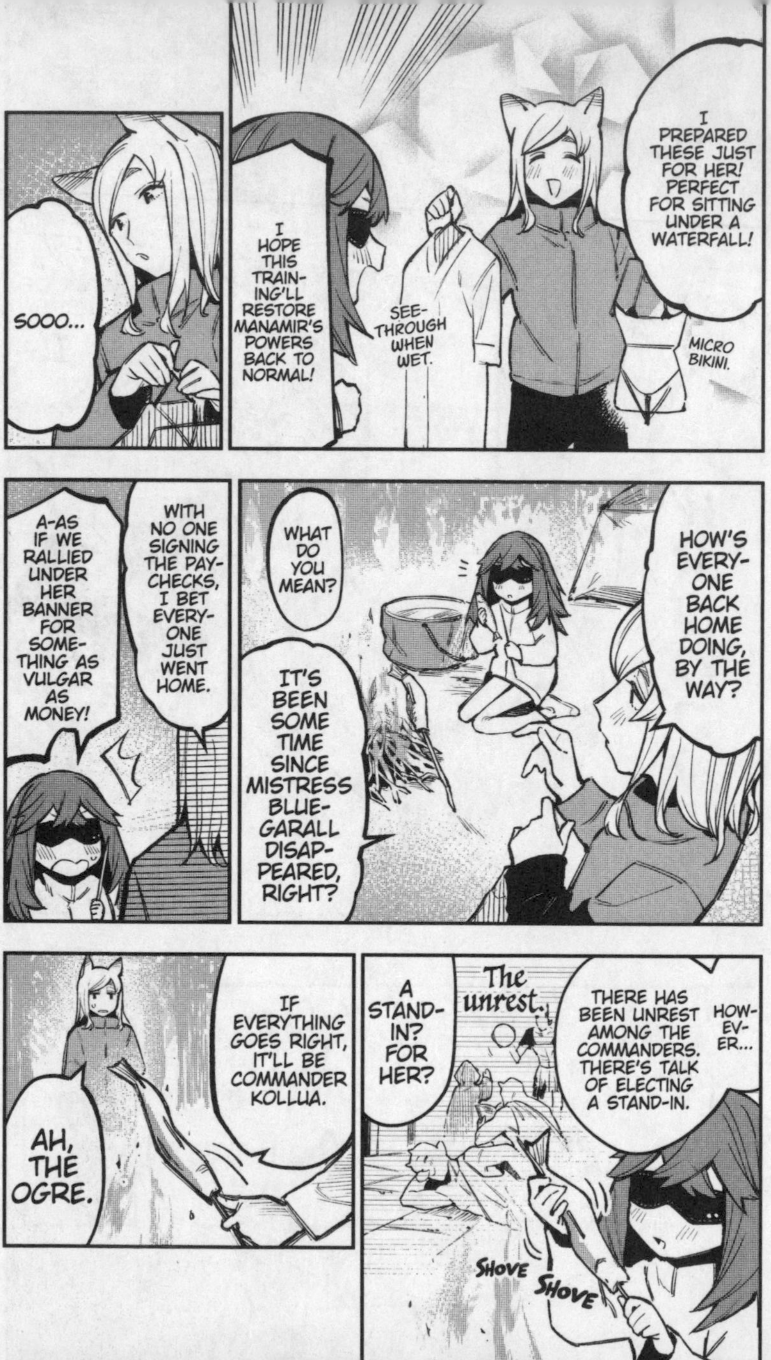
I PREPARED THESE JUST FOR HER! PERFECT FOR SITTING UNDER A WATERFALL!
MICRO BIKINI.
SEE-THROUGH WHEN WET.
I HOPE THIS TRAIN-ING'LL RESTORE MANAMIR'S POWERS BACK TO NORMAL!
SOOO...
HOW'S EVERY-ONE BACK HOME DOING, BY THE WAY?
WHAT DO YOU MEAN?
IT'S BEEN SOME TIME SINCE MISTRESS BLUE-GARALL DISAP-PEARED, RIGHT?
WITH NO ONE SIGNING THE PAY-CHECKS, I BET EVERY-ONE JUST WENT HOME.
A-AS IF WE RALLIED UNDER HER BANNER FOR SOME-THING AS VULGAR AS MONEY!
HOW-EV-ER...
THERE HAS BEEN UNREST AMONG THE COMMANDERS. THERE'S TALK OF ELECTING A STAND-IN.
The unrest.
A STAND-IN? FOR HER?
SHOVE
SHOVE
IF EVERYTHING GOES RIGHT, IT'LL BE COMMANDER KOLLUA.
AH, THE OGRE.

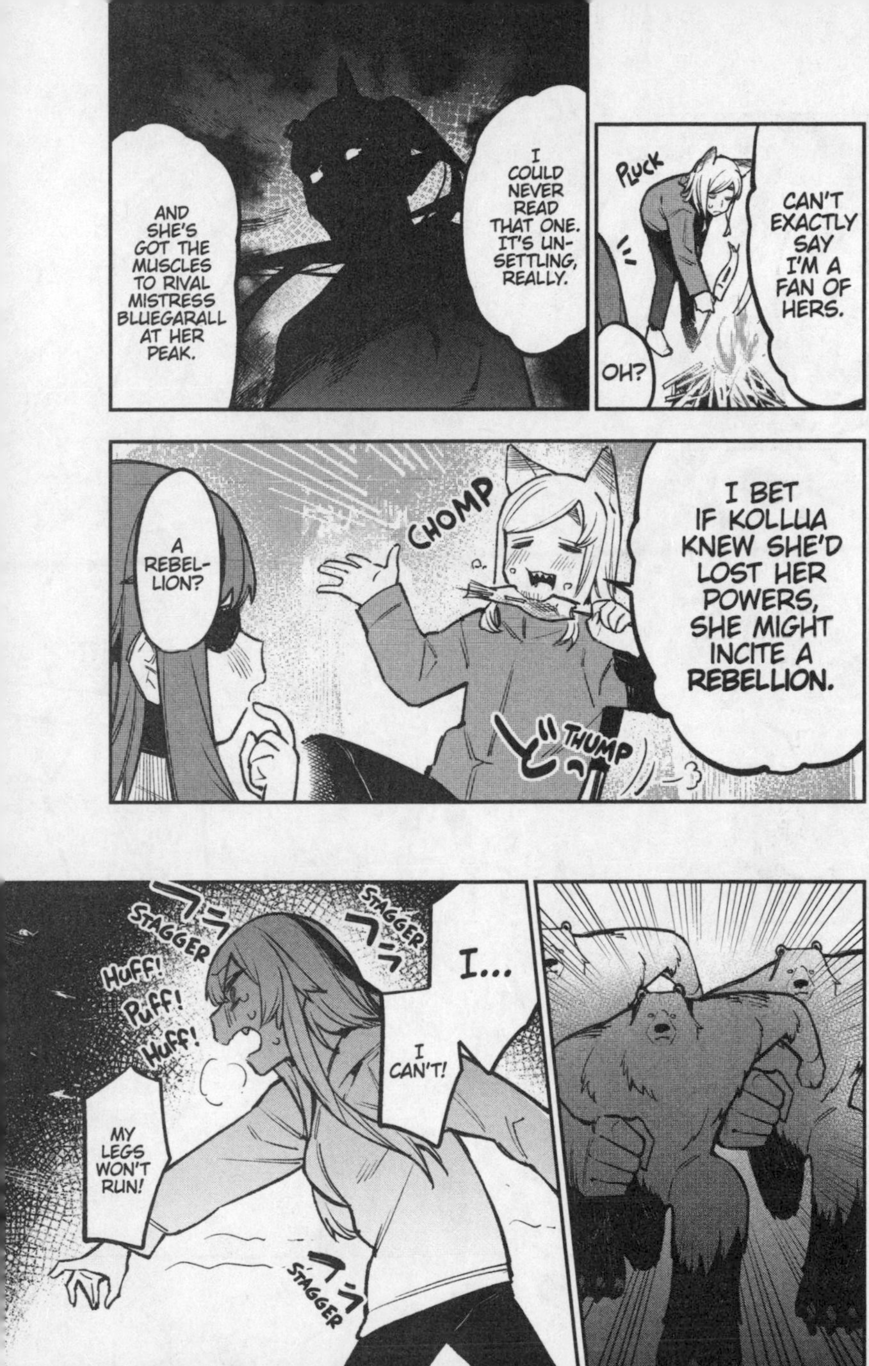
PLUCK
CAN'T EXACTLY SAY I'M A FAN OF HERS.
OH?
I COULD NEVER READ THAT ONE. IT'S UN-SETTLING, REALLY.
AND SHE'S GOT THE MUSCLES TO RIVAL MISTRESS BLUEGARALL AT HER PEAK.
I BET IF KOLLUA KNEW SHE'D LOST HER POWERS, SHE MIGHT INCITE A REBELLION.
CHOMP
THUMP
A REBEL-LION?
I...
STAGGER
I CAN'T!
STAGGER
Huff! Puff! Huff!
MY LEGS WON'T RUN!
STAGGER

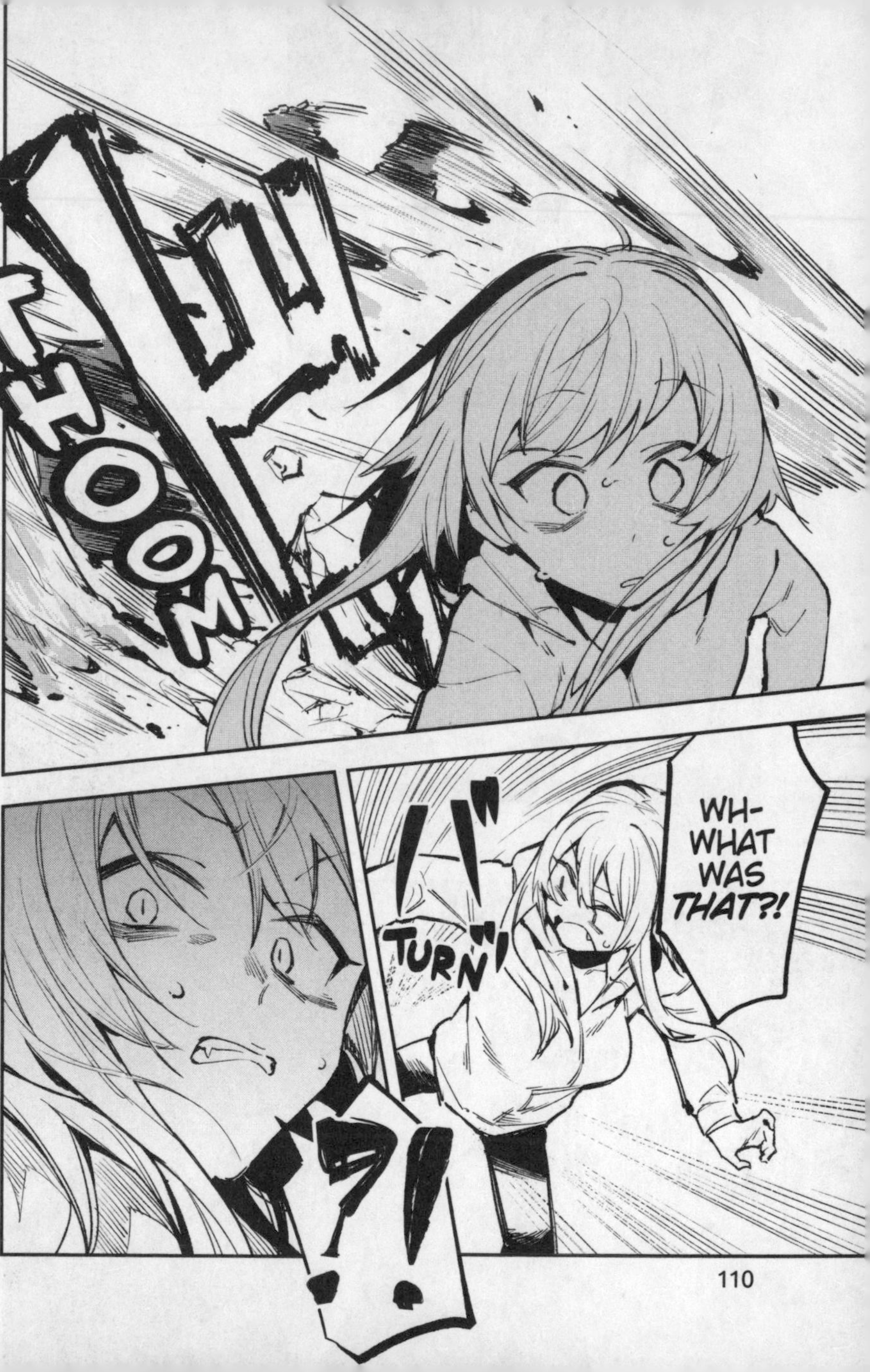
THOOM
WH-
WHAT
WAS
THAT?!
TURN
?!

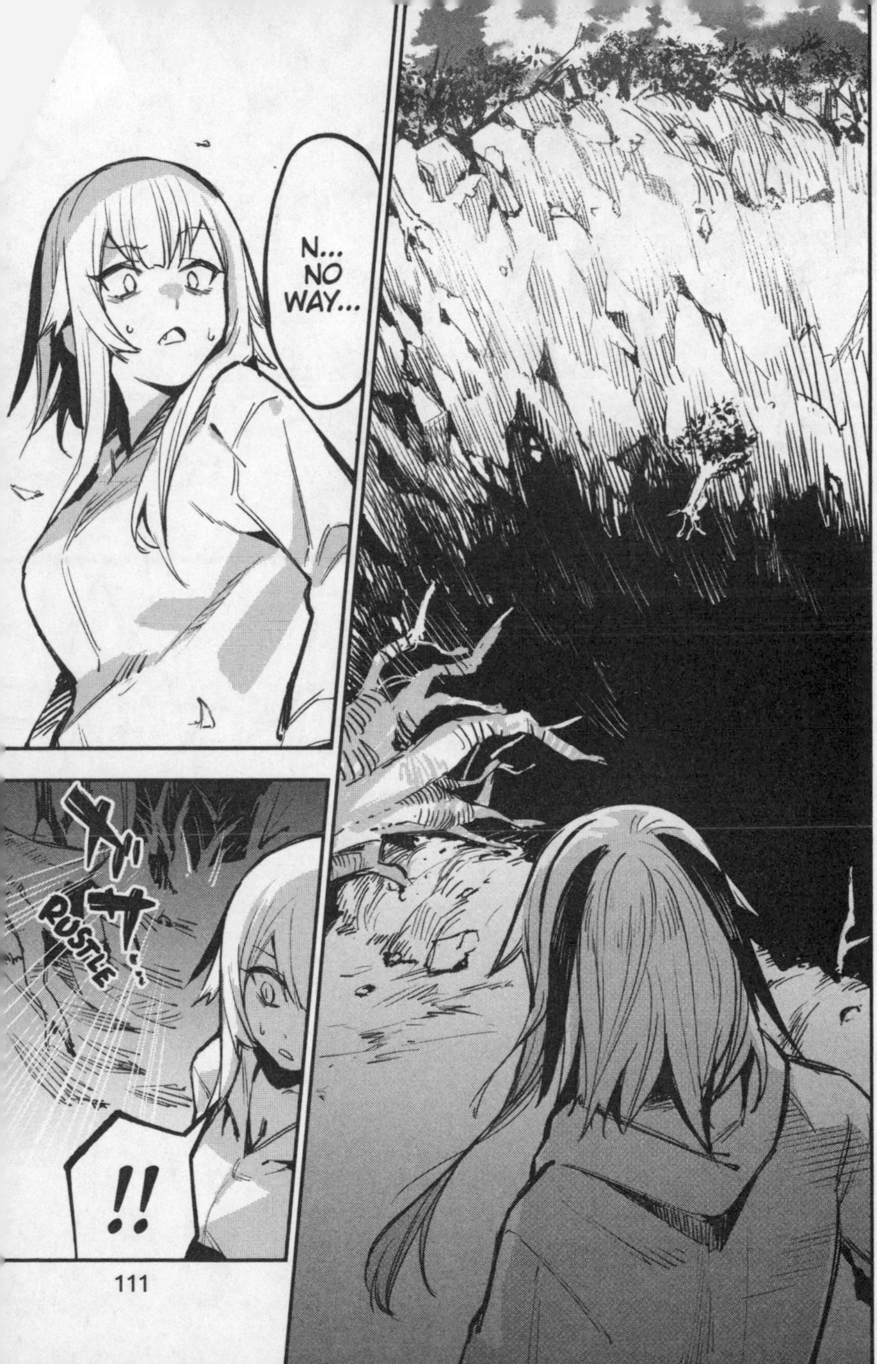
N... NO WAY...
RUSTLE
!!

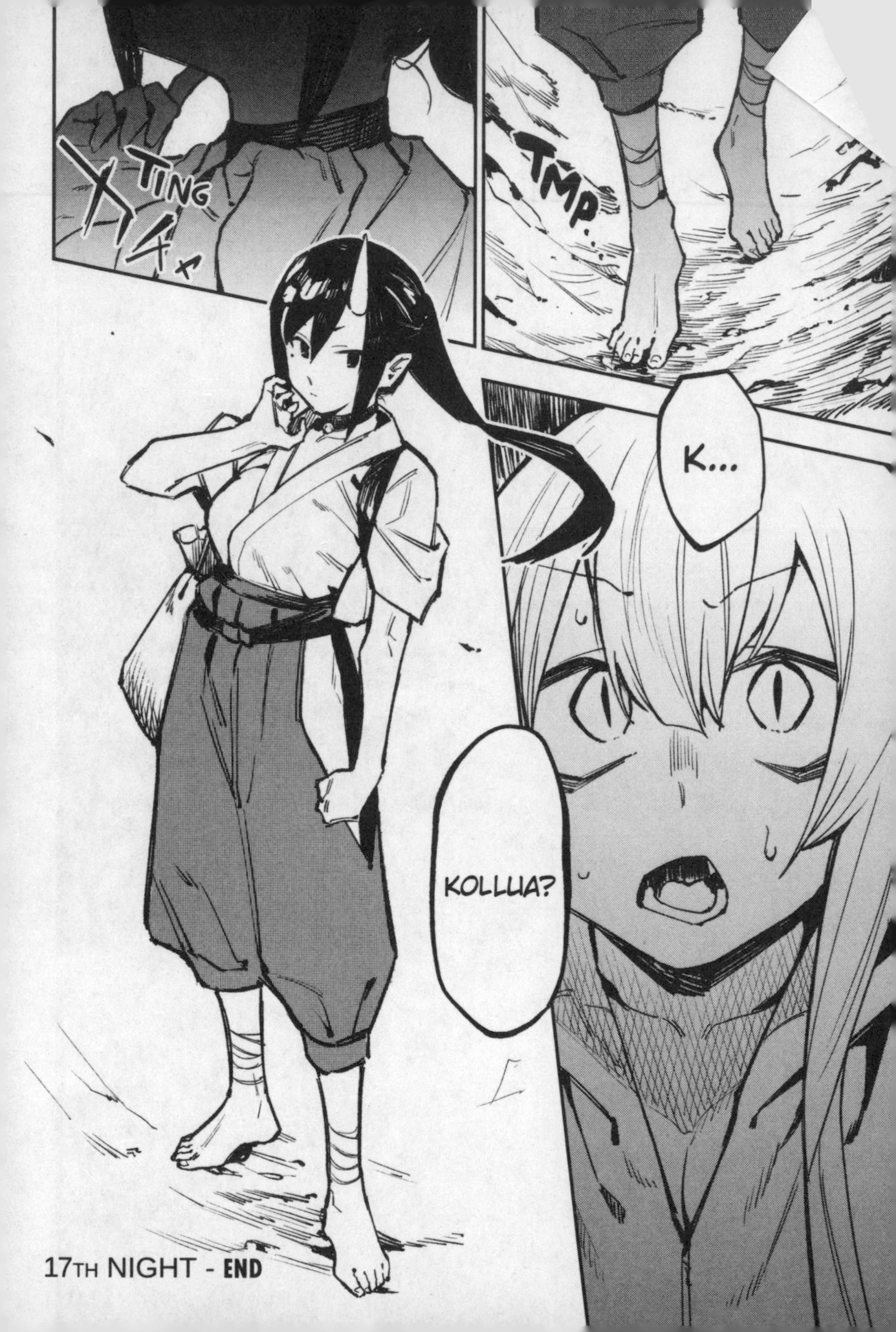
TMP
TING
K...
KOLLUA?

17TH NIGHT - END

18TH NIGHT DEADLY POISON MANTIS OF DEATH

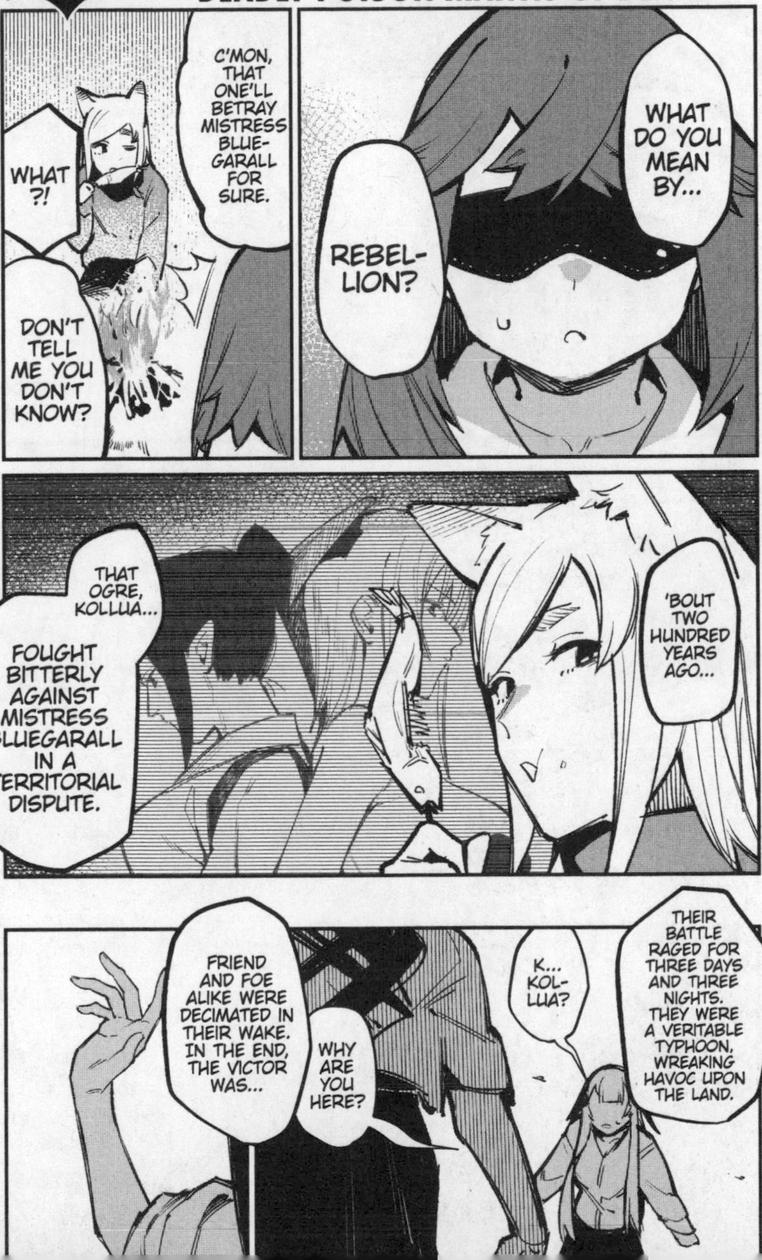
WHAT DO YOU MEAN BY...
REBEL-LION?
C'MON, THAT ONE'LL BETRAY MISTRESS BLUE-GARALL FOR SURE.
WHAT?!
DON'T TELL ME YOU DON'T KNOW?
'BOUT TWO HUNDRED YEARS AGO...
THAT OGRE, KOLLUA...
FOUGHT BITTERLY AGAINST MISTRESS BLUEGARALL IN A TERRITORIAL DISPUTE.
THEIR BATTLE RAGED FOR THREE DAYS AND THREE NIGHTS. THEY WERE A VERITABLE TYPHOON, WREAKING HAVOC UPON THE LAND.
K... KOL-LUA?
FRIEND AND FOE ALIKE WERE DECIMATED IN THEIR WAKE. IN THE END, THE VICTOR WAS...
WHY ARE YOU HERE?

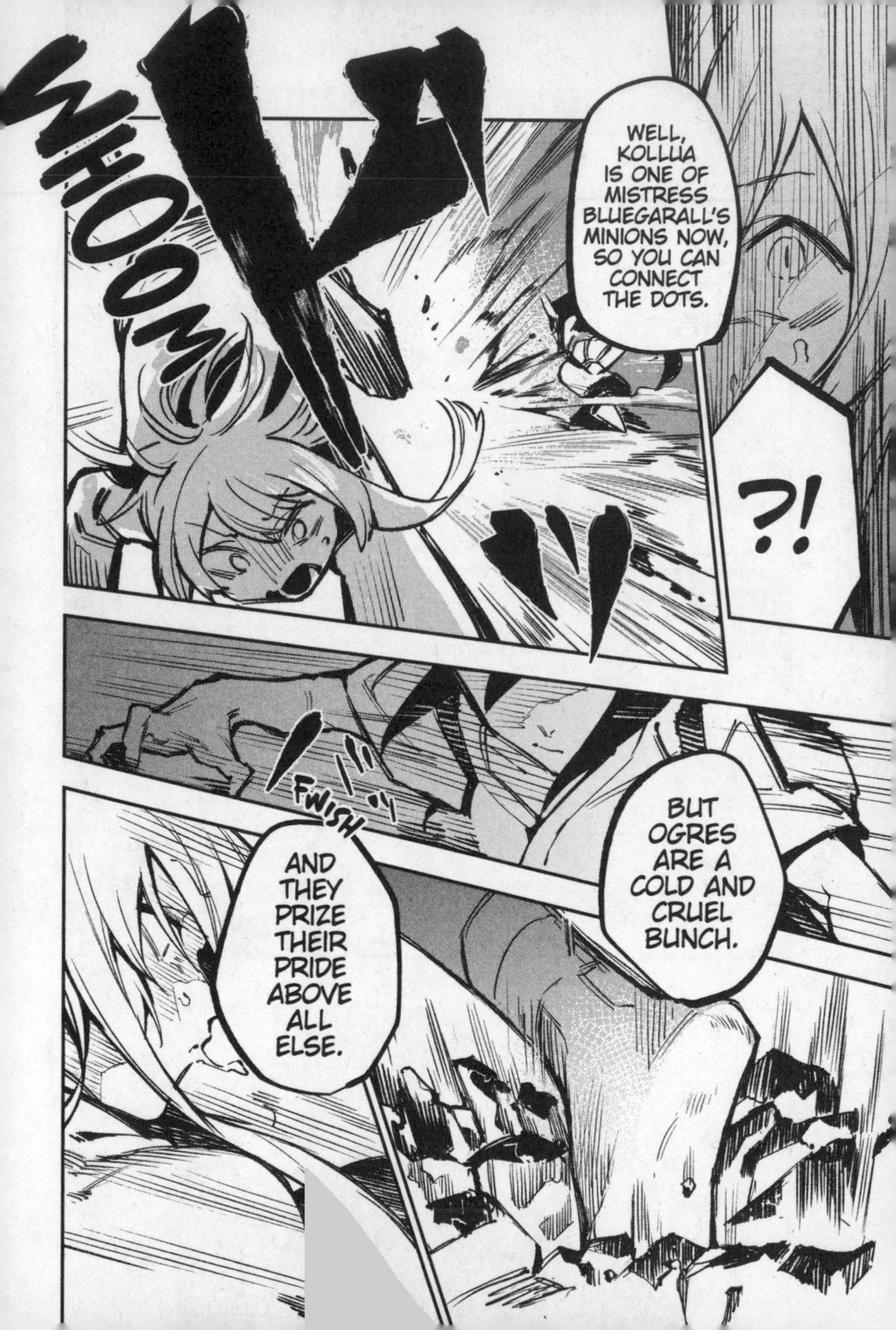
WELL, KOLLUA IS ONE OF MISTRESS BLUEGARALL'S MINIONS NOW, SO YOU CAN CONNECT THE DOTS.
?!
WHOOM
FWISH
BUT OGRES ARE A COLD AND CRUEL BUNCH.
AND THEY PRIZE THEIR PRIDE ABOVE ALL ELSE.

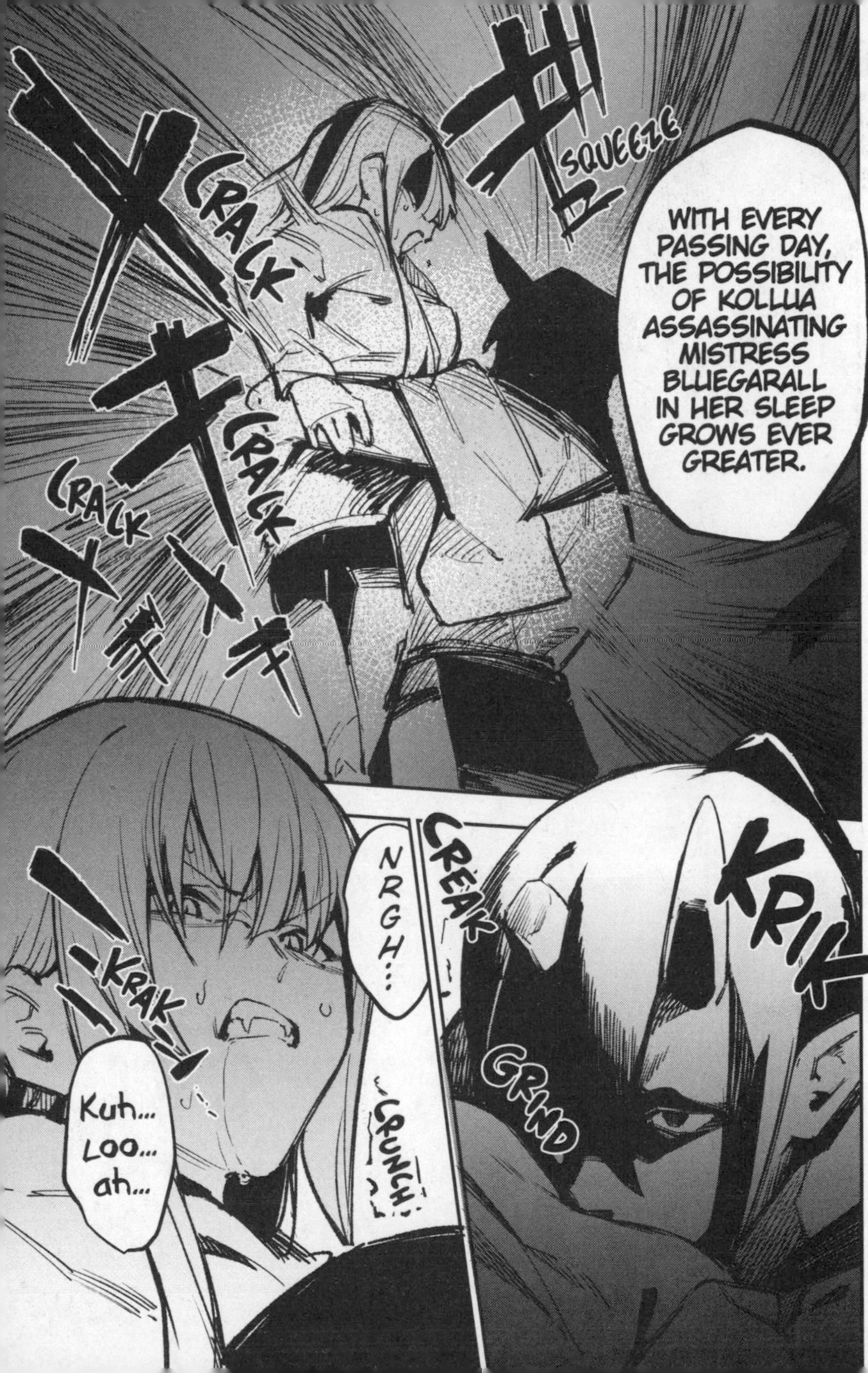
SQUEEZE
WITH EVERY PASSING DAY, THE POSSIBILITY OF KOLLUA ASSASSINATING MISTRESS BLUEGARALL IN HER SLEEP GROWS EVER GREATER.
CRACK
CRACK
CRACK
KRIK
CREAK
GRIND
NRGH...
CRUNCH
KRAK
Kuh... Loo... ah...

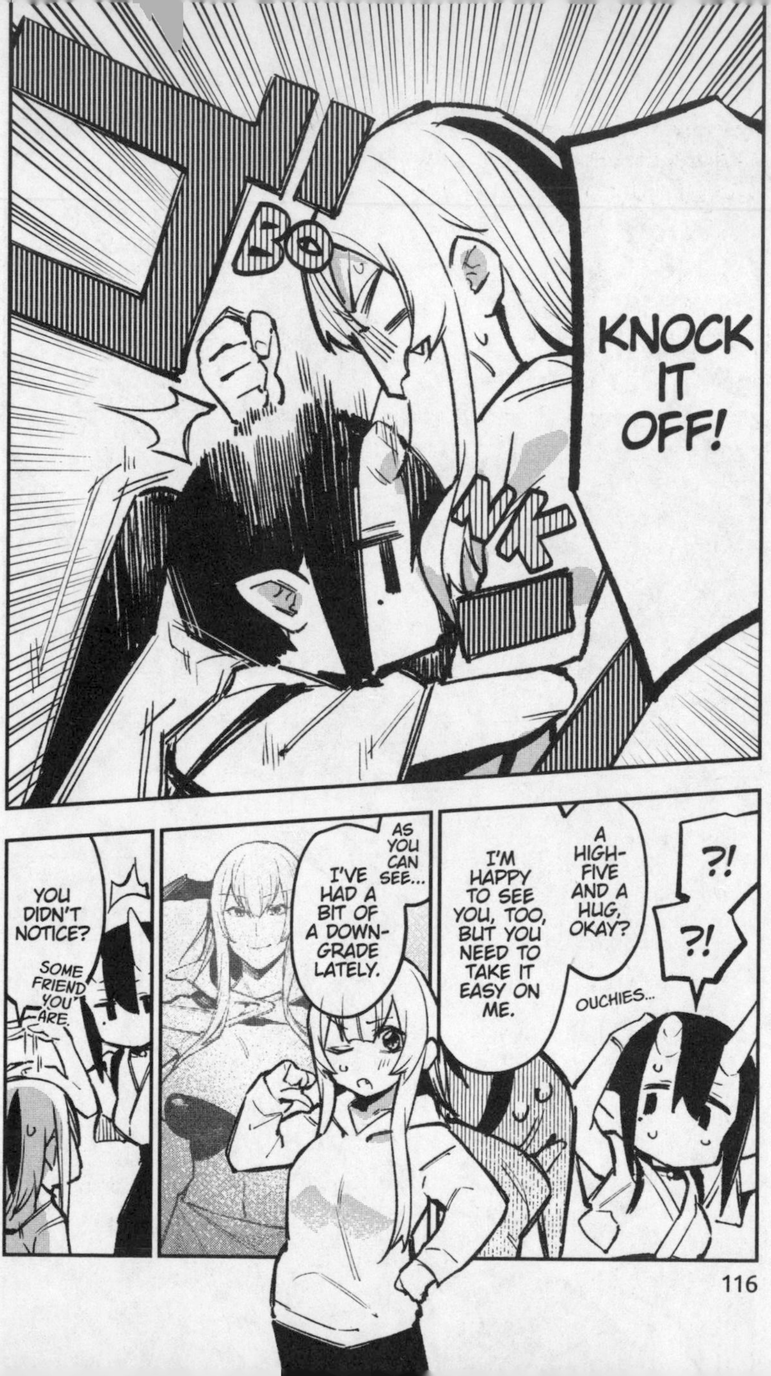
BO
KNOCK IT OFF!
?!
?!
OUCHIES...
A HIGH-FIVE AND A HUG, OKAY?
I'M HAPPY TO SEE YOU, TOO, BUT YOU NEED TO TAKE IT EASY ON ME.
AS YOU CAN SEE...
I'VE HAD A BIT OF A DOWNGRADE LATELY.
YOU DIDN'T NOTICE?
SOME FRIEND YOU ARE.

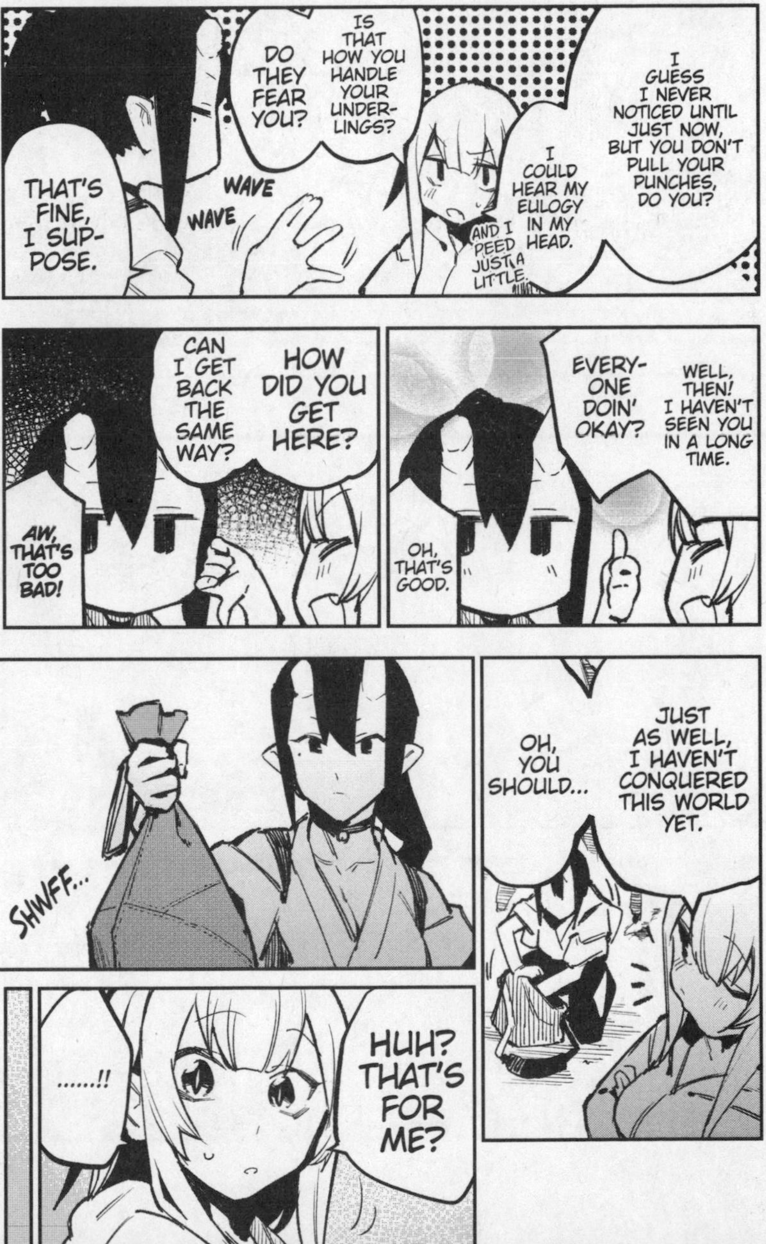
I GUESS I NEVER NOTICED UNTIL JUST NOW, BUT YOU DON'T PULL YOUR PUNCHES, DO YOU?
I COULD HEAR MY EULOGY IN MY HEAD.
AND I PEED JUST A LITTLE.
IS THAT HOW YOU HANDLE YOUR UNDER-LINGS?
DO THEY FEAR YOU?
WAVE
WAVE
THAT'S FINE, I SUP-POSE.
WELL, THEN! I HAVEN'T SEEN YOU IN A LONG TIME.
EVERY-ONE DOIN' OKAY?
OH, THAT'S GOOD.
HOW DID YOU GET HERE?
CAN I GET BACK THE SAME WAY?
AW, THAT'S TOO BAD!
JUST AS WELL, I HAVEN'T CONQUERED THIS WORLD YET.
OH, YOU SHOULD...
SHWFF...
HUH? THAT'S FOR ME?
......!!

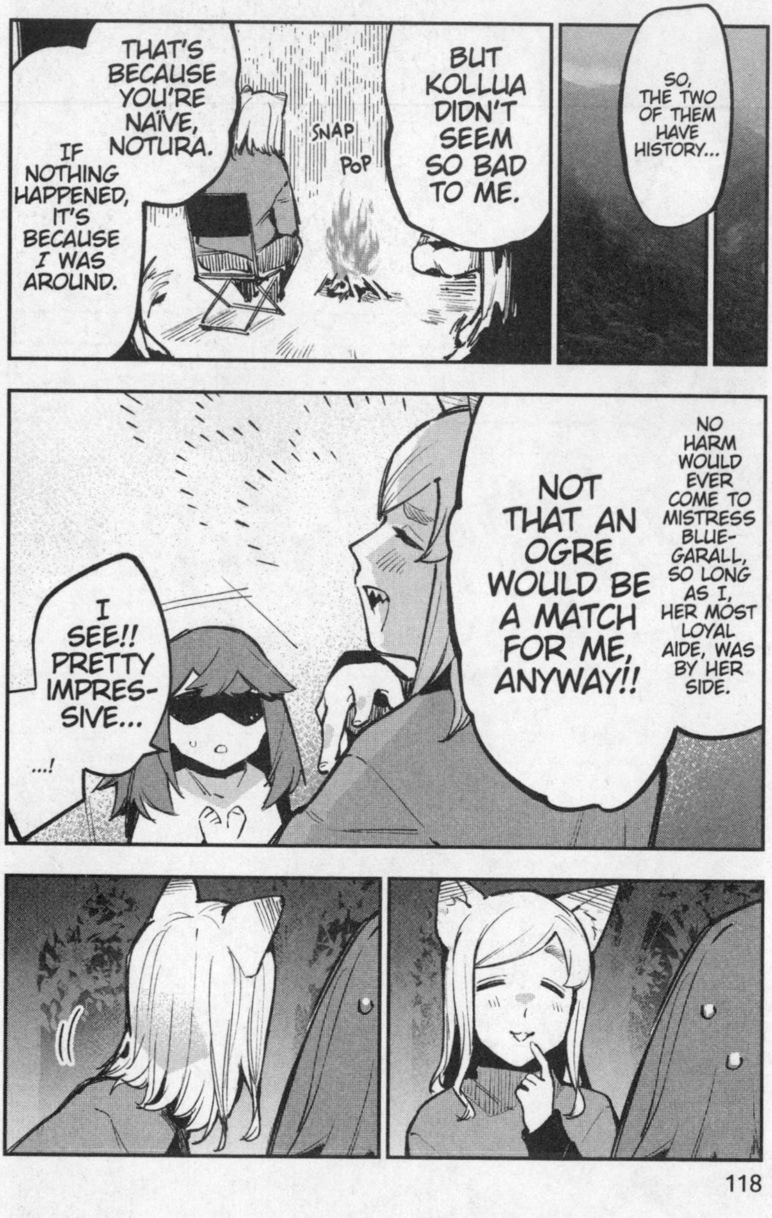
SO, THE TWO OF THEM HAVE HISTORY...
BUT KOLLUA DIDN'T SEEM SO BAD TO ME.
SNAP
POP
THAT'S BECAUSE YOU'RE NAÏVE, NOTURA.
IF NOTHING HAPPENED, IT'S BECAUSE *I* WAS AROUND.
NO HARM WOULD EVER COME TO MISTRESS BLUE-GARALL, SO LONG AS I, HER MOST LOYAL AIDE, WAS BY HER SIDE.
NOT THAT AN OGRE WOULD BE A MATCH FOR ME, ANYWAY!!
I SEE!! PRETTY IMPRESSIVE...
...!

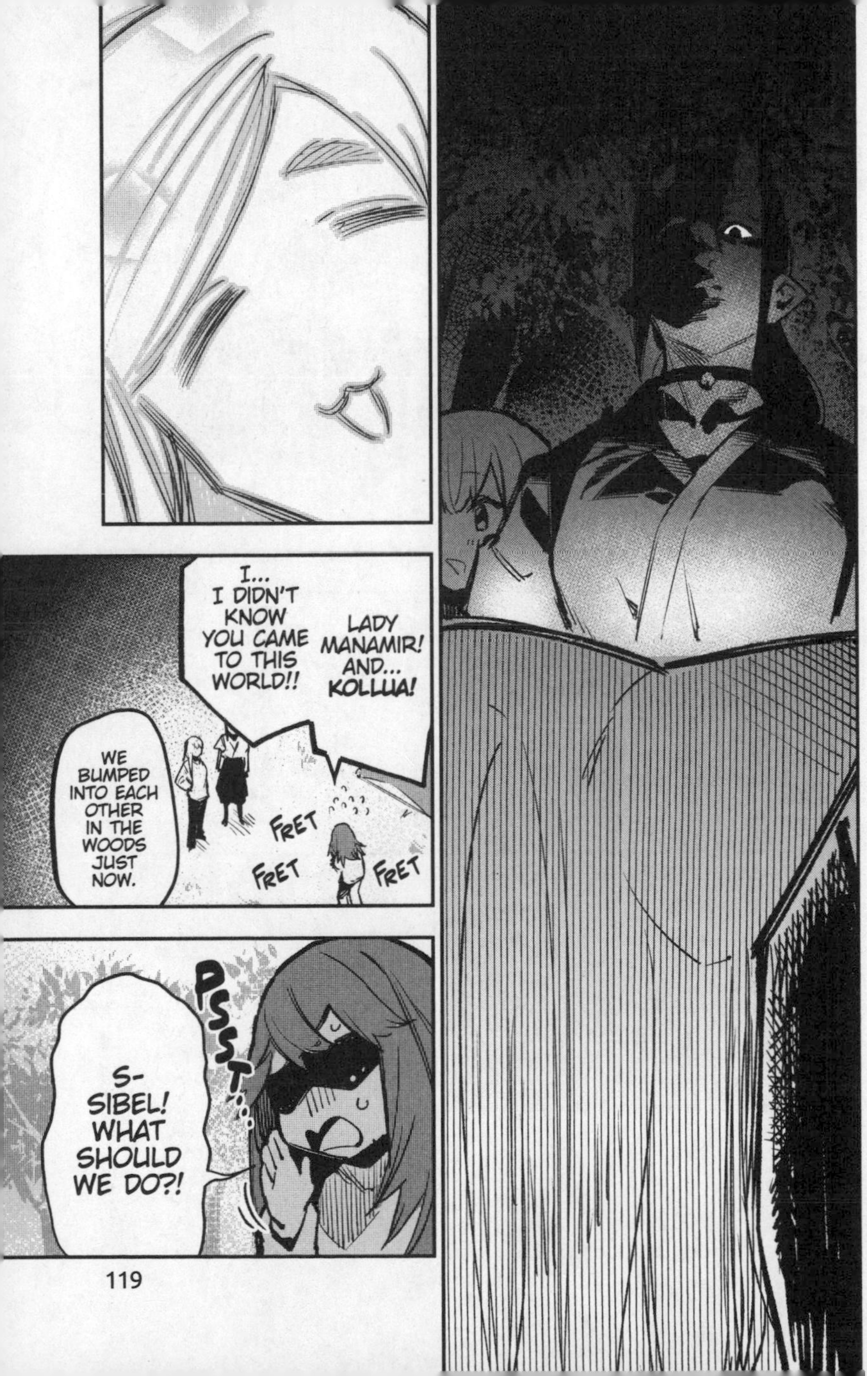
LADY MANAMIR! AND... KOLLUA!
I... I DIDN'T KNOW YOU CAME TO THIS WORLD!!
WE BUMPED INTO EACH OTHER IN THE WOODS JUST NOW.
FRET FRET FRET
PSST...
S-SIBEL! WHAT SHOULD WE DO?!

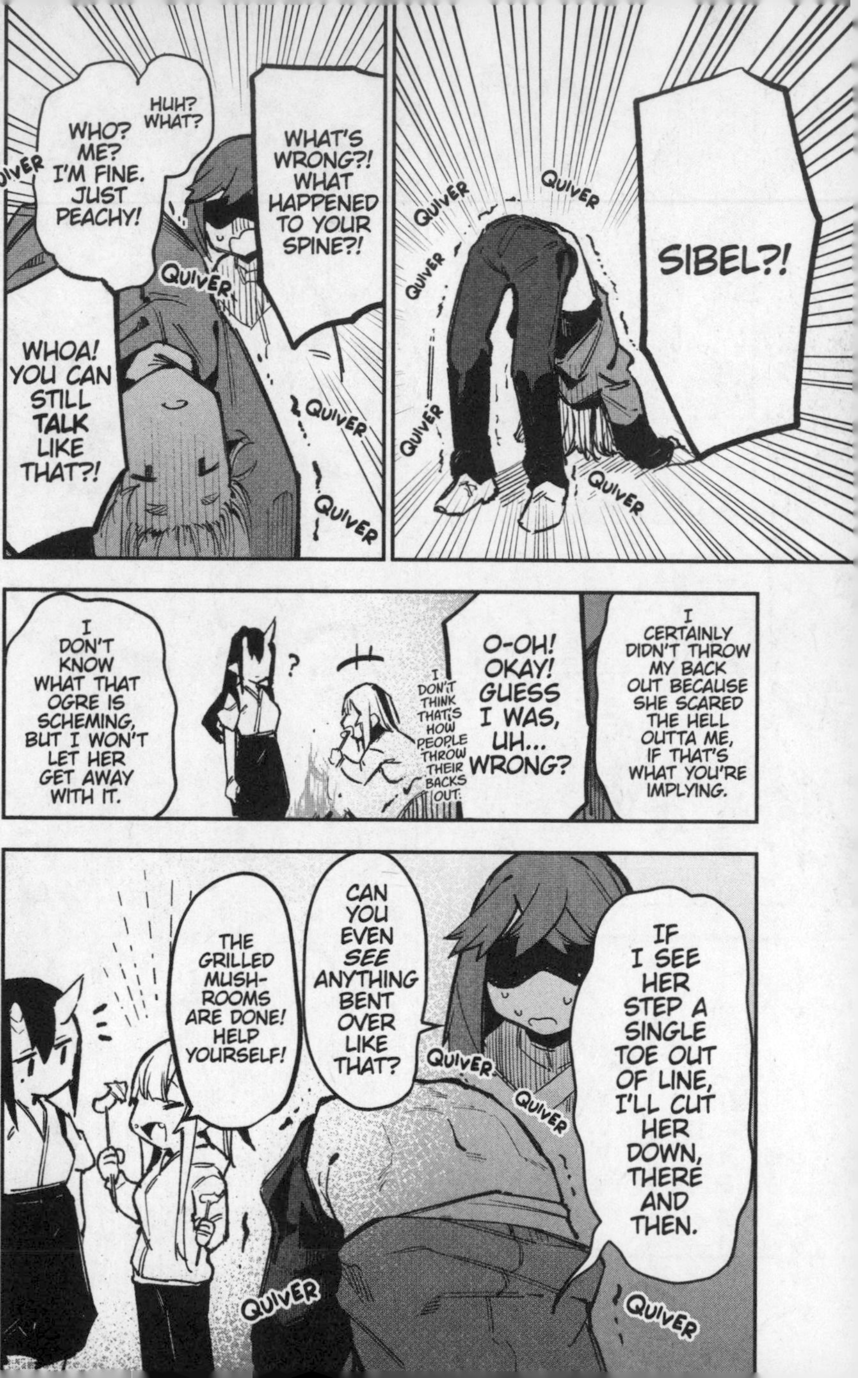
SIBEL?!
QUIVER
QUIVER
QUIVER
QUIVER
QUIVER
WHAT'S WRONG?! WHAT HAPPENED TO YOUR SPINE?!
HUH? WHAT?
WHO? ME? I'M FINE. JUST PEACHY!
QUIVER
QUIVER
WHOA! YOU CAN STILL TALK LIKE THAT?!
QUIVER
QUIVER
I CERTAINLY DIDN'T THROW MY BACK OUT BECAUSE SHE SCARED THE HELL OUTTA ME, IF THAT'S WHAT YOU'RE IMPLYING.
O-OH! OKAY! GUESS I WAS, UH... WRONG?
I DON'T THINK THAT'S HOW PEOPLE THROW THEIR BACKS OUT.
?
I DON'T KNOW WHAT THAT OGRE IS SCHEMING, BUT I WON'T LET HER GET AWAY WITH IT.
IF I SEE HER STEP A SINGLE TOE OUT OF LINE, I'LL CUT HER DOWN, THERE AND THEN.
QUIVER
QUIVER
QUIVER
CAN YOU EVEN *SEE* ANYTHING BENT OVER LIKE THAT?
THE GRILLED MUSH-ROOMS ARE DONE! HELP YOURSELF!
QUIVER

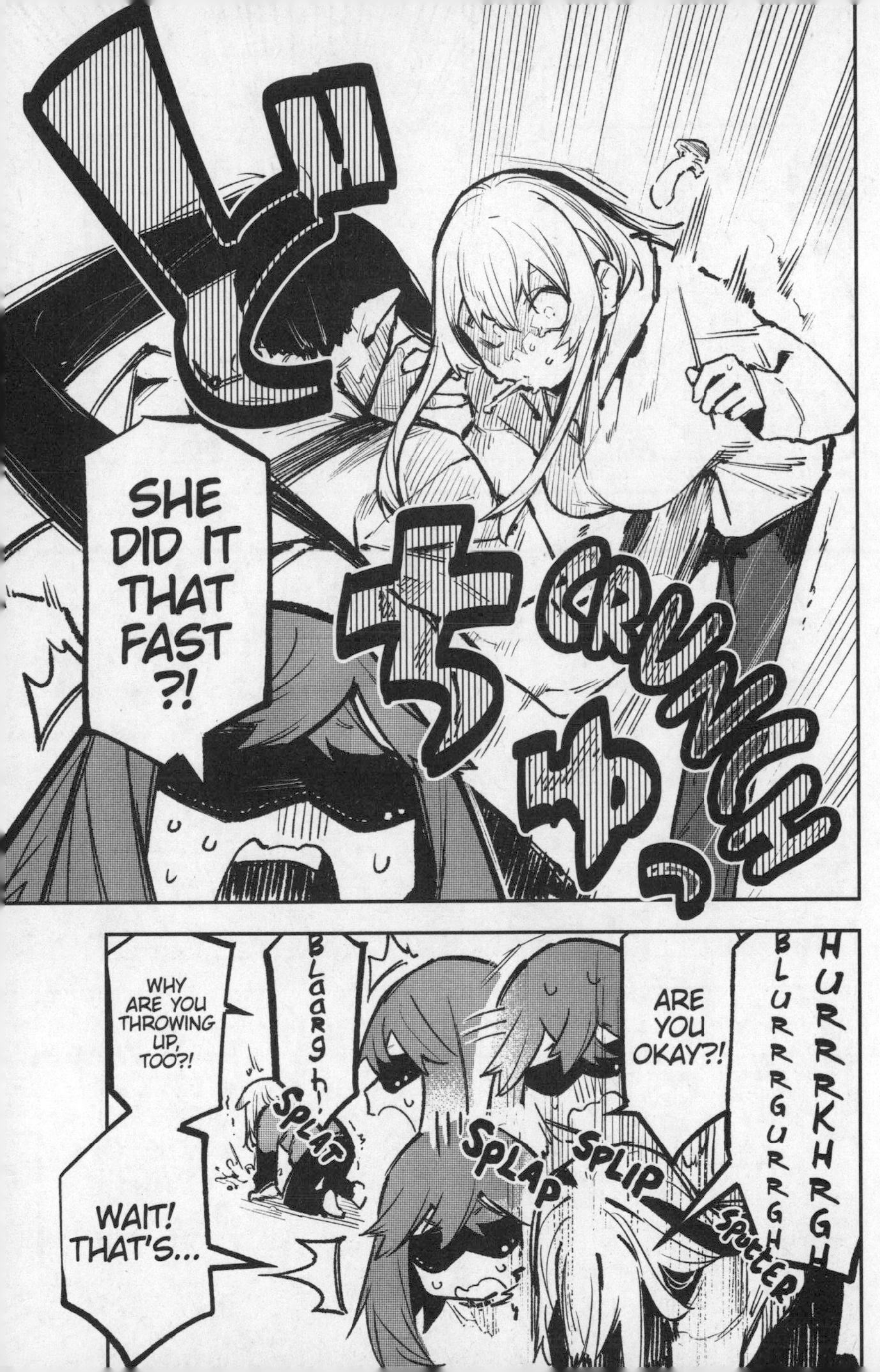
SHE DID IT THAT FAST?!
CRUNCH
HURRRKHRRGH
BLURRRGURRGH
ARE YOU OKAY?!
SPLIP
SPUTTER
SPLAP
Blaargh!
SPLAT
WHY ARE YOU THROWING UP, TOO?!
WAIT! THAT'S...

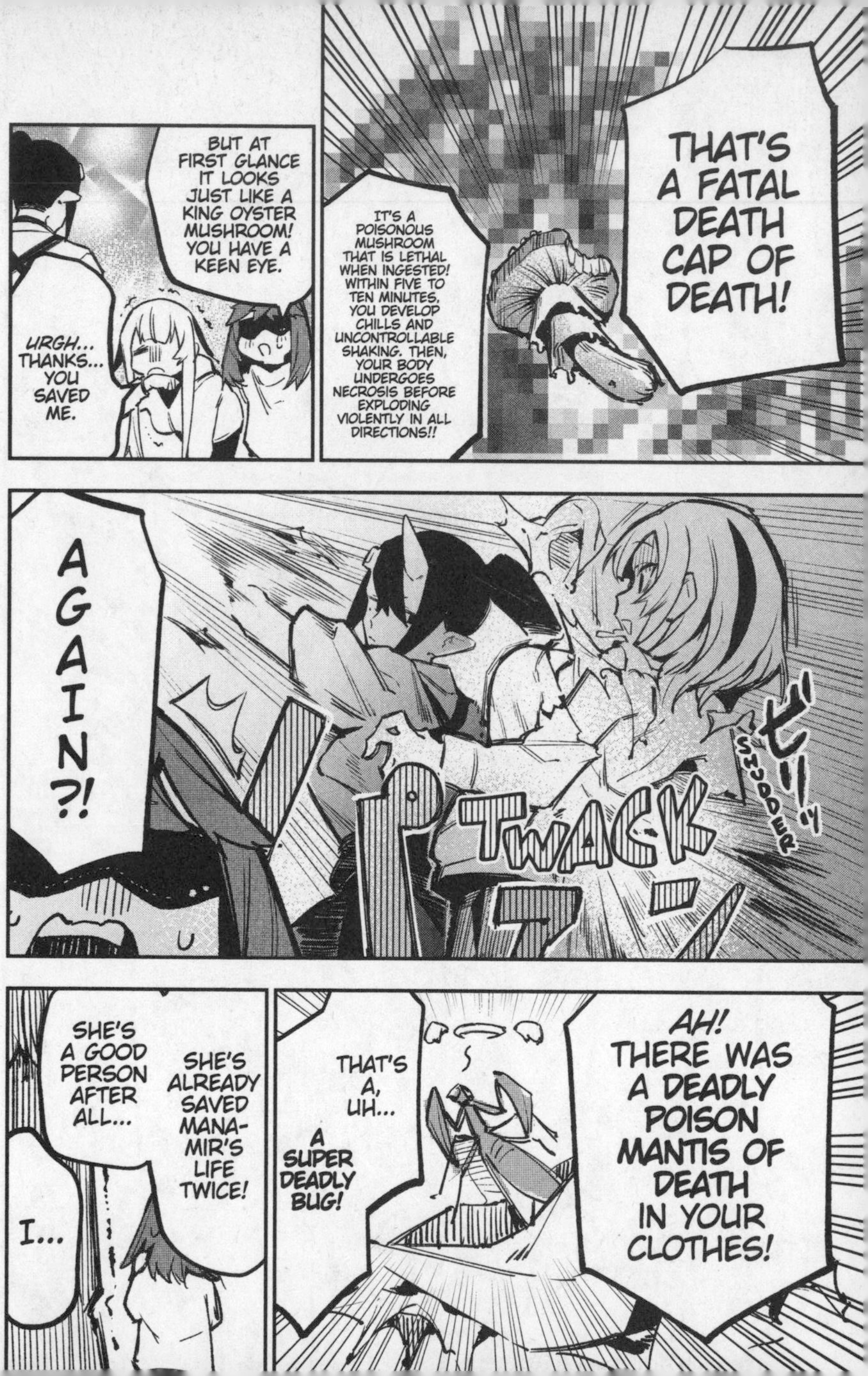
THAT'S A FATAL DEATH CAP OF DEATH!
IT'S A POISONOUS MUSHROOM THAT IS LETHAL WHEN INGESTED! WITHIN FIVE TO TEN MINUTES, YOU DEVELOP CHILLS AND UNCONTROLLABLE SHAKING. THEN, YOUR BODY UNDERGOES NECROSIS BEFORE EXPLODING VIOLENTLY IN ALL DIRECTIONS!!
BUT AT FIRST GLANCE IT LOOKS JUST LIKE A KING OYSTER MUSHROOM! YOU HAVE A KEEN EYE.
URGH... THANKS... YOU SAVED ME.
SHUDDER
TWACK
AGAIN?!
AH! THERE WAS A DEADLY POISON MANTIS OF DEATH IN YOUR CLOTHES!
THAT'S A, UH...
A SUPER DEADLY BUG!
SHE'S ALREADY SAVED MANA-MIR'S LIFE TWICE!
SHE'S A GOOD PERSON AFTER ALL...
I...

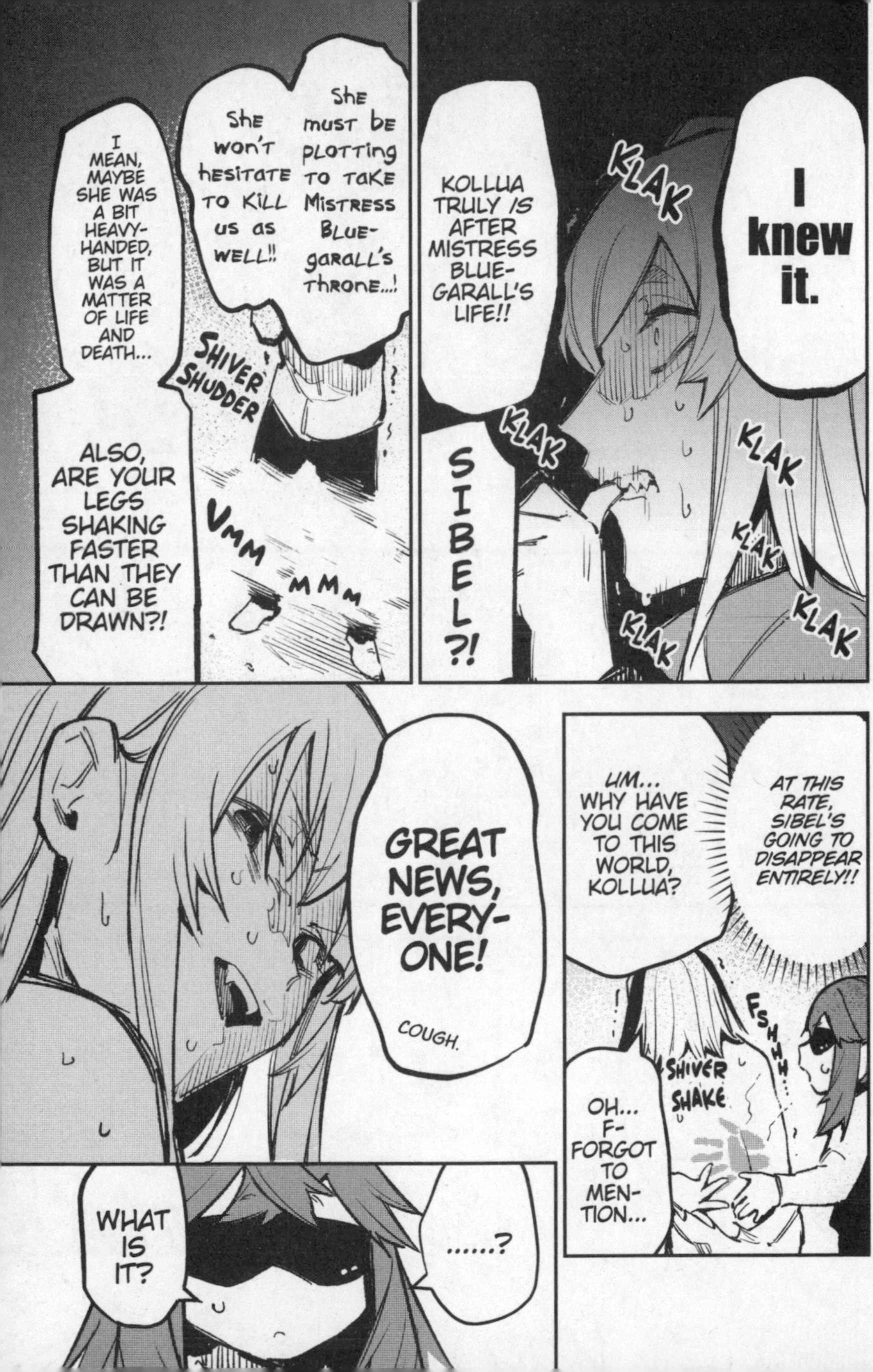
I knew it.
KLAK
KOLLUA TRULY IS AFTER MISTRESS BLUE-GARALL'S LIFE!!
KLAK
SIBEL?!
KLAK
KLAK
KLAK
KLAK
She must be plotting to take Mistress Blue-garall's throne...!
She won't hesitate to kill us as well!!
I MEAN, MAYBE SHE WAS A BIT HEAVY-HANDED, BUT IT WAS A MATTER OF LIFE AND DEATH...
SHIVER SHUDDER
ALSO, ARE YOUR LEGS SHAKING FASTER THAN THEY CAN BE DRAWN?!
VMM MMM
AT THIS RATE, SIBEL'S GOING TO DISAPPEAR ENTIRELY!!
UM... WHY HAVE YOU COME TO THIS WORLD, KOLLUA?
FSHHH...
SHIVER SHAKE
OH... F-FORGOT TO MENTION...
GREAT NEWS, EVERY-ONE!
COUGH.
......?
WHAT IS IT?

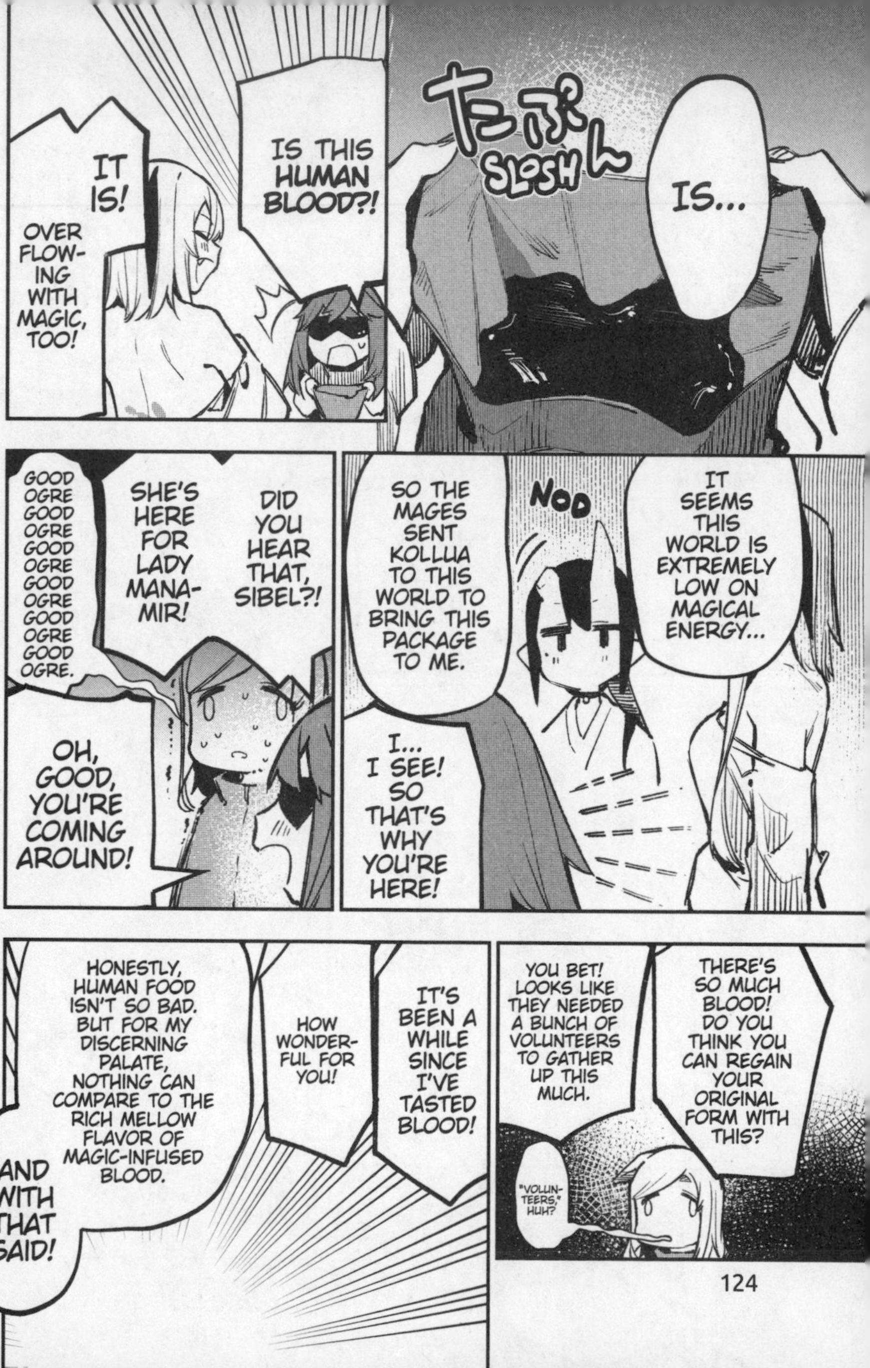
たぷん
SLOSH
IS...
IS THIS HUMAN BLOOD?!
IT IS!
OVERFLOWING WITH MAGIC, TOO!
IT SEEMS THIS WORLD IS EXTREMELY LOW ON MAGICAL ENERGY...
NOD
SO THE MAGES SENT KOLLUA TO THIS WORLD TO BRING THIS PACKAGE TO ME.
I... I SEE! SO THAT'S WHY YOU'RE HERE!
DID YOU HEAR THAT, SIBEL?!
SHE'S HERE FOR LADY MANAMIR!
GOOD OGRE GOOD OGRE GOOD OGRE GOOD OGRE GOOD OGRE GOOD OGRE GOOD OGRE.
OH, GOOD, YOU'RE COMING AROUND!
THERE'S SO MUCH BLOOD! DO YOU THINK YOU CAN REGAIN YOUR ORIGINAL FORM WITH THIS?
YOU BET! LOOKS LIKE THEY NEEDED A BUNCH OF VOLUNTEERS TO GATHER UP THIS MUCH.
"VOLUNTEERS," HUH?
IT'S BEEN A WHILE SINCE I'VE TASTED BLOOD!
HOW WONDERFUL FOR YOU!
HONESTLY, HUMAN FOOD ISN'T SO BAD. BUT FOR MY DISCERNING PALATE, NOTHING CAN COMPARE TO THE RICH MELLOW FLAVOR OF MAGIC-INFUSED BLOOD.
AND WITH THAT SAID!

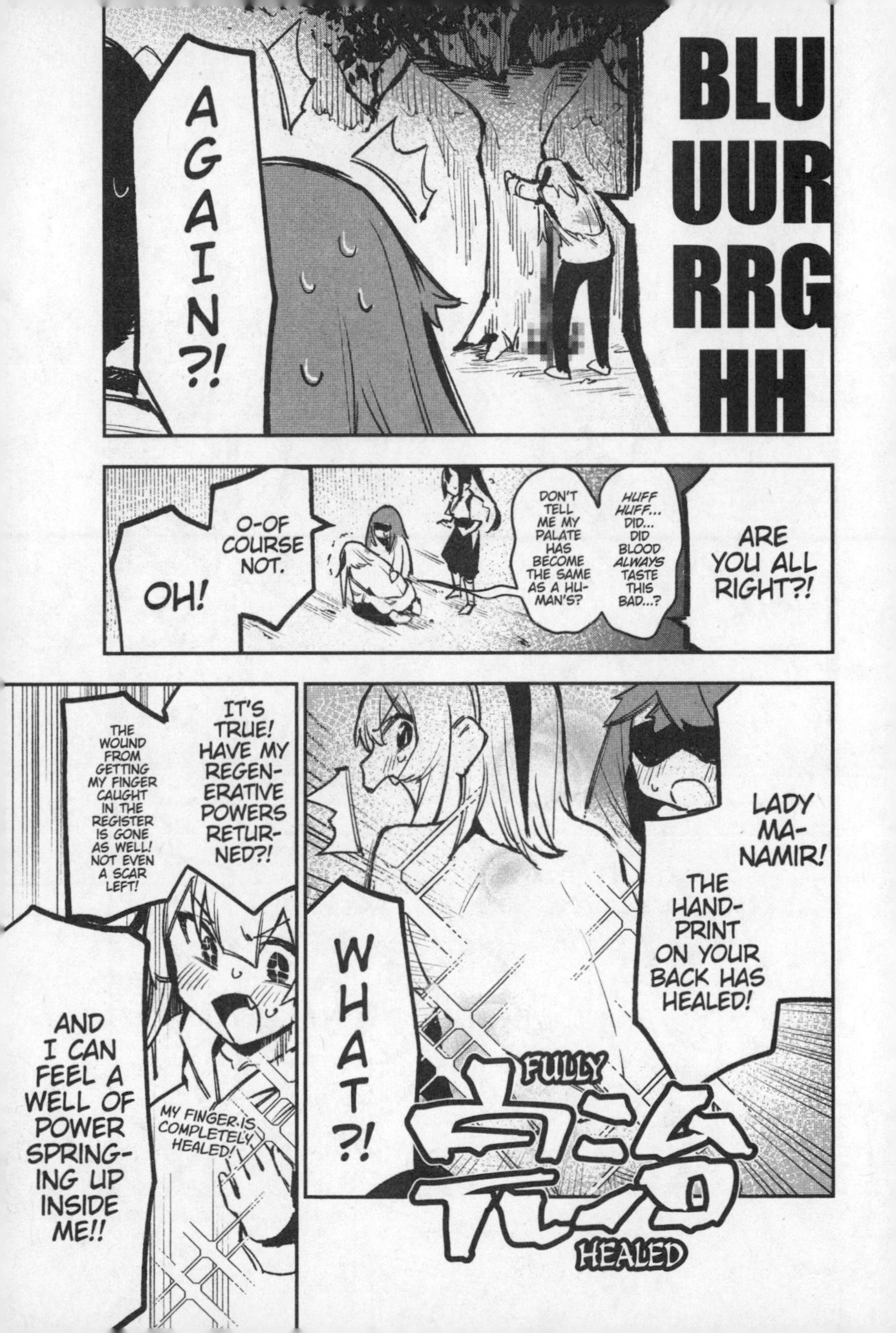
BLUURRGHH
AGAIN?!
ARE YOU ALL RIGHT?!
HUFF HUFF... DID... DID BLOOD ALWAYS TASTE THIS BAD...?
DON'T TELL ME MY PALATE HAS BECOME THE SAME AS A HUMAN'S?
O-OF COURSE NOT.
OH!
LADY MANAMIR!
THE HANDPRINT ON YOUR BACK HAS HEALED!
WHAT?!
FULLY HEALED
IT'S TRUE! HAVE MY REGENERATIVE POWERS RETURNED?!
THE WOUND FROM GETTING MY FINGER CAUGHT IN THE REGISTER IS GONE AS WELL! NOT EVEN A SCAR LEFT!
MY FINGER IS COMPLETELY HEALED!
AND I CAN FEEL A WELL OF POWER SPRINGING UP INSIDE ME!!

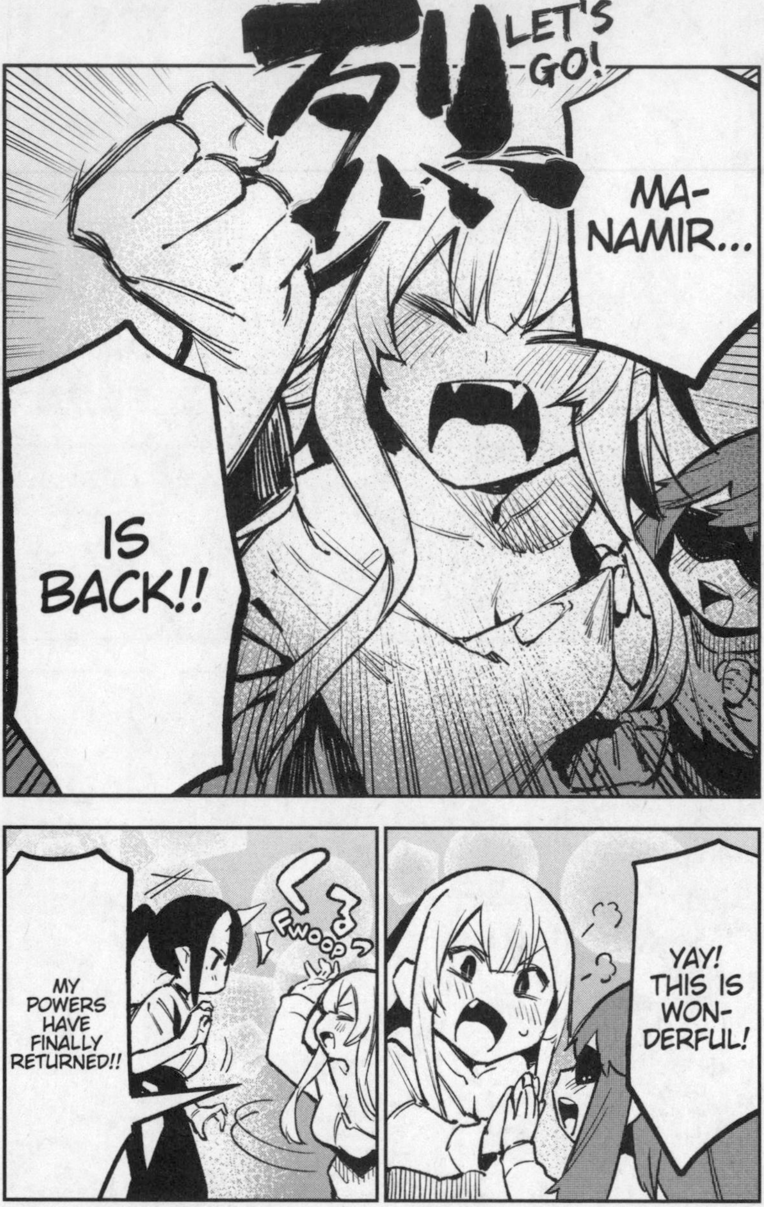
LET'S GO!
MA-NAMIR...
IS BACK!!
YAY! THIS IS WON-DERFUL!
MY POWERS HAVE FINALLY RETURNED!!
FWOOP

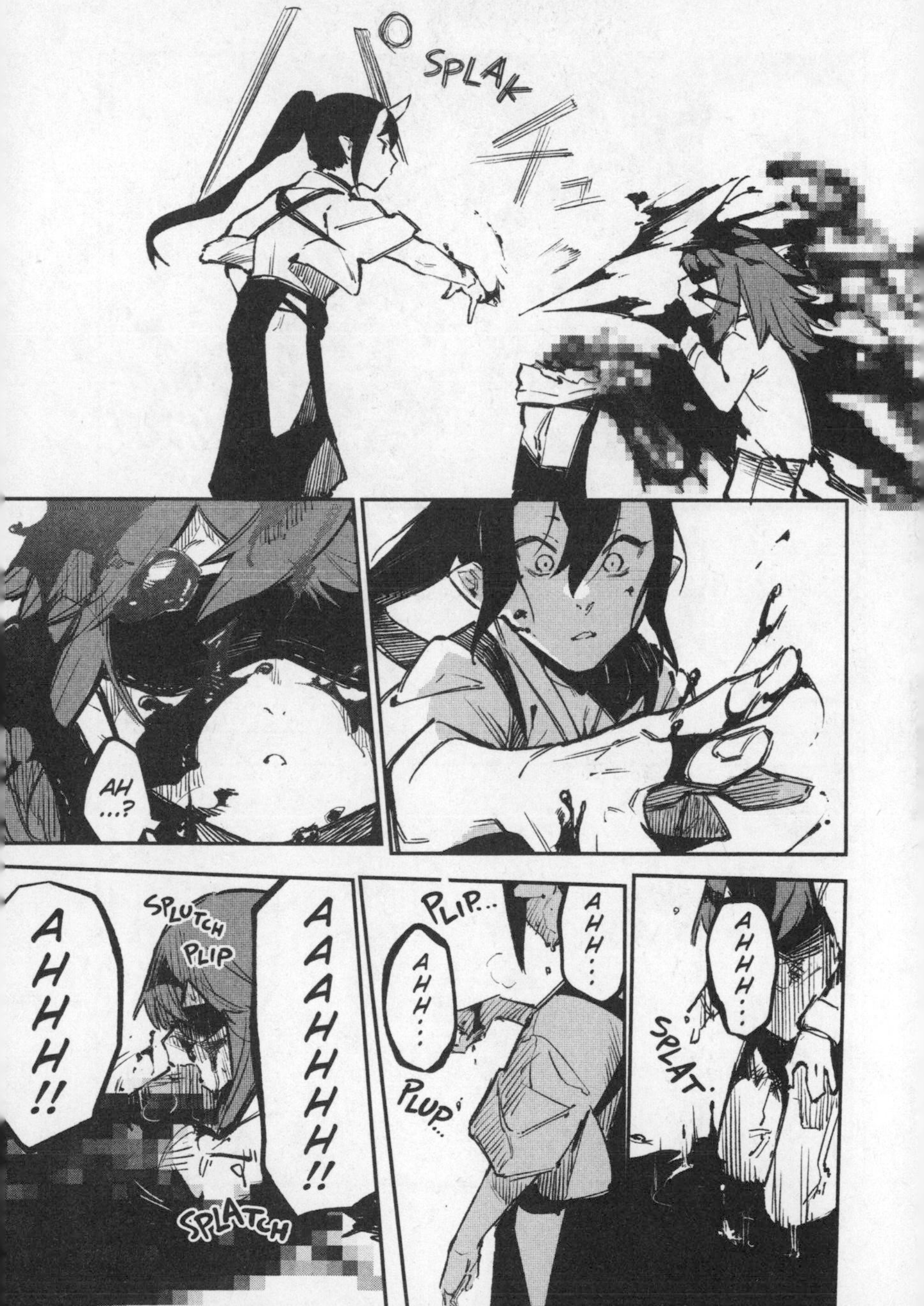
SPLAK
AH ...?
AHHH...
SPLAT
AHH...
PLIP...
AHH...
PLUP...
AAAAHHHHH!!
SPLUTCH
PLIP
AHHHH!!
SPLATCH

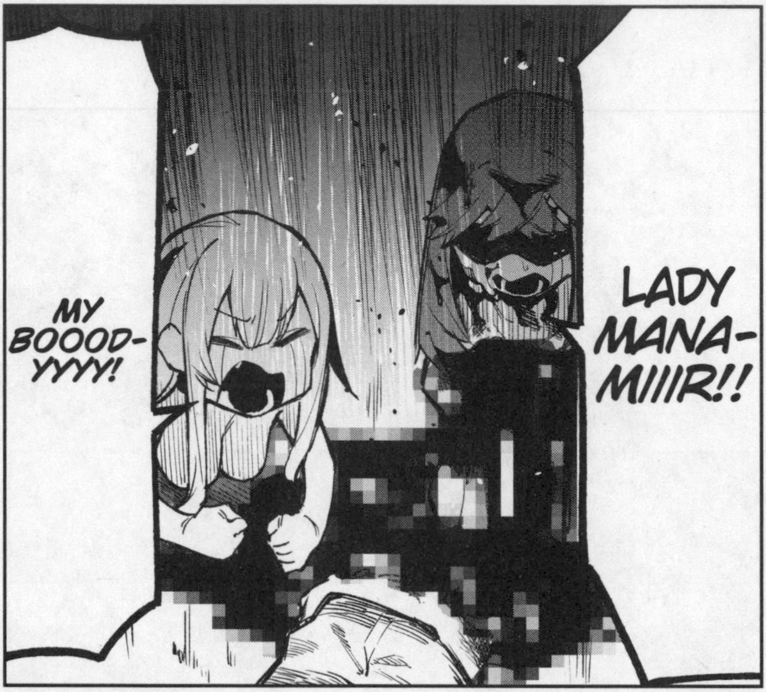
LADY MANA-MIIIR!!
MY BOOOD-YYYY!

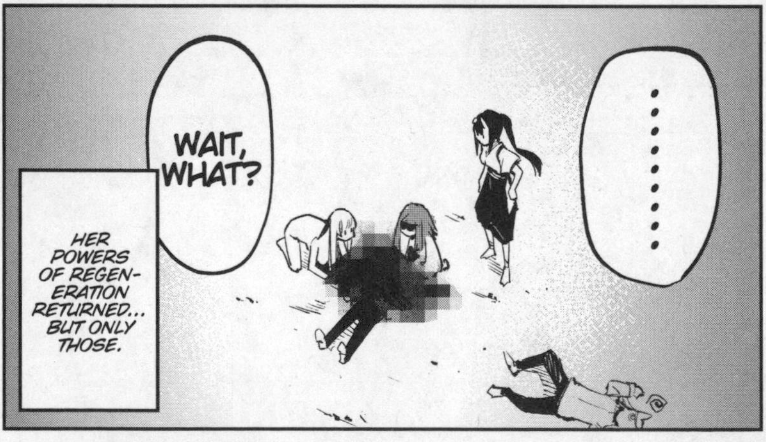
......
WAIT, WHAT?
HER POWERS OF REGEN-ERATION RETURNED... BUT ONLY THOSE.

Gathering up
chunks of flesh is
LEWD.

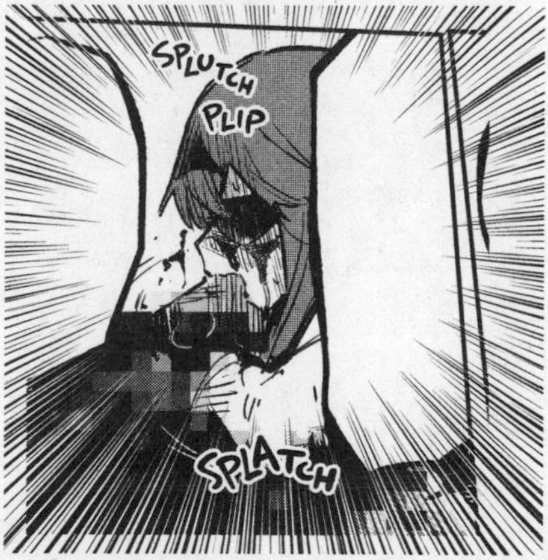
SPLUTCH
PLIP
SPLATCH

It's Just Not My Night!

Tale of a Fallen Vampire Queen

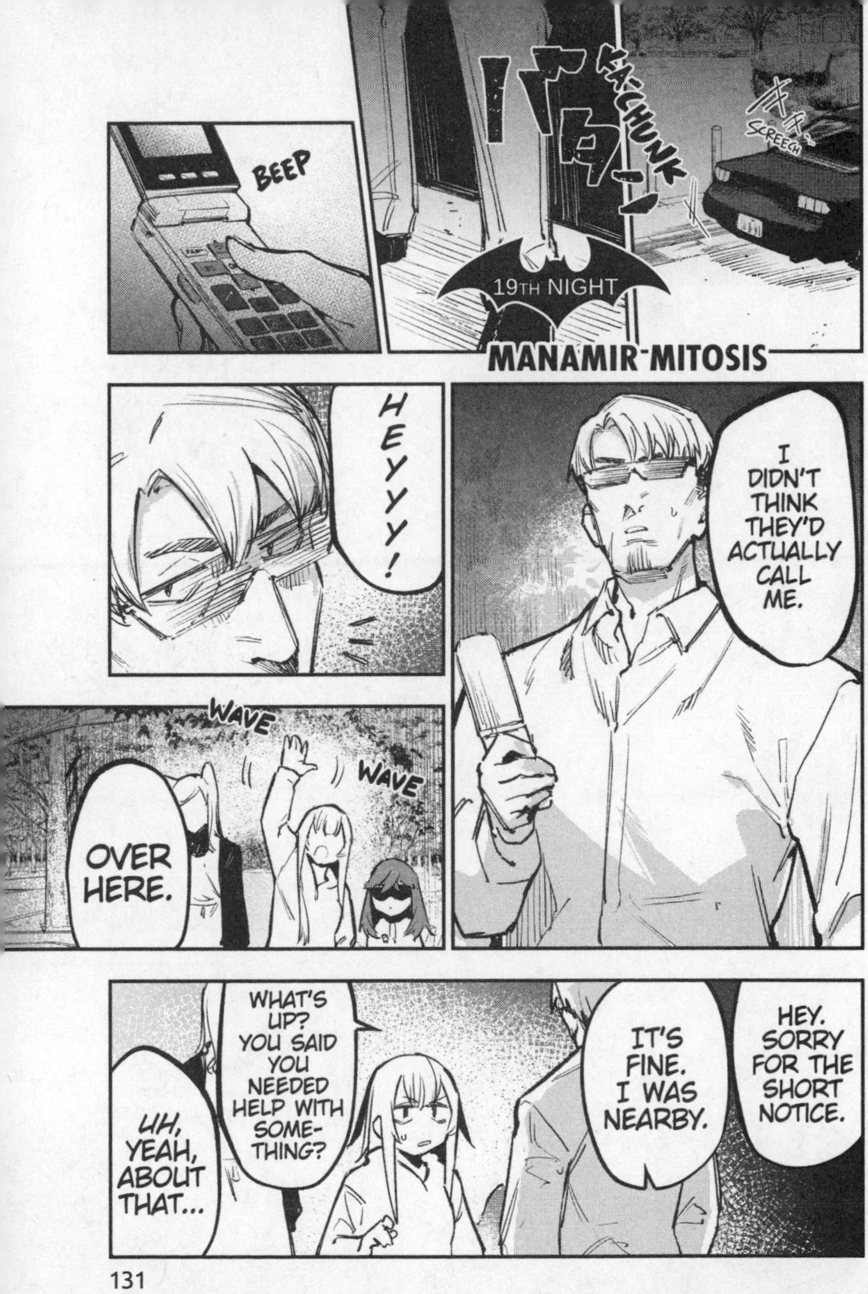
KA-CHUNK
SCREECH
19TH NIGHT
MANAMIR MITOSIS
BEEP
I DIDN'T THINK THEY'D ACTUALLY CALL ME.
HEYYY!
WAVE
WAVE
OVER HERE.
HEY. SORRY FOR THE SHORT NOTICE.
IT'S FINE. I WAS NEARBY.
WHAT'S UP? YOU SAID YOU NEEDED HELP WITH SOME-THING?
UH, YEAH, ABOUT THAT...

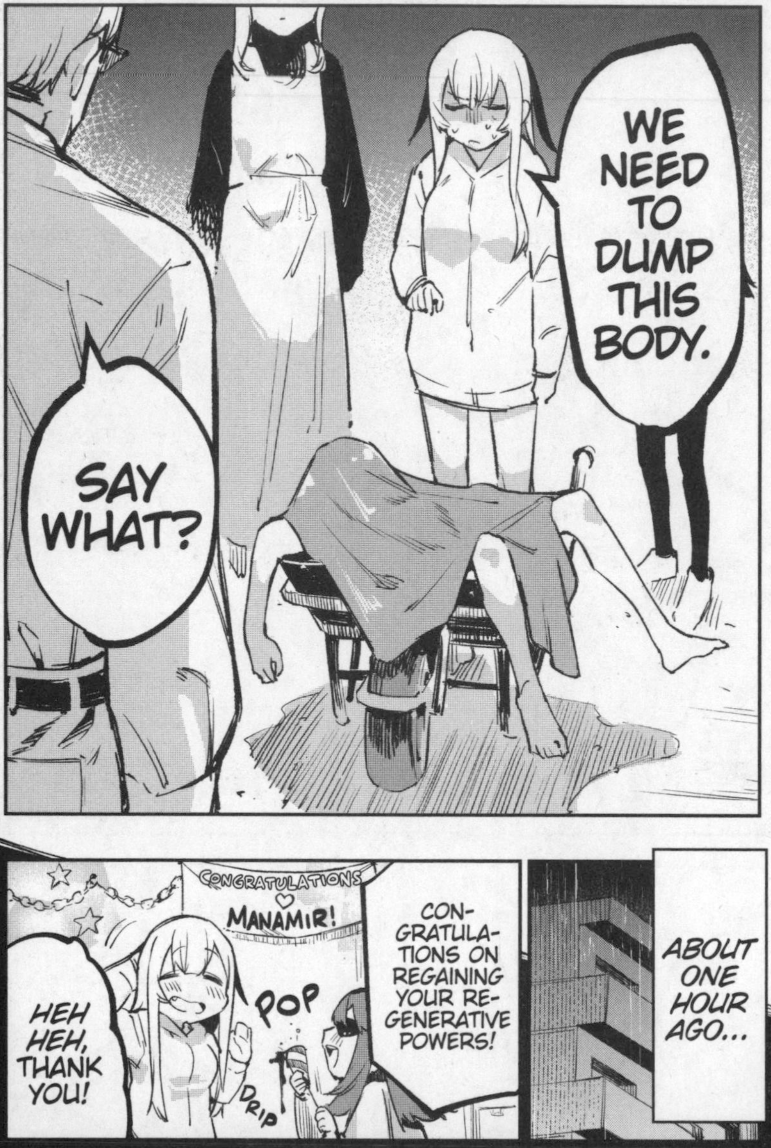
WE NEED TO DUMP THIS BODY.
SAY WHAT?
ABOUT ONE HOUR AGO...
CON-GRATULA-TIONS ON REGAINING YOUR RE-GENERATIVE POWERS!
CONGRATULATIONS ♡ MANAMIR!
POP
HEH HEH, THANK YOU!
DRIP

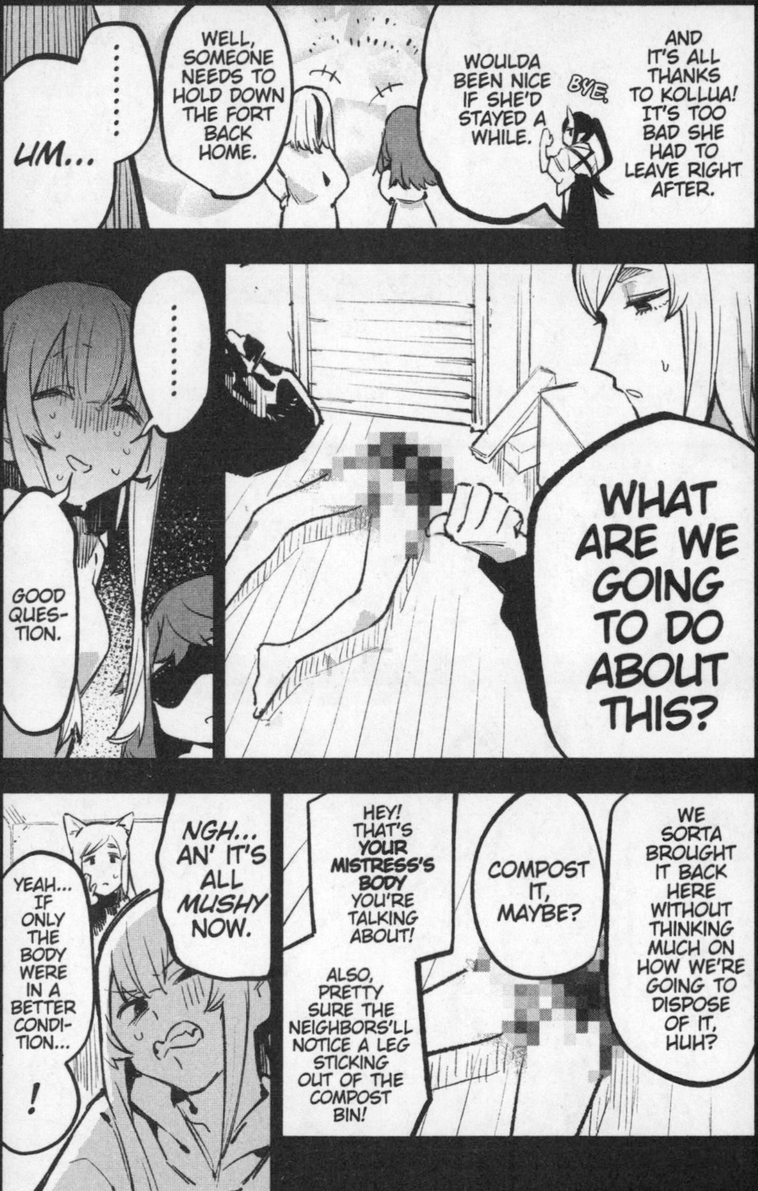
AND IT'S ALL THANKS TO KOLLUA! IT'S TOO BAD SHE HAD TO LEAVE RIGHT AFTER.
BYE.
WOULDA BEEN NICE IF SHE'D STAYED A WHILE.
WELL, SOMEONE NEEDS TO HOLD DOWN THE FORT BACK HOME.
......
UM...
WHAT ARE WE GOING TO DO ABOUT THIS?
......
GOOD QUES-TION.
WE SORTA BROUGHT IT BACK HERE WITHOUT THINKING MUCH ON HOW WE'RE GOING TO DISPOSE OF IT, HUH?
COMPOST IT, MAYBE?
HEY! THAT'S YOUR MISTRESS'S BODY YOU'RE TALKING ABOUT!
ALSO, PRETTY SURE THE NEIGHBORS'LL NOTICE A LEG STICKING OUT OF THE COMPOST BIN!
NGH... AN' IT'S ALL MUSHY NOW.
YEAH... IF ONLY THE BODY WERE IN A BETTER CONDI-TION...
!

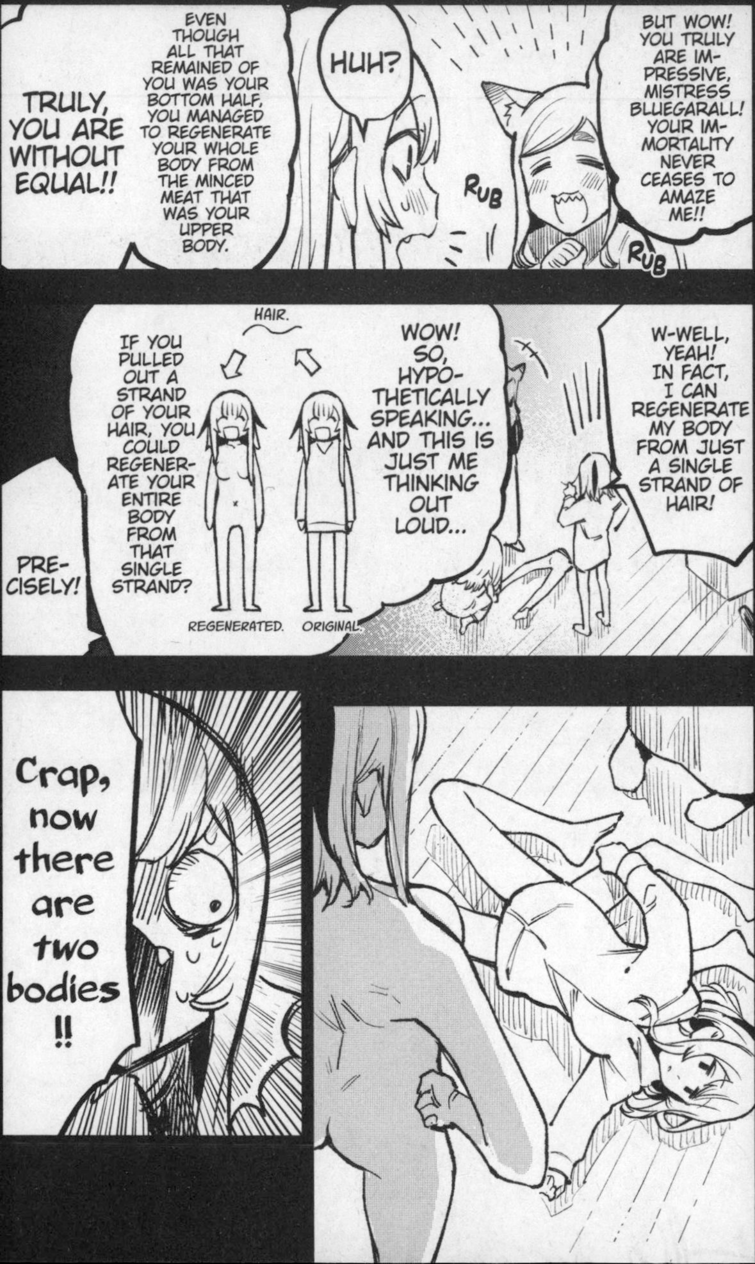
BUT WOW! YOU TRULY ARE IMPRESSIVE, MISTRESS BLUEGARALL! YOUR IMMORTALITY NEVER CEASES TO AMAZE ME!!
RUB
RUB
HUH?
EVEN THOUGH ALL THAT REMAINED OF YOU WAS YOUR BOTTOM HALF, YOU MANAGED TO REGENERATE YOUR WHOLE BODY FROM THE MINCED MEAT THAT WAS YOUR UPPER BODY.
TRULY, YOU ARE WITHOUT EQUAL!!
W-WELL, YEAH! IN FACT, I CAN REGENERATE MY BODY FROM JUST A SINGLE STRAND OF HAIR!
WOW! SO, HYPOTHETICALLY SPEAKING... AND THIS IS JUST ME THINKING OUT LOUD...
HAIR.
IF YOU PULLED OUT A STRAND OF YOUR HAIR, YOU COULD REGENERATE YOUR ENTIRE BODY FROM THAT SINGLE STRAND?
ORIGINAL.
REGENERATED.
PRECISELY!
Crap, now there are two bodies!!

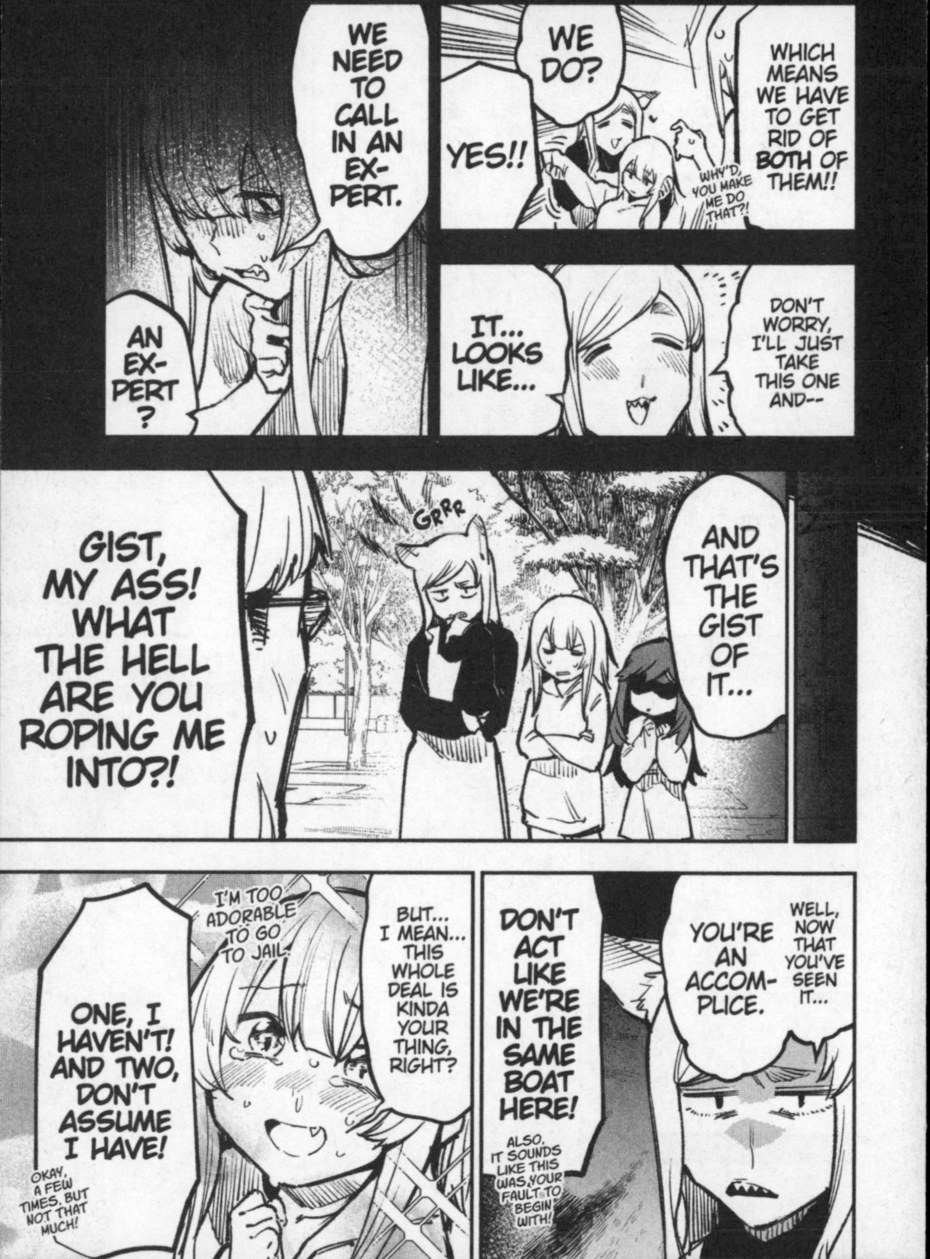
WHICH MEANS WE HAVE TO GET RID OF BOTH OF THEM!!
WE DO?
YES!!
WHY'D YOU MAKE ME DO THAT?!
DON'T WORRY, I'LL JUST TAKE THIS ONE AND--
IT... LOOKS LIKE...
WE NEED TO CALL IN AN EX-PERT.
AN EX-PERT?
AND THAT'S THE GIST OF IT...
GRRR
GIST, MY ASS! WHAT THE HELL ARE YOU ROPING ME INTO?!
WELL, NOW THAT YOU'VE SEEN IT...
YOU'RE AN ACCOM-PLICE.
DON'T ACT LIKE WE'RE IN THE SAME BOAT HERE!
ALSO, IT SOUNDS LIKE THIS WAS YOUR FAULT TO BEGIN WITH!
BUT... I MEAN... THIS WHOLE DEAL IS KINDA YOUR THING, RIGHT?
I'M TOO ADORABLE TO GO TO JAIL.
ONE, I HAVEN'T! AND TWO, DON'T ASSUME I HAVE!
OKAY, A FEW TIMES, BUT NOT THAT MUCH!

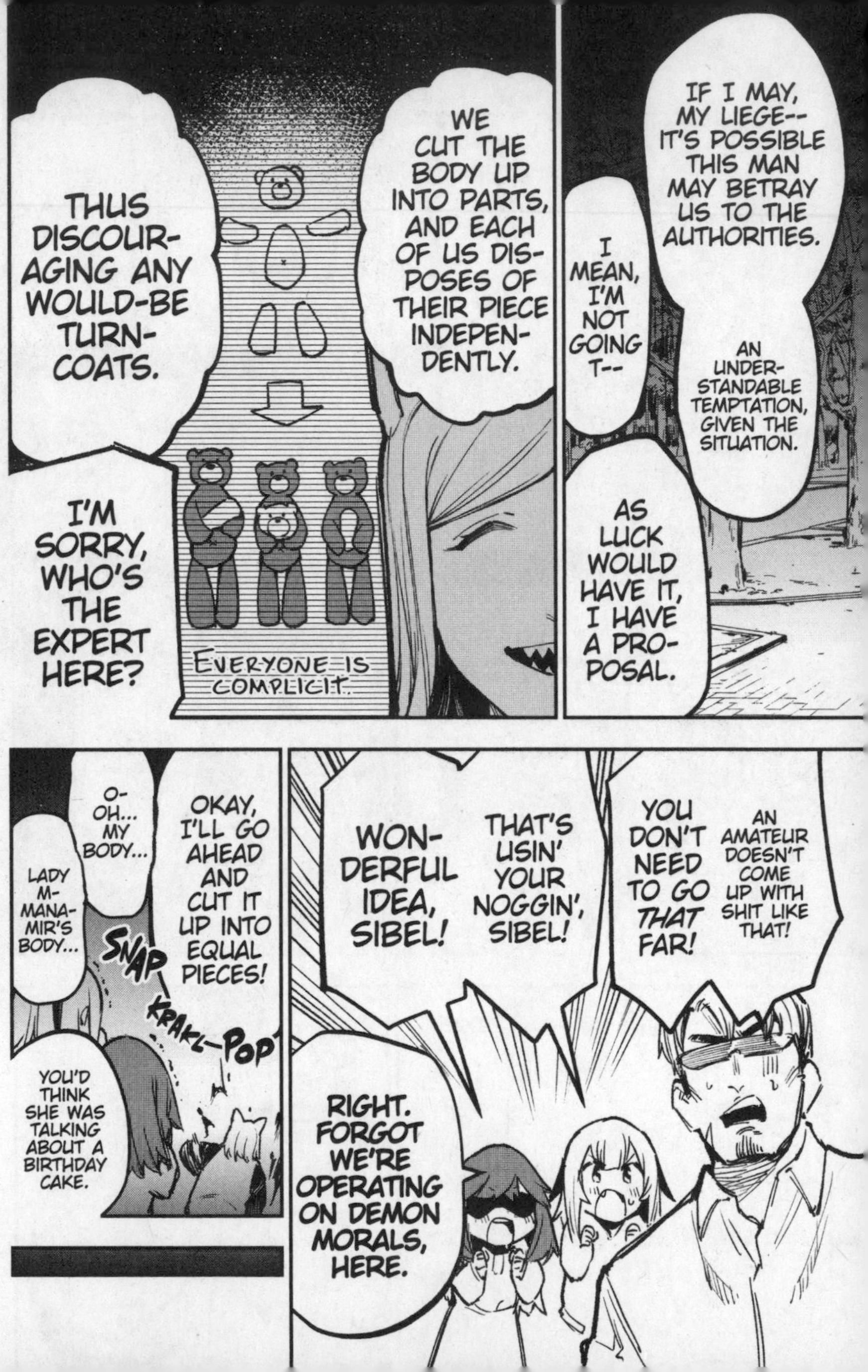
IF I MAY, MY LIEGE-- IT'S POSSIBLE THIS MAN MAY BETRAY US TO THE AUTHORITIES.
I MEAN, I'M NOT GOING T--
AN UNDERSTANDABLE TEMPTATION, GIVEN THE SITUATION.
AS LUCK WOULD HAVE IT, I HAVE A PROPOSAL.
WE CUT THE BODY UP INTO PARTS, AND EACH OF US DISPOSES OF THEIR PIECE INDEPENDENTLY.
THUS DISCOURAGING ANY WOULD-BE TURNCOATS.
EVERYONE IS COMPLICIT.
I'M SORRY, WHO'S THE EXPERT HERE?
AN AMATEUR DOESN'T COME UP WITH SHIT LIKE THAT!
YOU DON'T NEED TO GO *THAT* FAR!
THAT'S USIN' YOUR NOGGIN', SIBEL!
WONDERFUL IDEA, SIBEL!
RIGHT. FORGOT WE'RE OPERATING ON DEMON MORALS, HERE.
OKAY, I'LL GO AHEAD AND CUT IT UP INTO EQUAL PIECES!
O-OH... MY BODY...
LADY M-MANAMIR'S BODY...
SNAP
KRAKL-POP
YOU'D THINK SHE WAS TALKING ABOUT A BIRTHDAY CAKE.

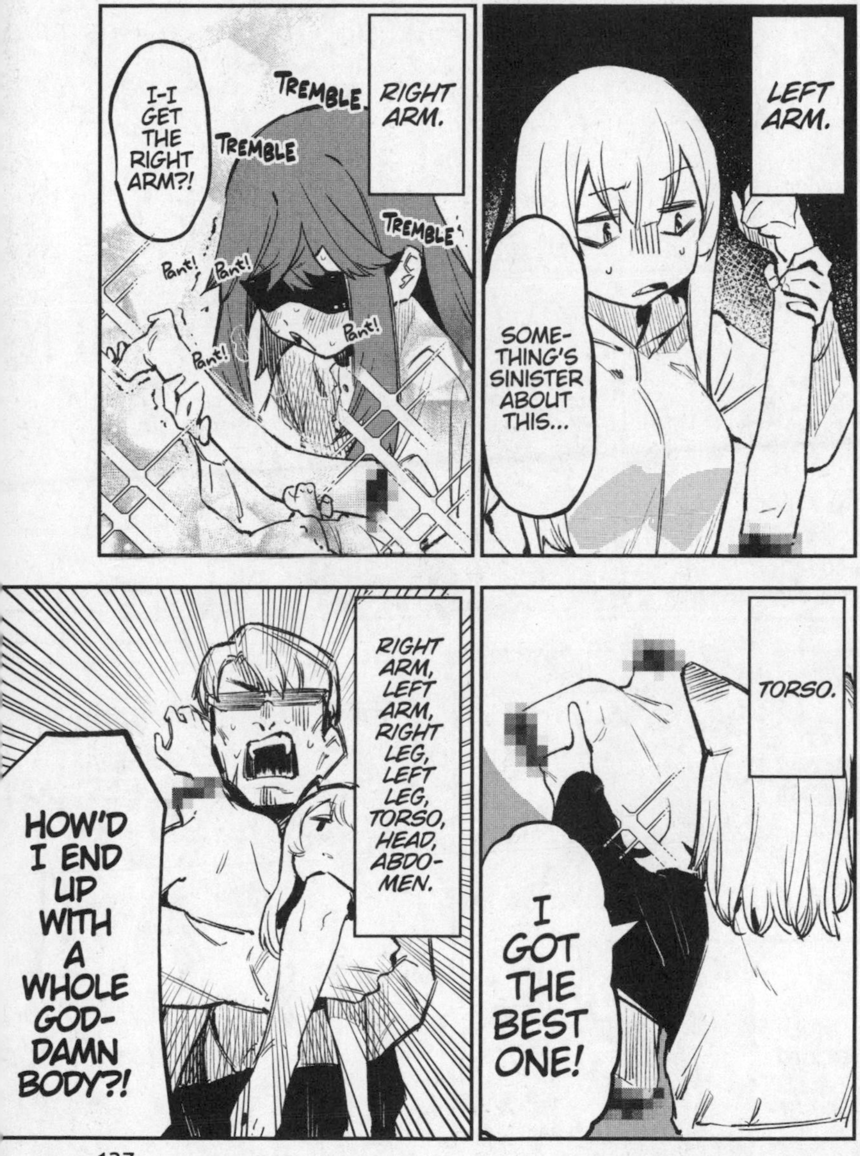
LEFT ARM.
SOME-THING'S SINISTER ABOUT THIS...
RIGHT ARM.
TREMBLE
I-I GET THE RIGHT ARM?!
TREMBLE
TREMBLE
Pant! Pant!
Pant!
Pant!
TORSO.
I GOT THE BEST ONE!
RIGHT ARM, LEFT ARM, RIGHT LEG, LEFT LEG, TORSO, HEAD, ABDO-MEN.
HOW'D I END UP WITH A WHOLE GOD-DAMN BODY?!

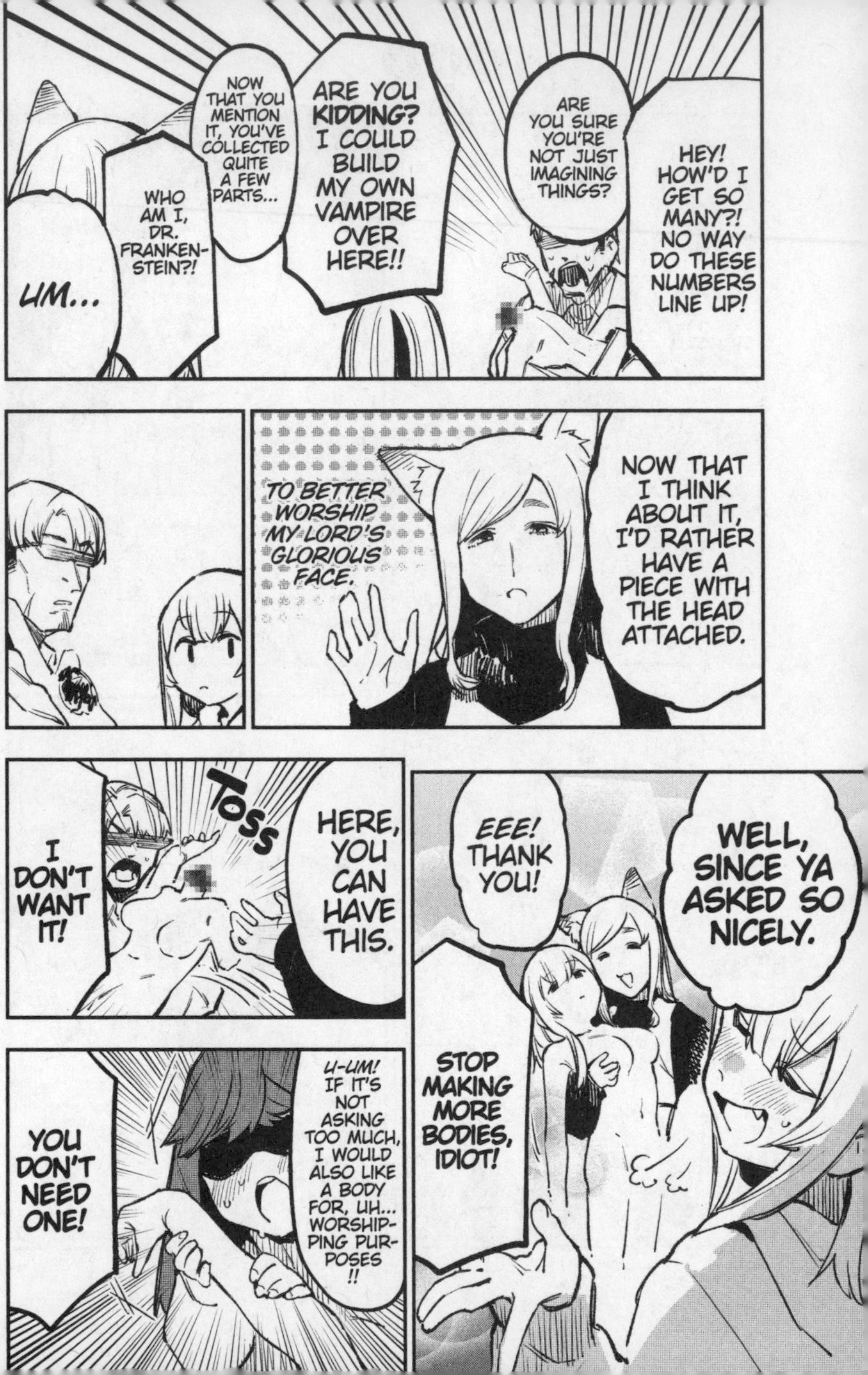
HEY! HOW'D I GET SO MANY?! NO WAY DO THESE NUMBERS LINE UP!
ARE YOU SURE YOU'RE NOT JUST IMAGINING THINGS?
ARE YOU KIDDING? I COULD BUILD MY OWN VAMPIRE OVER HERE!!
NOW THAT YOU MENTION IT, YOU'VE COLLECTED QUITE A FEW PARTS...
WHO AM I, DR. FRANKEN-STEIN?!
UM...
NOW THAT I THINK ABOUT IT, I'D RATHER HAVE A PIECE WITH THE HEAD ATTACHED.
TO BETTER WORSHIP MY LORD'S GLORIOUS FACE.
WELL, SINCE YA ASKED SO NICELY.
EEE! THANK YOU!
STOP MAKING MORE BODIES, IDIOT!
TOSS
HERE, YOU CAN HAVE THIS.
I DON'T WANT IT!
U-UM! IF IT'S NOT ASKING TOO MUCH, I WOULD ALSO LIKE A BODY FOR, UH... WORSHIP-PING PUR-POSES!!
YOU DON'T NEED ONE!

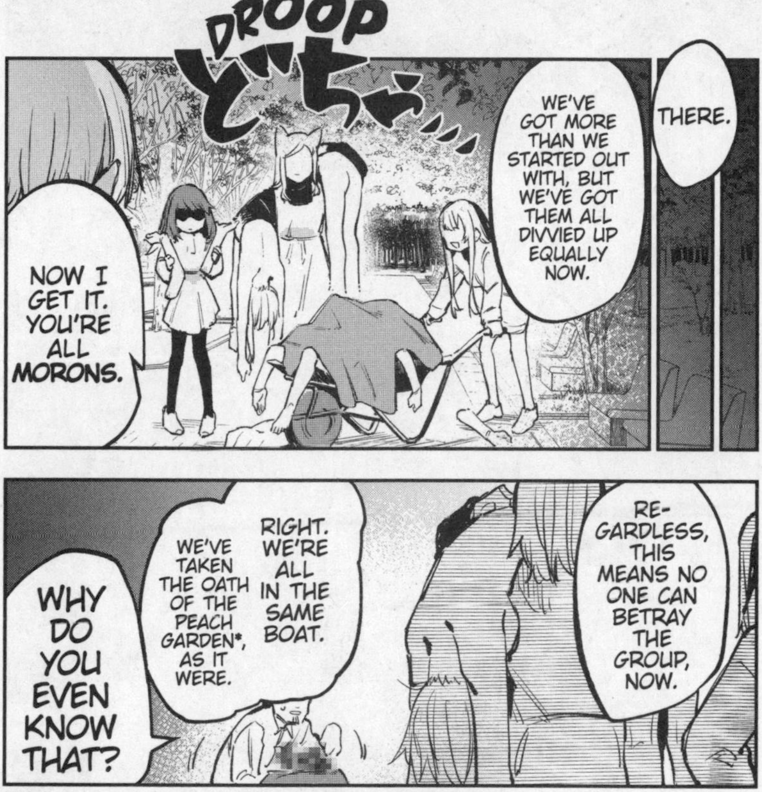
THERE.
WE'VE GOT MORE THAN WE STARTED OUT WITH, BUT WE'VE GOT THEM ALL DIVVIED UP EQUALLY NOW.
DROOP
どちゃ...
NOW I GET IT. YOU'RE ALL MORONS.
RE-GARDLESS, THIS MEANS NO ONE CAN BETRAY THE GROUP, NOW.
RIGHT. WE'RE ALL IN THE SAME BOAT.
WE'VE TAKEN THE OATH OF THE PEACH GARDEN*, AS IT WERE.
WHY DO YOU EVEN KNOW THAT?

*This is a legendary oath between three sworn brothers in ancient China.

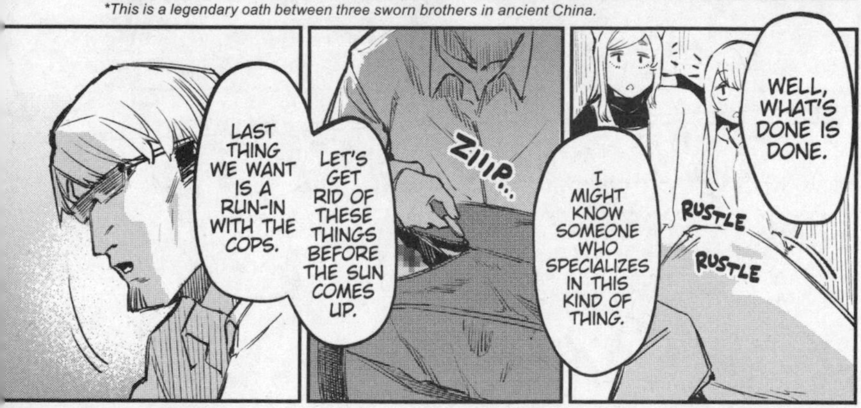
WELL, WHAT'S DONE IS DONE.
I MIGHT KNOW SOMEONE WHO SPECIALIZES IN THIS KIND OF THING.
RUSTLE
RUSTLE
ZIIIP...
LET'S GET RID OF THESE THINGS BEFORE THE SUN COMES UP.
LAST THING WE WANT IS A RUN-IN WITH THE COPS.

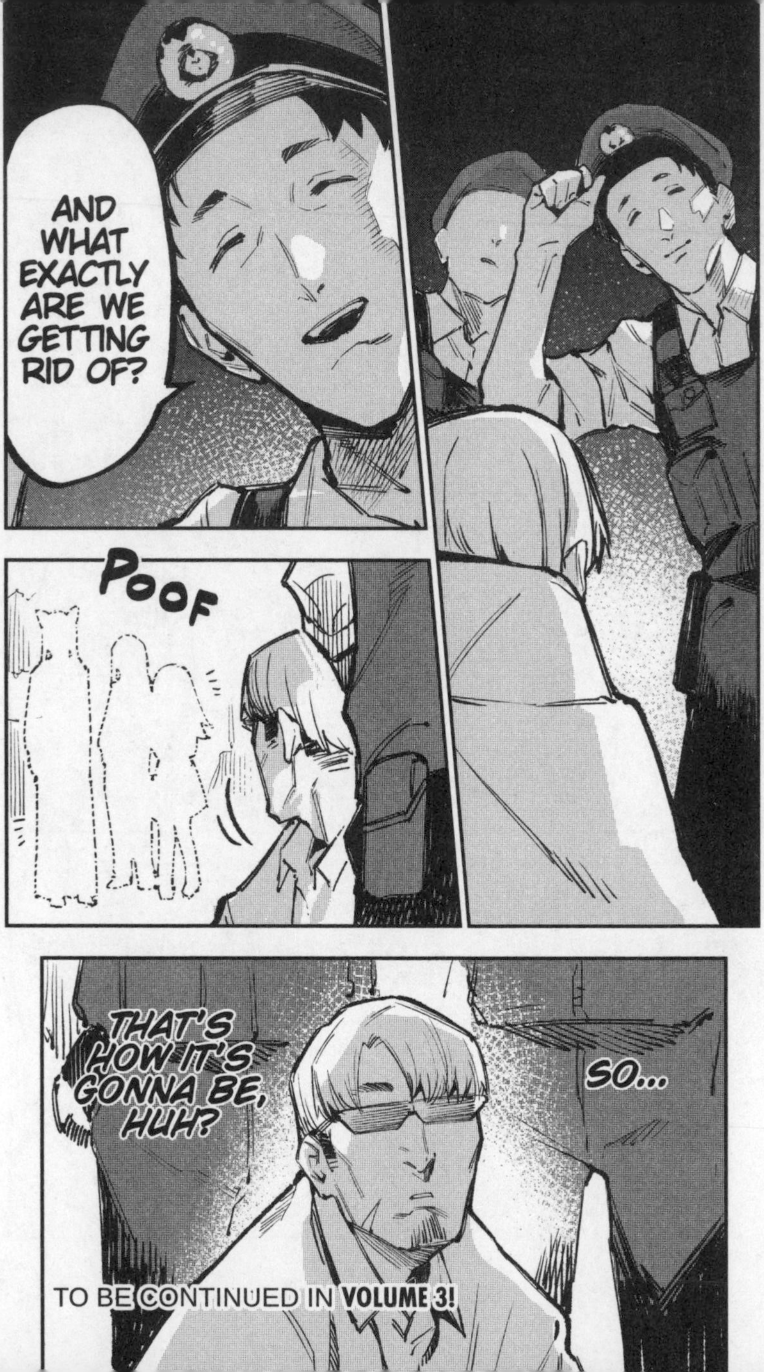
AND WHAT EXACTLY ARE WE GETTING RID OF?
POOF
SO...
THAT'S HOW IT'S GONNA BE, HUH?
TO BE CONTINUED IN VOLUME 3!

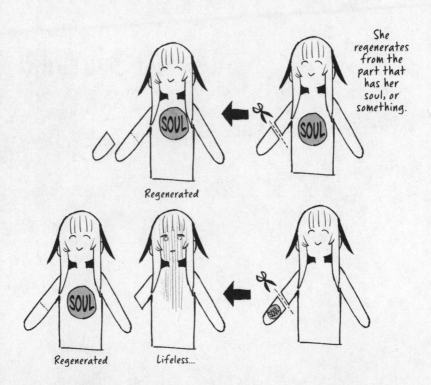

She regenerates from the part that has her soul, or something.

Regenerated

Regenerated   Lifeless...

It's Just Not My Night!

Tale of a Fallen Vampire Queen

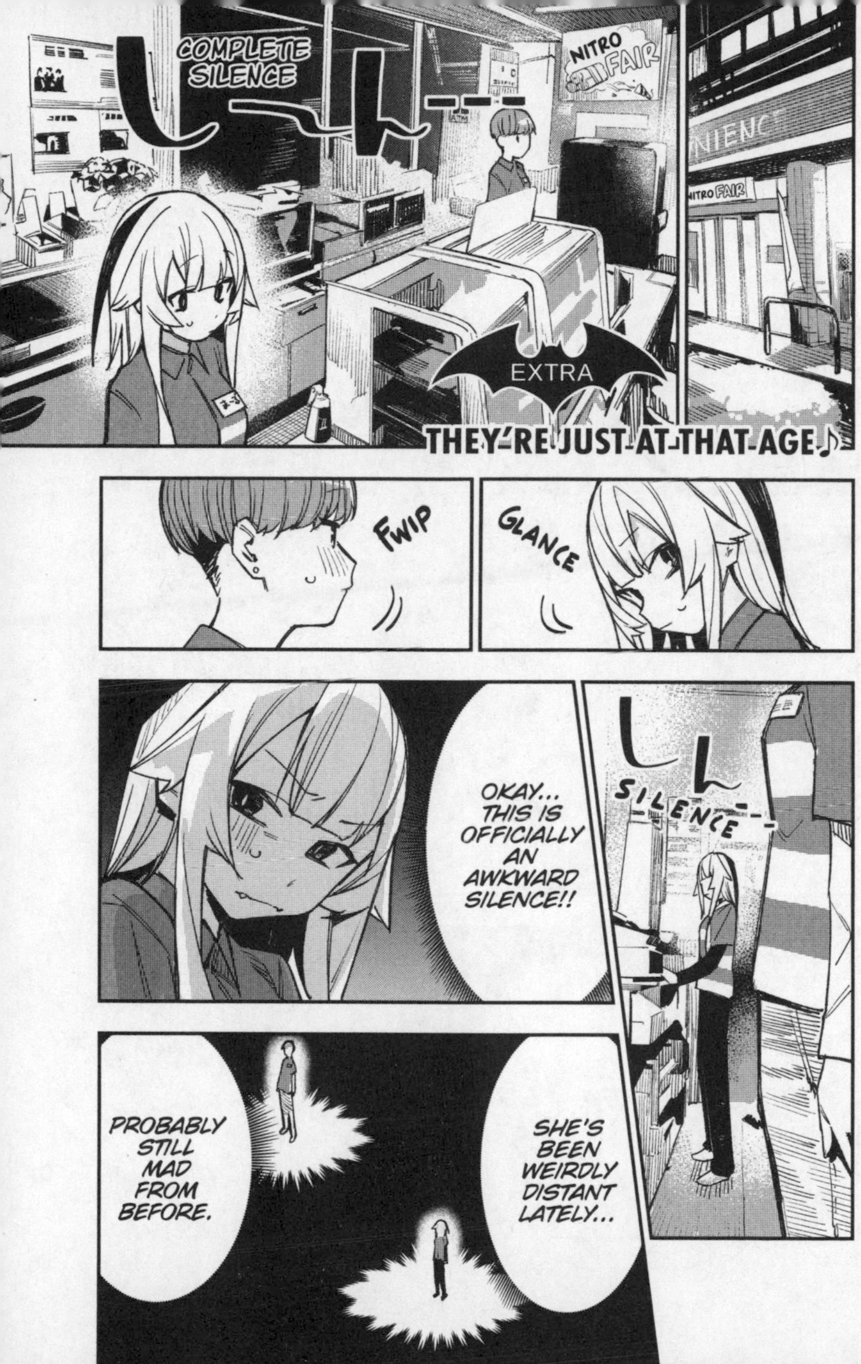
COMPLETE SILENCE
EXTRA
THEY'RE JUST AT THAT AGE♪
GLANCE
FWIP
SILENCE
OKAY... THIS IS OFFICIALLY AN AWKWARD SILENCE!!
SHE'S BEEN WEIRDLY DISTANT LATELY...
PROBABLY STILL MAD FROM BEFORE.

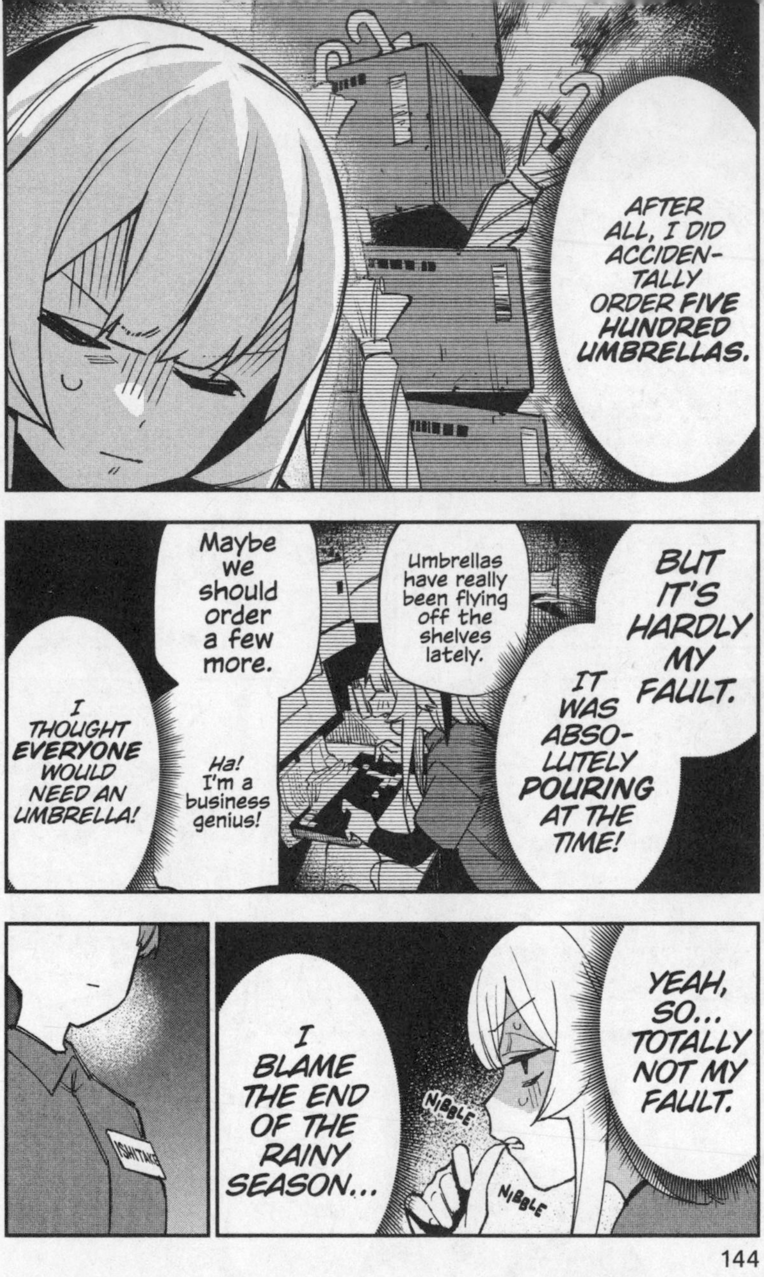
AFTER ALL, I DID ACCIDENTALLY ORDER FIVE HUNDRED UMBRELLAS.
BUT IT'S HARDLY MY FAULT.
IT WAS ABSOLUTELY POURING AT THE TIME!
Umbrellas have really been flying off the shelves lately.
Maybe we should order a few more.
Ha! I'm a business genius!
I THOUGHT EVERYONE WOULD NEED AN UMBRELLA!
YEAH, SO... TOTALLY NOT MY FAULT.
I BLAME THE END OF THE RAINY SEASON...
NIBBLE
NIBBLE
ISHITAKE

DID MANAMIR-SAN END UP BUY-ING...

ALL THOSE ADULT TOYS?

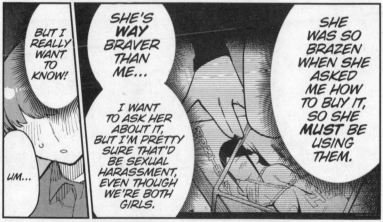

SHE WAS SO BRAZEN WHEN SHE ASKED ME HOW TO BUY IT, SO SHE *MUST* BE USING THEM.

SHE'S *WAY* BRAVER THAN ME...

I WANT TO ASK HER ABOUT IT, BUT I'M PRETTY SURE THAT'D BE SEXUAL HARASSMENT, EVEN THOUGH WE'RE BOTH GIRLS.

BUT I REALLY WANT TO KNOW!

UM...

H-HEY, MANAMIR-SAN...

ABOUT THE UH, **STUFF** FROM BEFORE.

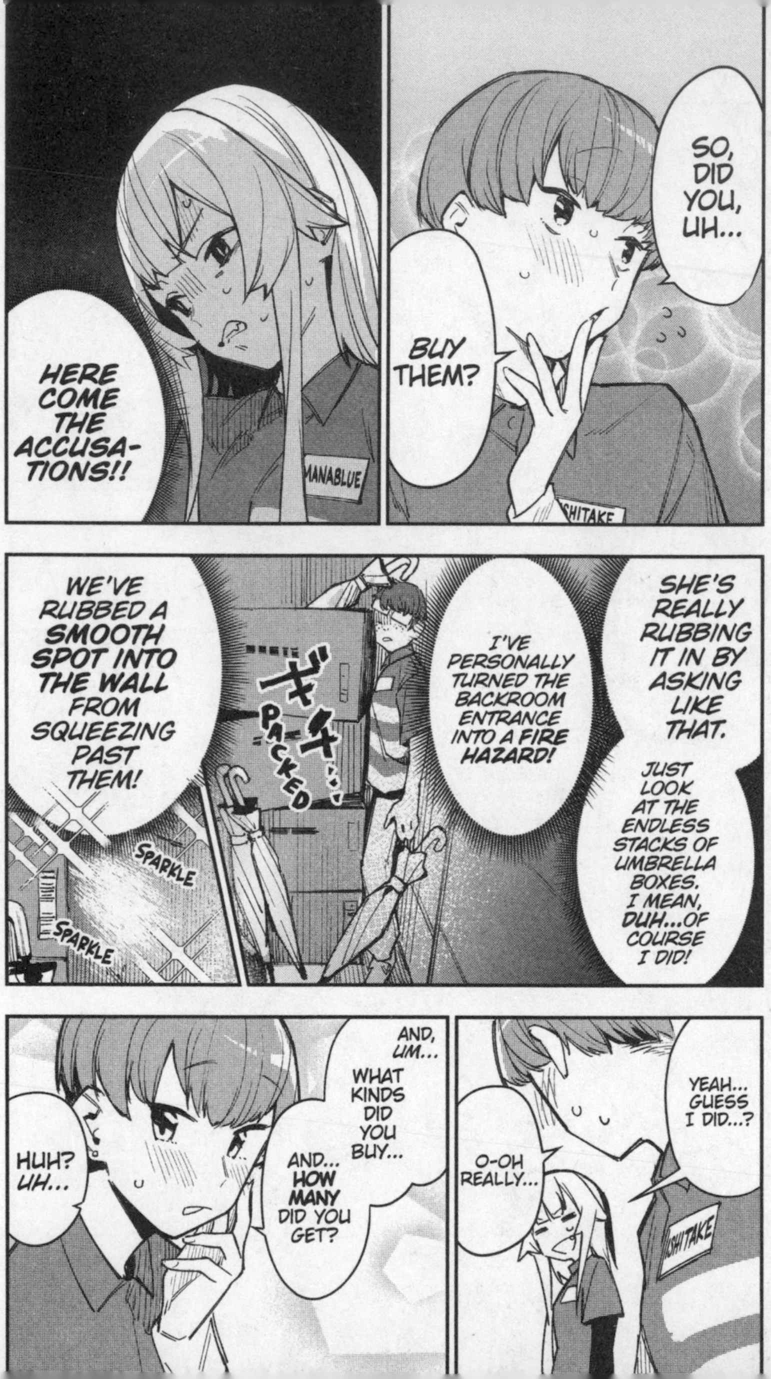
SO, DID YOU, UH...
BUY THEM?
SHITAKE
HERE COME THE ACCUSATIONS!!
MANABLUE
SHE'S REALLY RUBBING IT IN BY ASKING LIKE THAT.
JUST LOOK AT THE ENDLESS STACKS OF UMBRELLA BOXES. I MEAN, DUH...OF COURSE I DID!
I'VE PERSONALLY TURNED THE BACKROOM ENTRANCE INTO A FIRE HAZARD!
PACKED
WE'VE RUBBED A SMOOTH SPOT INTO THE WALL FROM SQUEEZING PAST THEM!
SPARKLE
SPARKLE
YEAH... GUESS I DID...?
O-OH REALLY...
SHITAKE
AND, UM...
WHAT KINDS DID YOU BUY...
AND... HOW MANY DID YOU GET?
HUH? UH...

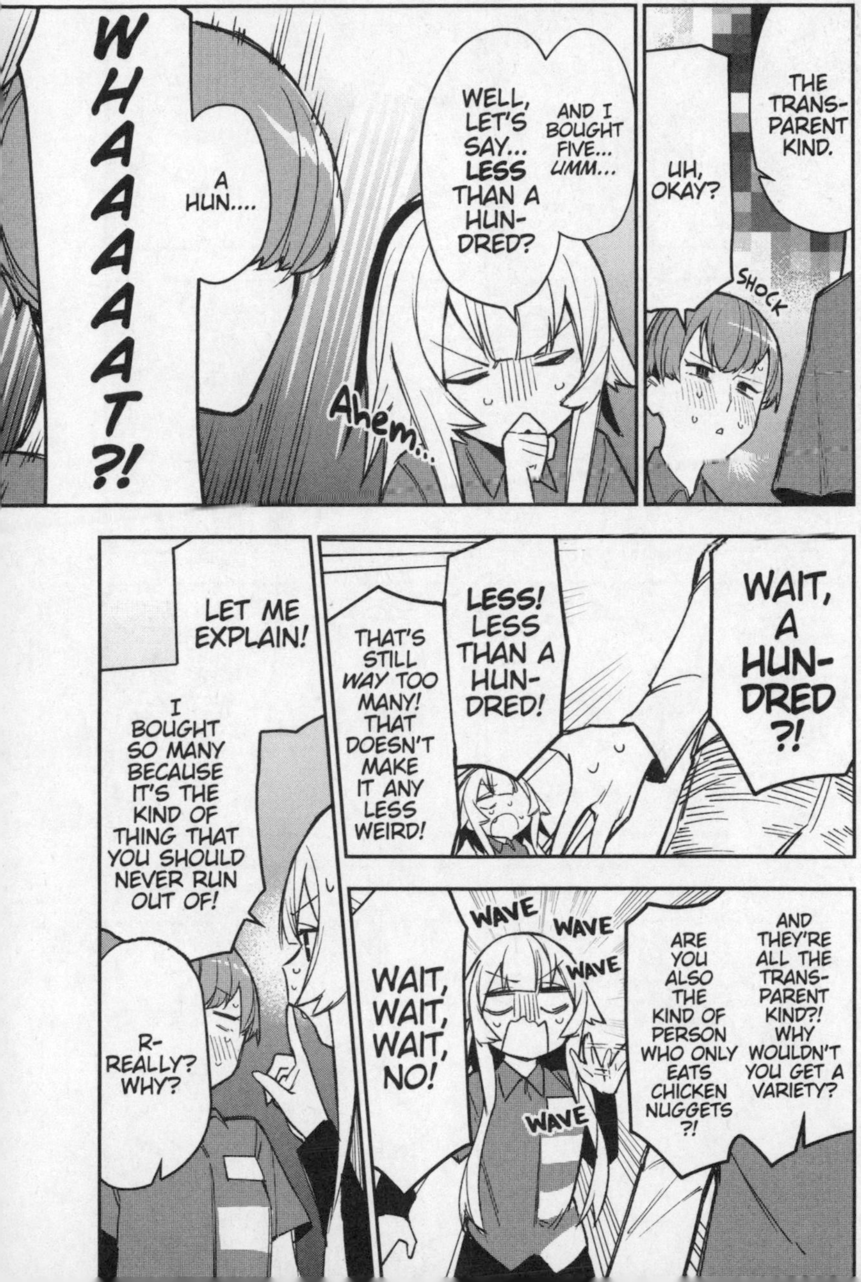
THE TRANS-PARENT KIND.
UH, OKAY?
SHOCK
AND I BOUGHT FIVE... UMM...
WELL, LET'S SAY... LESS THAN A HUN-DRED?
Ahem...
A HUN....
WHAAAAAT?!
WAIT, A HUN-DRED?!
LESS! LESS THAN A HUN-DRED!
THAT'S STILL WAY TOO MANY! THAT DOESN'T MAKE IT ANY LESS WEIRD!
AND THEY'RE ALL THE TRANS-PARENT KIND?! WHY WOULDN'T YOU GET A VARIETY?
ARE YOU ALSO THE KIND OF PERSON WHO ONLY EATS CHICKEN NUGGETS?!
WAVE
WAVE
WAVE
WAIT, WAIT, WAIT, NO!
WAVE
LET ME EXPLAIN!
I BOUGHT SO MANY BECAUSE IT'S THE KIND OF THING THAT YOU SHOULD NEVER RUN OUT OF!
R-REALLY? WHY?

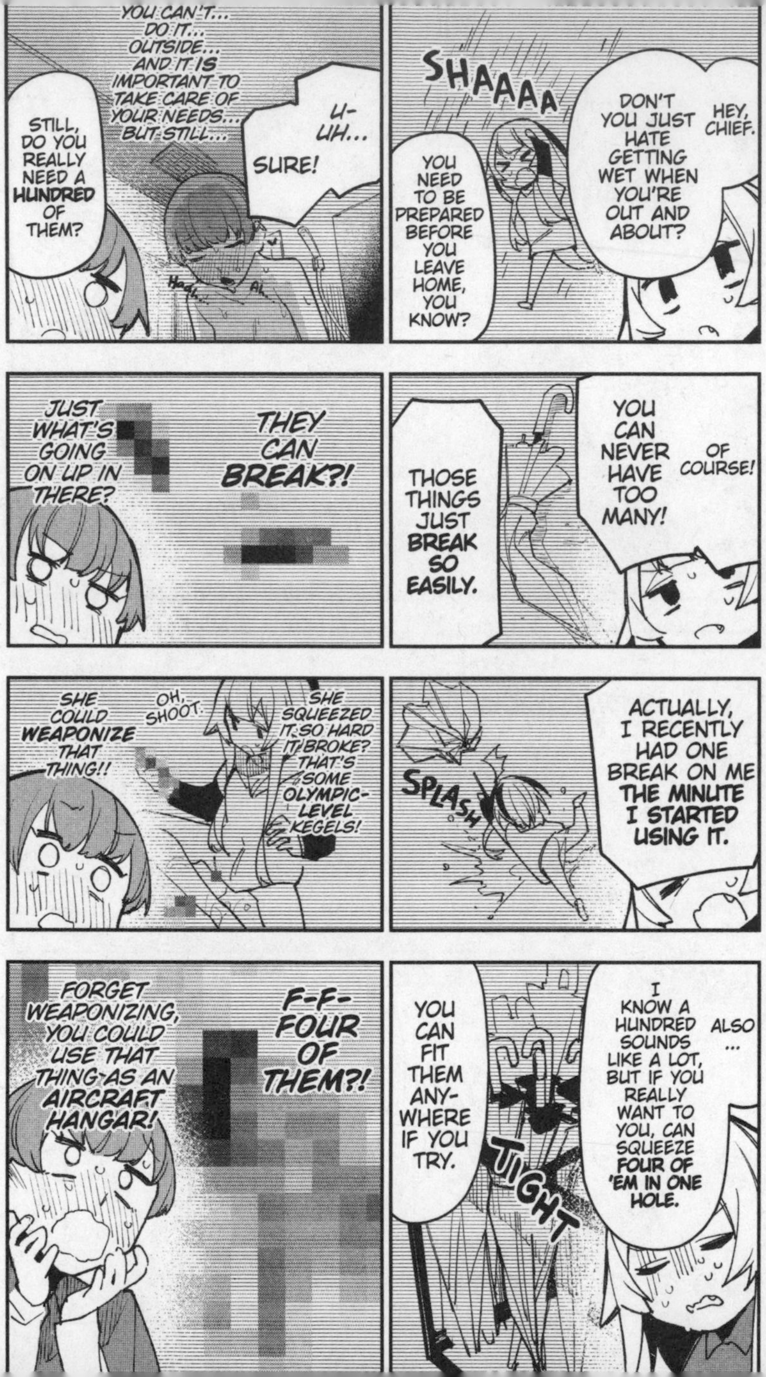
HEY, CHIEF.
DON'T YOU JUST HATE GETTING WET WHEN YOU'RE OUT AND ABOUT?
SHAAAA
YOU NEED TO BE PREPARED BEFORE YOU LEAVE HOME, YOU KNOW?
U-UH... SURE!
YOU CAN'T... DO IT... OUTSIDE... AND IT IS IMPORTANT TO TAKE CARE OF YOUR NEEDS... BUT STILL...
STILL, DO YOU REALLY NEED A HUNDRED OF THEM?
OF COURSE!
YOU CAN NEVER HAVE TOO MANY!
THOSE THINGS JUST BREAK SO EASILY.
THEY CAN BREAK?!
JUST WHAT'S GOING ON UP IN THERE?
ACTUALLY, I RECENTLY HAD ONE BREAK ON ME THE MINUTE I STARTED USING IT.
SPLASH
SHE SQUEEZED IT SO HARD IT BROKE? THAT'S SOME OLYMPIC-LEVEL KEGELS!
OH, SHOOT.
SHE COULD WEAPONIZE THAT THING!!
ALSO...
I KNOW A HUNDRED SOUNDS LIKE A LOT, BUT IF YOU REALLY WANT TO YOU, CAN SQUEEZE FOUR OF 'EM IN ONE HOLE.
TIGHT
YOU CAN FIT THEM ANYWHERE IF YOU TRY.
F-F-FOUR OF THEM?!
FORGET WEAPONIZING, YOU COULD USE THAT THING AS AN AIRCRAFT HANGAR!

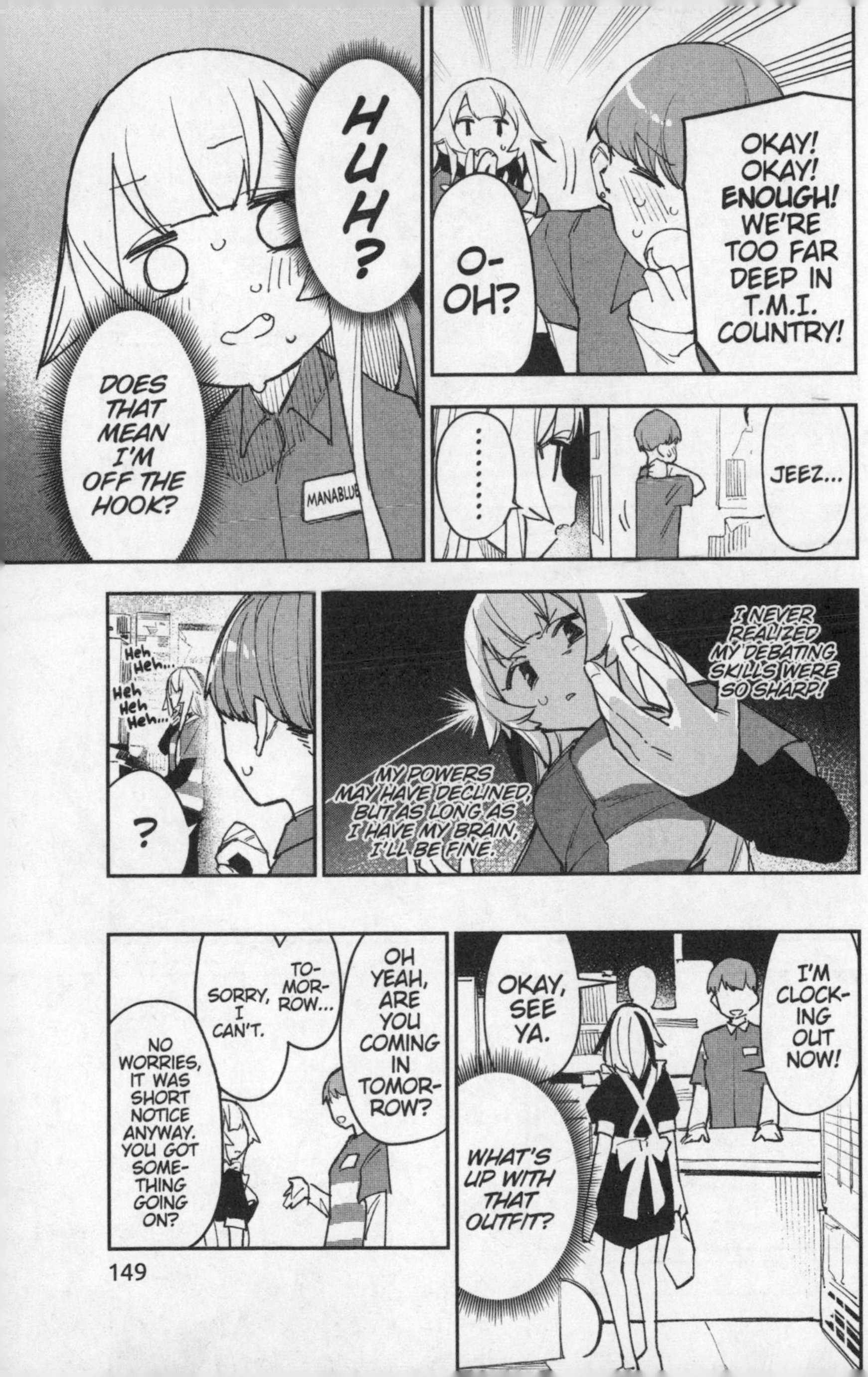
OKAY! OKAY! ENOUGH! WE'RE TOO FAR DEEP IN T.M.I. COUNTRY!
O-OH?
JEEZ...
......
HUH?
DOES THAT MEAN I'M OFF THE HOOK?
MANABLUE
I NEVER REALIZED MY DEBATING SKILLS WERE SO SHARP!
MY POWERS MAY HAVE DECLINED, BUT AS LONG AS I HAVE MY BRAIN, I'LL BE FINE.
Heh Heh... Heh Heh Heh...
?
I'M CLOCKING-ING OUT NOW!
OKAY, SEE YA.
WHAT'S UP WITH THAT OUTFIT?
OH YEAH, ARE YOU COMING IN TOMORROW?
TO-MOR-ROW...
SORRY, I CAN'T.
NO WORRIES, IT WAS SHORT NOTICE ANYWAY. YOU GOT SOME-THING GOING ON?

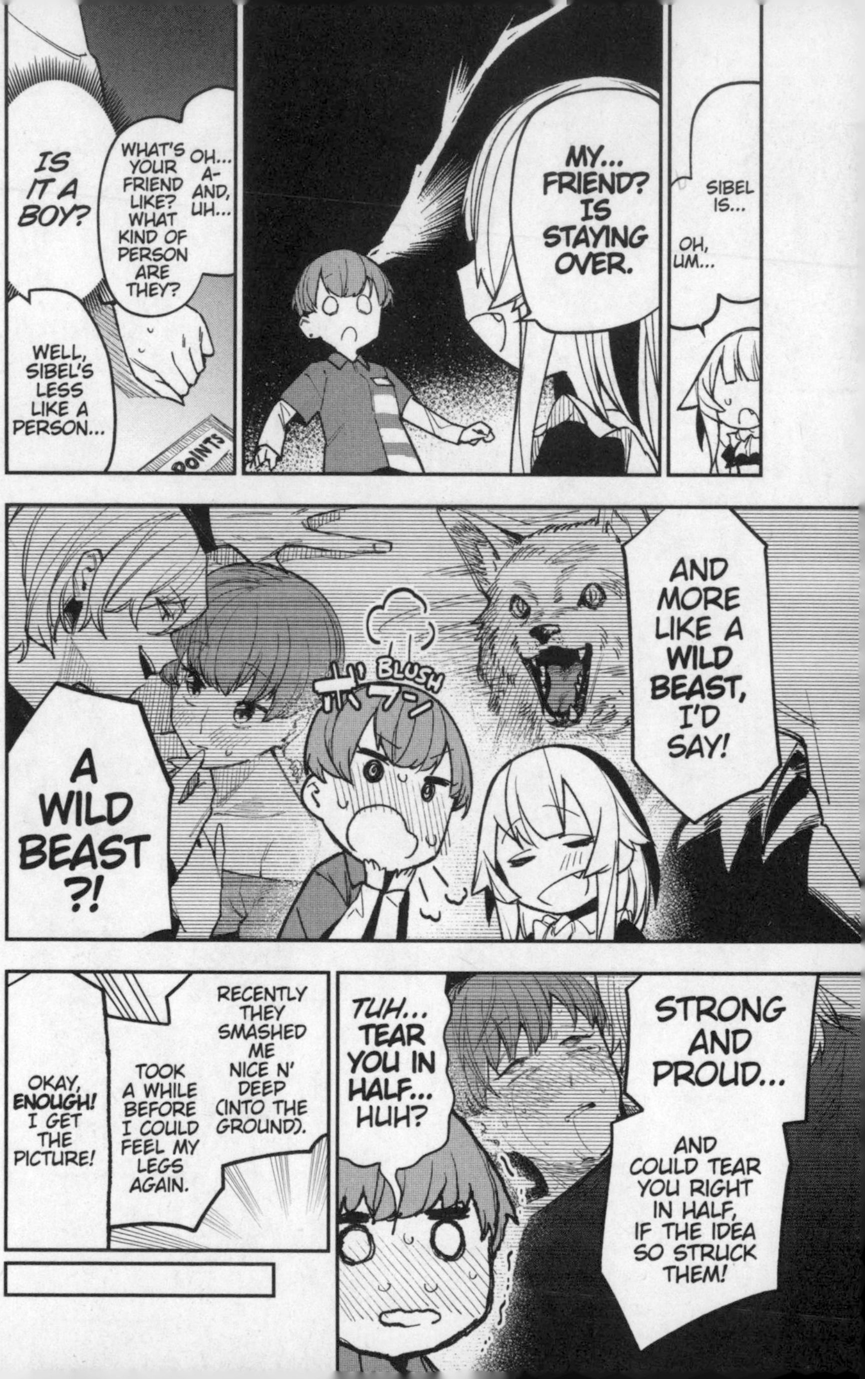
SIBEL IS...
OH, UM...
MY... FRIEND? IS STAYING OVER.
OH... A-AND, UH...
WHAT'S YOUR FRIEND LIKE? WHAT KIND OF PERSON ARE THEY?
IS IT A BOY?
WELL, SIBEL'S LESS LIKE A PERSON...
POINTS
AND MORE LIKE A WILD BEAST, I'D SAY!
BLUSH
A WILD BEAST ?!
STRONG AND PROUD...
AND COULD TEAR YOU RIGHT IN HALF, IF THE IDEA SO STRUCK THEM!
TUH... TEAR YOU IN HALF... HUH?
RECENTLY THEY SMASHED ME NICE N' DEEP (INTO THE GROUND).
TOOK A WHILE BEFORE I COULD FEEL MY LEGS AGAIN.
OKAY, ENOUGH! I GET THE PICTURE!

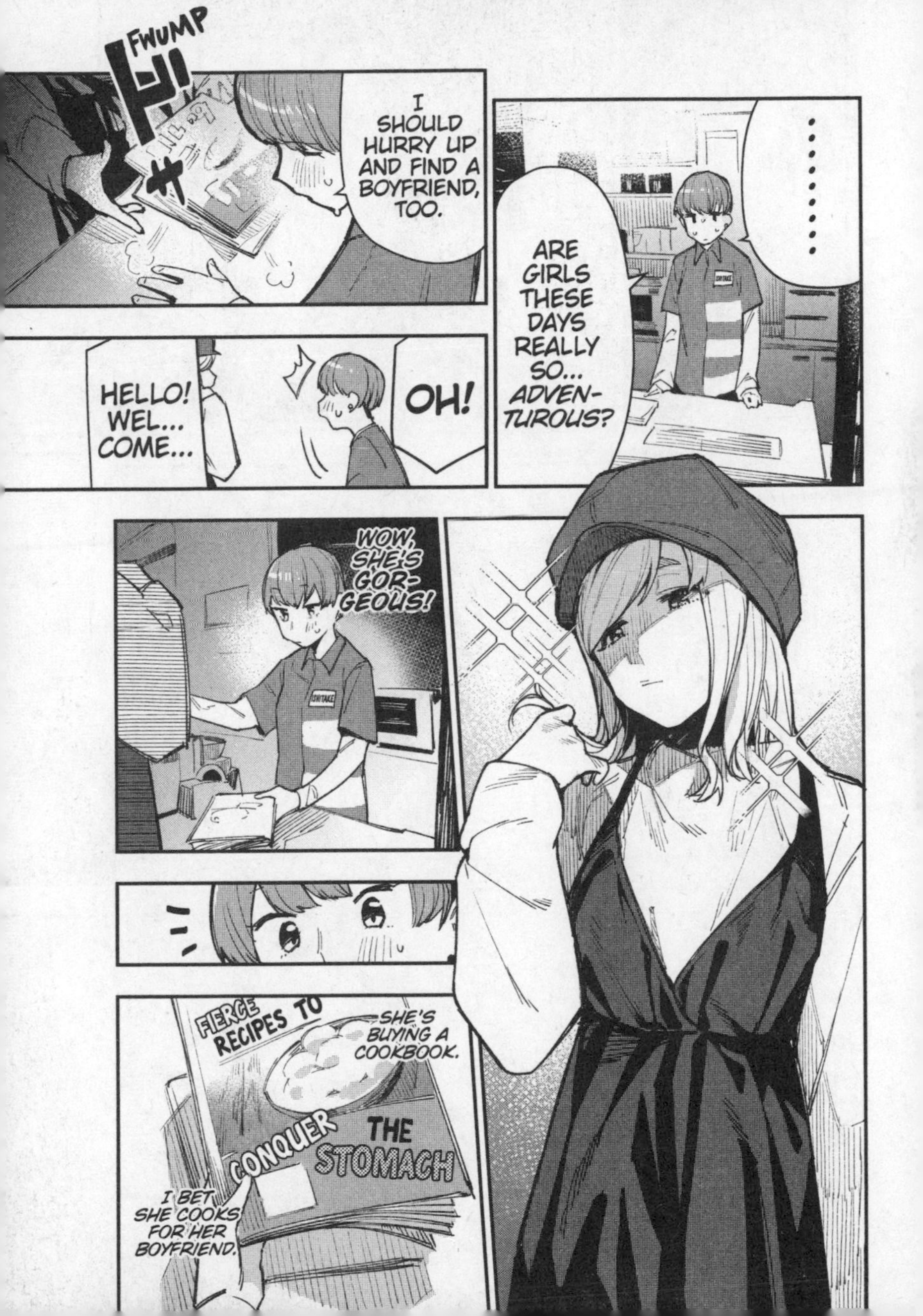

......
ARE GIRLS THESE DAYS REALLY SO... ADVENTUROUS?
FWUMP
I SHOULD HURRY UP AND FIND A BOYFRIEND, TOO.
OH!
HELLO! WEL... COME...
WOW, SHE'S GORGEOUS!
FIERCE RECIPES TO CONQUER THE STOMACH
SHE'S BUYING A COOKBOOK.
I BET SHE COOKS FOR HER BOYFRIEND.

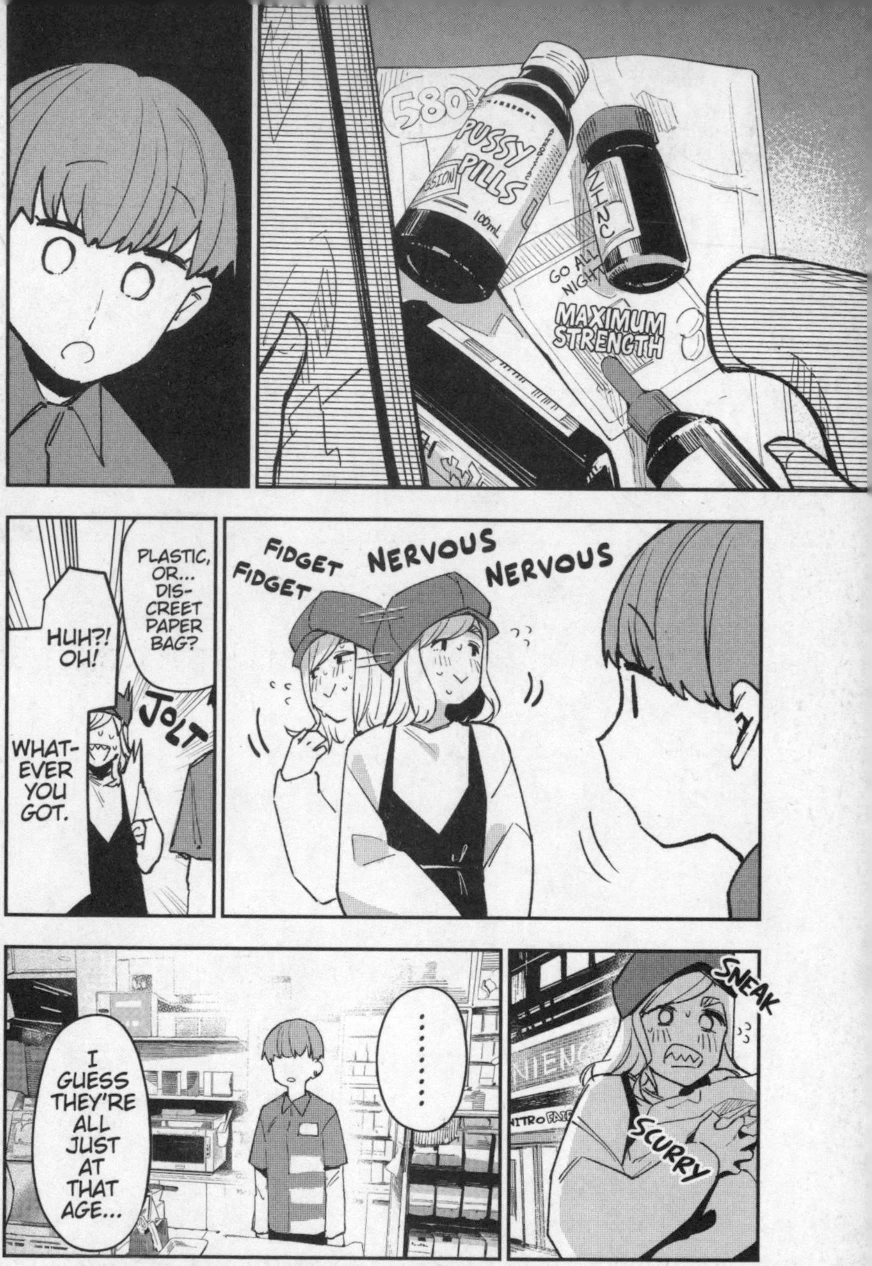
PUSSY PILLS
100mL
ZINC
GO ALL NIGHT
MAXIMUM STRENGTH
FIDGET FIDGET
NERVOUS NERVOUS
PLASTIC, OR... DIS-CREET PAPER BAG?
HUH?! OH!
JOLT
WHAT-EVER YOU GOT.
SNEAK
SCURRY
....
I GUESS THEY'RE ALL JUST AT THAT AGE...

BONUS ①

THE POWER OF SUGGESTION

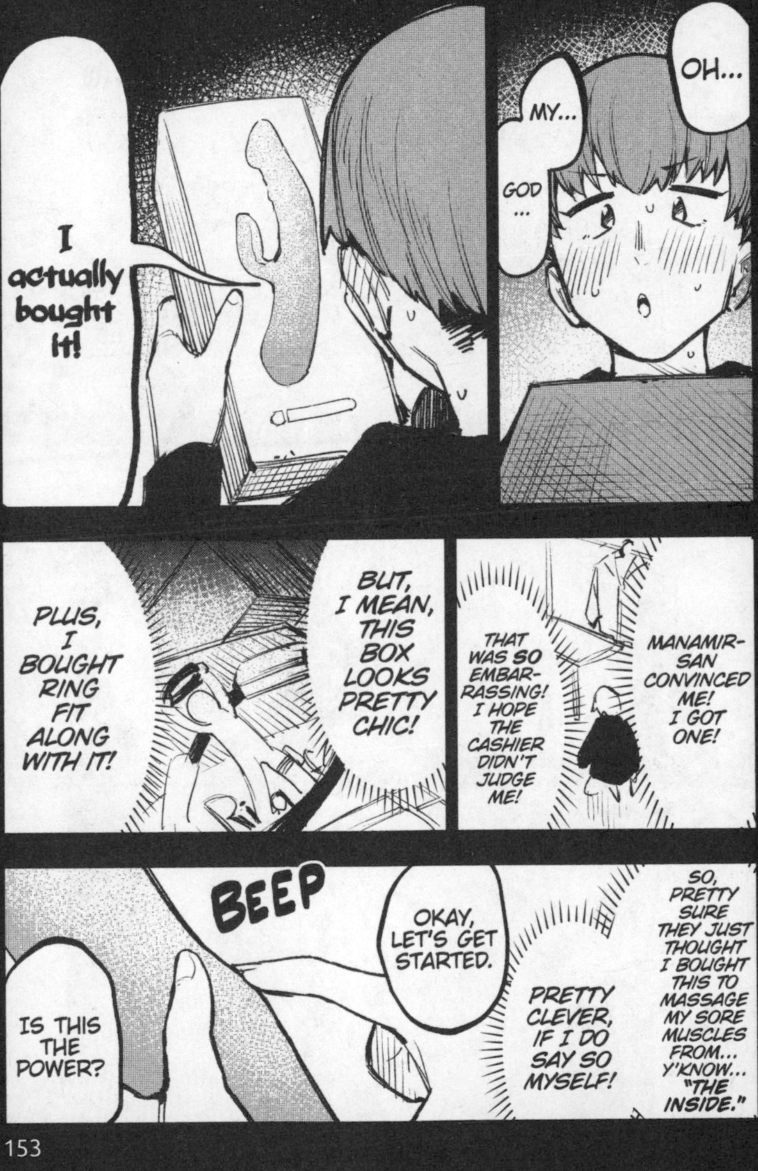
OH...
MY...
GOD...
I actually bought it!
MANAMIR-SAN CONVINCED ME! I GOT ONE!
THAT WAS SO EMBARRASSING! I HOPE THE CASHIER DIDN'T JUDGE ME!
BUT, I MEAN, THIS BOX LOOKS PRETTY CHIC!
PLUS, I BOUGHT RING FIT ALONG WITH IT!
SO, PRETTY SURE THEY JUST THOUGHT I BOUGHT THIS TO MASSAGE MY SORE MUSCLES FROM... Y'KNOW... "THE INSIDE."
PRETTY CLEVER, IF I DO SAY SO MYSELF!
OKAY, LET'S GET STARTED.
BEEP
IS THIS THE POWER?

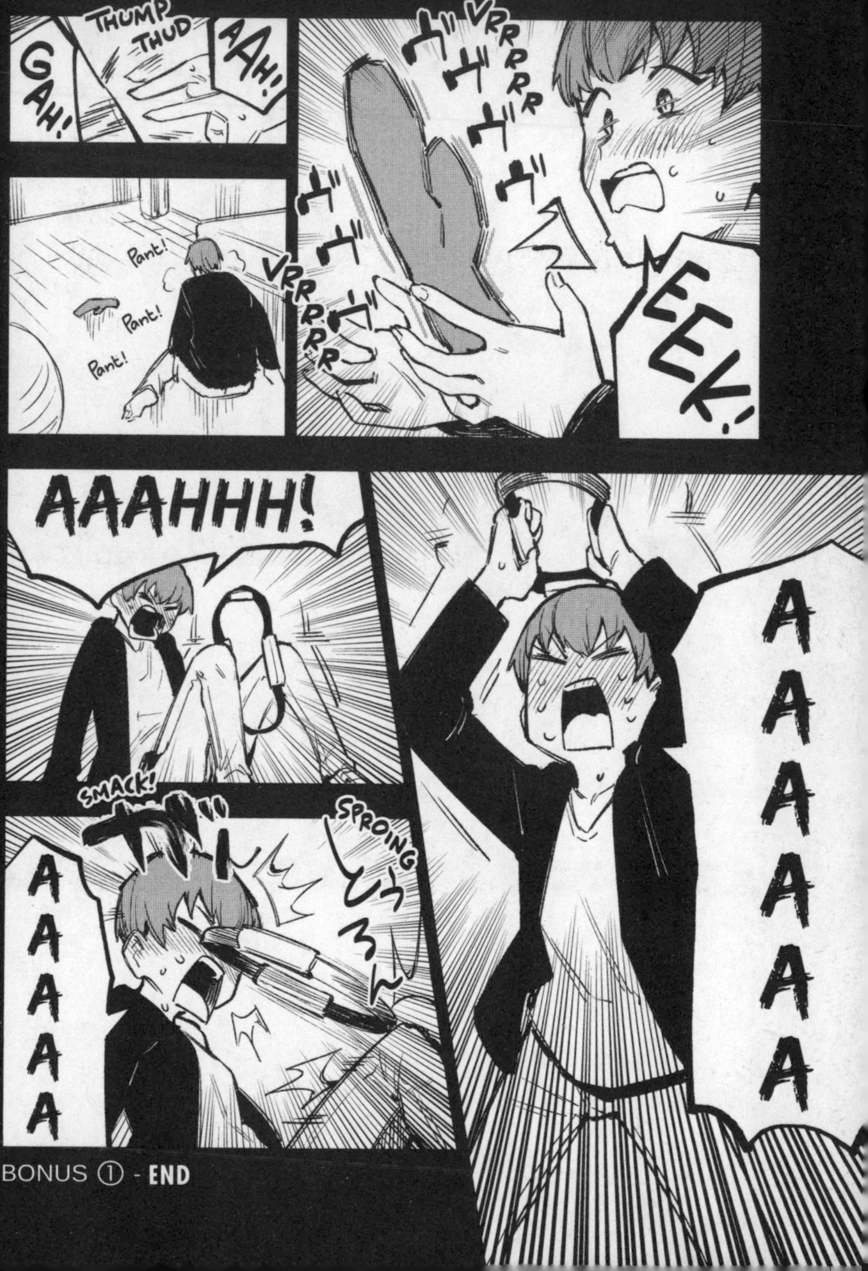
VRRRRRR
VRRRRRRR
EEK!
GAH!
AAH!
THUMP
THUD
Pant!
Pant!
Pant!
AAAA
AAAA
AAAHHH!
SMACK!
SPROING
AAAA
AAAA

BONUS ① - **END**

BONUS ②

THE NIGHT BEFORE THE 15TH NIGHT

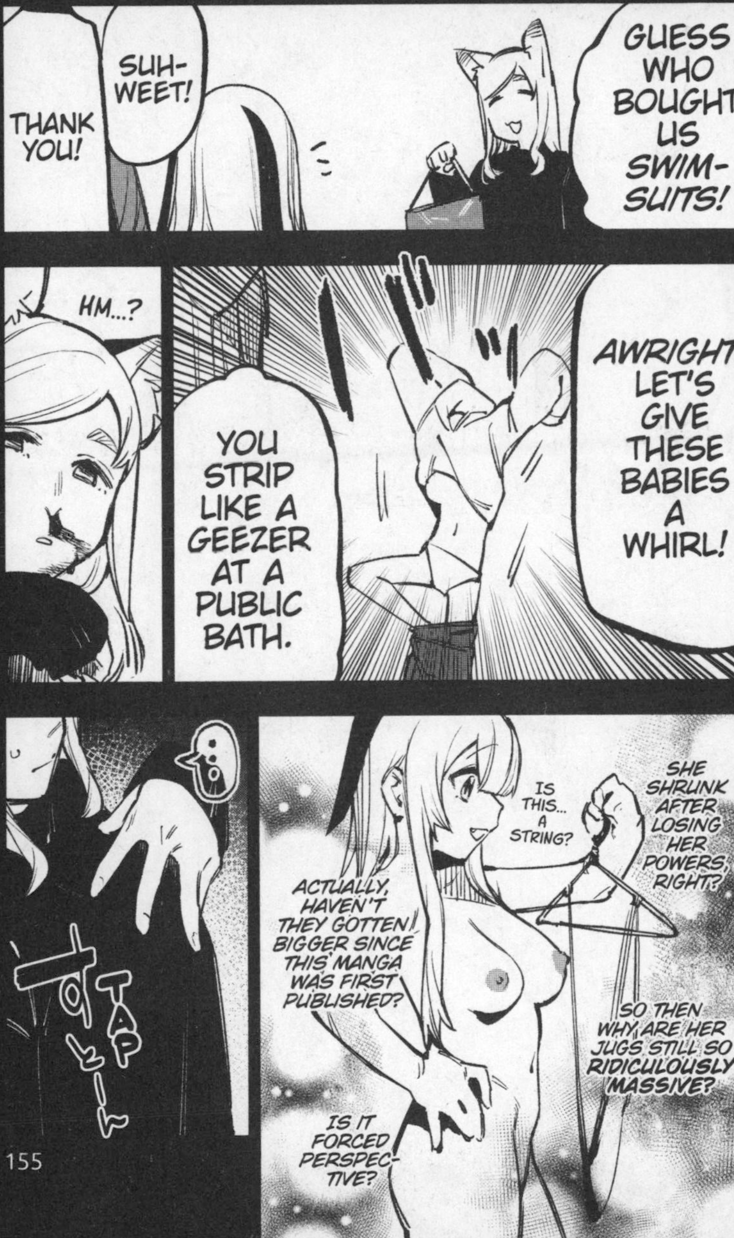
GUESS WHO BOUGHT US SWIM-SUITS!
SUH-WEET!
THANK YOU!
AWRIGHT! LET'S GIVE THESE BABIES A WHIRL!
YOU STRIP LIKE A GEEZER AT A PUBLIC BATH.
HM...?
IS THIS... A STRING?
SHE SHRUNK AFTER LOSING HER POWERS, RIGHT?
SO THEN WHY ARE HER JUGS STILL SO RIDICULOUSLY MASSIVE?
ACTUALLY, HAVEN'T THEY GOTTEN BIGGER SINCE THIS MANGA WAS FIRST PUBLISHED?
IS IT FORCED PERSPECTIVE?
TAP

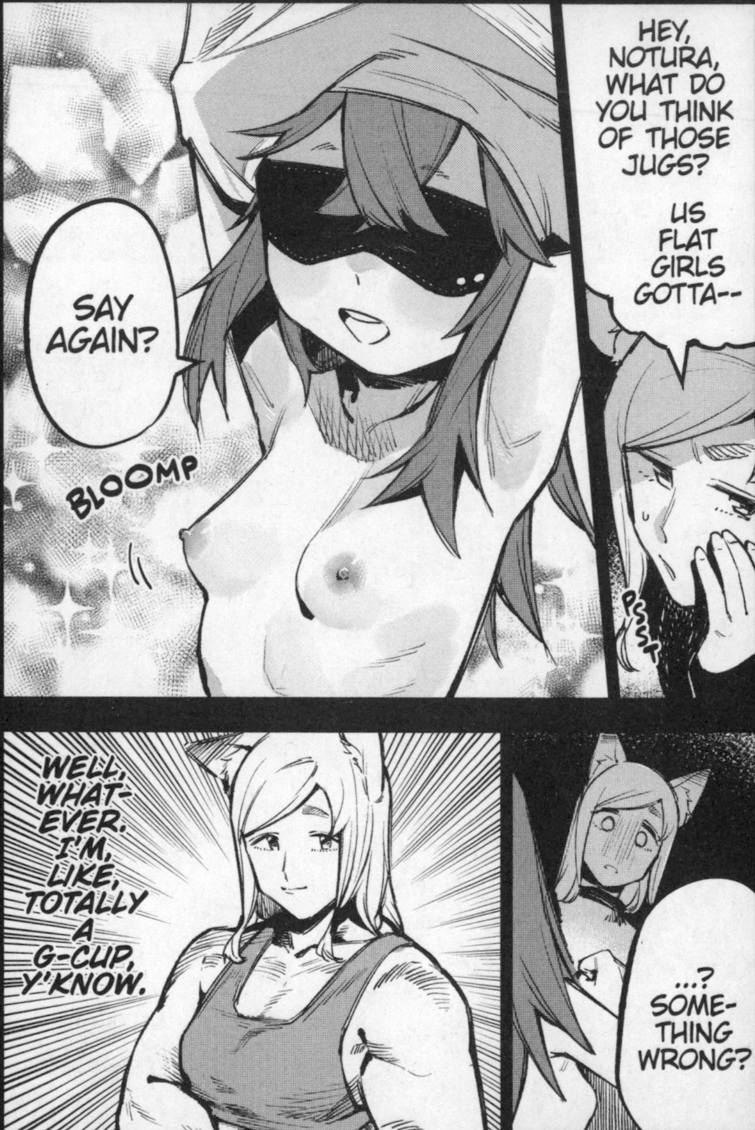
HEY, NOTURA, WHAT DO YOU THINK OF THOSE JUGS?
US FLAT GIRLS GOTTA--
PSST
SAY AGAIN?
BLOOMP
...? SOME-THING WRONG?
WELL, WHAT-EVER. I'M, LIKE, TOTALLY A G-CUP, Y'KNOW.

BONUS ② - **END**

BONUS ③ **ACTUAL BONUS STUFF**

REJECTED BOOK COVERS

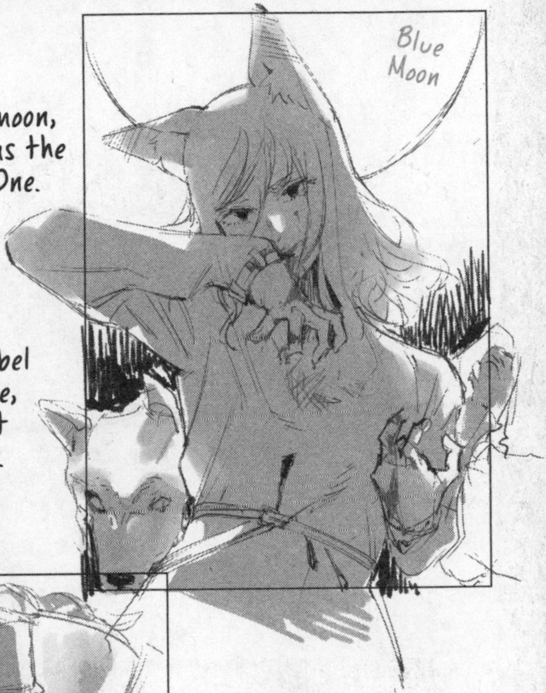
Blue Moon

Sibel under a blue moon, with a similar vibe as the cover for Volume One.

We don't really get to see demon Sibel much in this volume, so I wanted to put that on the cover.

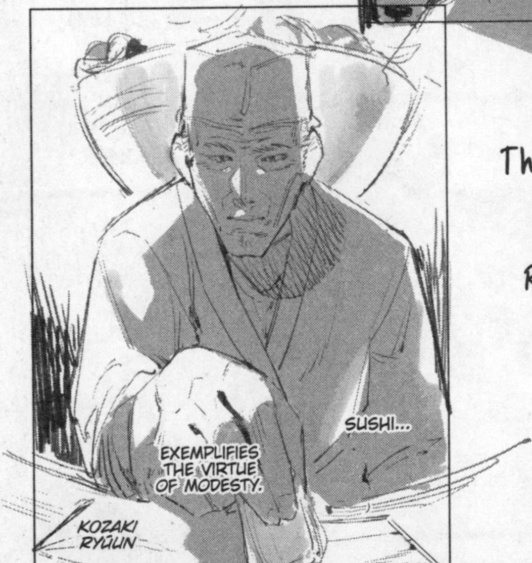
SUSHI...
EXEMPLIFIES THE VIRTUE OF MODESTY.
KOZAKI RYŪUN

The Chef

Reason for rejection:

Who the hell is this?

Afterword

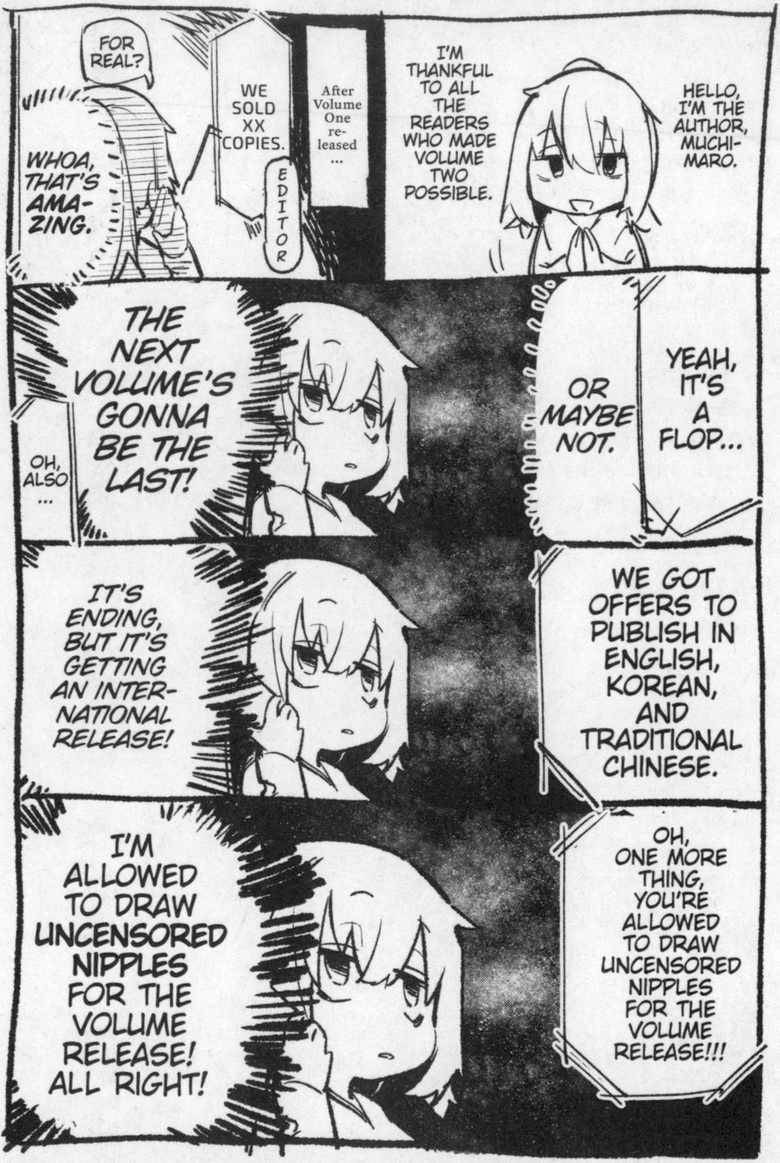
HELLO, I'M THE AUTHOR, MUCHIMARO.
I'M THANKFUL TO ALL THE READERS WHO MADE VOLUME TWO POSSIBLE.
After Volume One released ...
WE SOLD XX COPIES.
EDITOR
FOR REAL?
WHOA, THAT'S **AMAZING.**
YEAH, IT'S A FLOP...
OR MAYBE NOT.
THE NEXT VOLUME'S GONNA BE THE LAST!
OH, ALSO ...
WE GOT OFFERS TO PUBLISH IN ENGLISH, KOREAN, AND TRADITIONAL CHINESE.
IT'S ENDING, BUT IT'S GETTING AN INTERNATIONAL RELEASE!
OH, ONE MORE THING, YOU'RE ALLOWED TO DRAW UNCENSORED NIPPLES FOR THE VOLUME RELEASE!!!
I'M ALLOWED TO DRAW UNCENSORED NIPPLES FOR THE VOLUME RELEASE! ALL RIGHT!

It's Just Not My Night! 3

OLD YAKUZA DUDE VS. THE POLICE!

I DIDN'T KILL NOBODY!
WE GOT ALL THE PROOF WE NEED RIGHT HERE!
SO QUIT RESISTING AND GET IN THE CAR!!
IT AIN'T EVEN A CORPSE, IT'S...
WHY ARE YOU HOLDING HANDS WITH IT?!
ARE YOU MESSIN' WITH ME RIGHT NOW?!

THEIR BATTLE BEGINS!!

INNOCENT BYSTANDERS GET DRAWN INTO THE CHAOS WHEN BODY PARTS START SPREADING ALL OVER THE CITY AT SUPER HIGH SPEED!

WH-WHOSE IS THAT...?
DID YOU...
DID YOU REGAIN YOUR MEMORIES OF YOUR MERCENARY DAYS?!
HEY, DAD, LOOK WHAT I GOT!
HM? WHAT DID...
IS THAT A SEX DOLL?!
YO-SHIO-SAN ...?

AAAAH! IT'S A CORPSE CARRYING MORE CORPSES!!

DESPERATION

DESCENDS UPON MANABLUE...

WHAT WILL BE HER FATE?!!

SEE YOU NEXT TIME!!

SEVEN SEAS' GHOST SHIP PRESENTS

It's Just Not My Night!

Tale of a Fallen Vampire Queen

story and art by **MUCHIMARO**

VOLUME 2

TRANSLATION
Alan Cheng & Rowena Chen

ADAPTATION
David Lumsdon

LETTERING
Mo Harrison

COVER AND LOGO DESIGN
H. Qi

PROOFREADER
Leighanna DeRouen

COPY EDITOR
B. Lillian Martin

SENIOR EDITOR
J.P. Sullivan

PREPRESS TECHNICIAN
Melanie Ujimori

PRINT MANAGER
Rhiannon Rasmussen-Silverstein

PRODUCTION DESIGNER
George Panella

PRODUCTION MANAGER
Lissa Pattillo

EDITOR-IN-CHIEF
Julie Davis

ASSOCIATE PUBLISHER
Adam Arnold

PUBLISHER
Jason DeAngelis

Yo ga yo nara! Vol. 2

First published in Japan in 2021 by Kodansha Ltd., Tokyo.
Publication rights for this English edition arranged through Kodansha Ltd., Tokyo.

Seven Seas press and purchase enquiries can be sent to Marketing Manager Lianne Sentar at press@gomanga.com. Information regarding the distribution and purchase of digital editions is available from Digital Manager CK Russell at digital@gomanga.com.

ISBN: 978-1-63858-678-4
Printed in Canada
First Printing: October 2022
10 9 8 7 6 5 4 3 2 1

READING DIRECTIONS

This book reads from ***right to left***, Japanese style. If this is your first time reading manga, you start reading from the top right panel on each page and take it from there. If you get lost, just follow the numbered diagram here. It may seem backwards at first, but you'll get the hang of it! Have fun!!

1
2
3
4
5
6
7
8
9

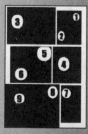

Follow us online: www.GhostShipManga.com